To Run a School

To Run a School

Administrative Organization and Learning

Christopher A. Simon

Westport, Connecticut
London

Library of Congress Cataloging-in-Publication Data

Simon, Christopher A., 1968–
    To run a school : administrative organization and learning / Christopher A. Simon.
        p. cm.
    Includes bibliographical references and index.
    ISBN 0–275–96834–0 (alk. paper)
    1. School management and organization—United States. 2. Education and state—United
States. 3. Public schools—United States—Administration. I. Title.
    LB2805.S589 2001
    371.2′00973—dc21   00–061166

British Library Cataloguing in Publication Data is available.

Library of Congress Catalog Card Number: 00–061166
ISBN: 0–275–96834–0

First published in 2001

Praeger Publishers, 88 Post Road West, Westport, CT 06881
An imprint of Greenwood Publishing Group, Inc.
www.praeger.com

Printed in the United States of America

The paper used in this book complies with the
Permanent Paper Standard issued by the National
Information Standards Organization (Z39.48–1984).

10 9 8 7 6 5 4 3 2 1

Contents

Preface

There is a quiet revolution occurring in public education policy. The debate surrounds the issue of how best to go about educating America's youth in the modern (some would say postmodern) world. With the election of Ronald Reagan, U.S. public education policy was introduced to the concept of privatization. The move was largely built on the premise that the less government involvement in the lives of individual denizens the better. The privatization movement was built on ideologically well-prepared soil and the debate that followed was played out on what appears to be fairly stark ideological lines. Public school apologists are generally of the belief that elementary and secondary education is a public good, without which citizens would not be able to participate equally in our democratic institutions. Public education also means the pursuit of equal opportunity in the workforce. Private school advocates make their point on the grounds of economic efficiency, effectiveness, and individual freedom. Privatization scholars have argued repeatedly that public schools waste a tremendous amount of the fiscal resources provided them. Teachers' unions actively grab for larger salaries and better benefits. Most importantly, the privatization scholars argue that the outcome—student performance—is dismal. For these scholars, school choice means freedom to pursue outcomes that are best for each individual; rather than focusing on equal outcomes for the collective.

This book is not an attempt to sort out the question of "Who is correct." It is impossible to answer the question with empirical analysis because the question is in fact normative, deeply embedded in centuries-old philosophic debate. My main concern at the moment is not to pursue the debate itself, but focus instead on what public school organization tells us about outcomes. I argue that public schools are "open systems" organizations, continually reacting to a changing environment and to evolving internal organizational conditions.

The structure of public schools has not changed dramatically, but the organizational priorities have and will continue to change. Our public schools are complex mechanisms that cannot be easily manipulated to produce a "quick fix" to perceived problems—they are in fact delicate human-made organisms that can only produce positive change with the benefit of careful nurturing. The book does not respond to the debate, as I have already mentioned, but it does remind us that the debate should not be couched (as it has been) in the premise that there's something irreparably wrong with our public schools as organizations. It is quite possible that the problem (if there is one) lies to a greater extent in the organizational environment of schools and to a lesser extent in public schools as a system.

Public schools face a growing public consensus that private school competition will lead to improved outcomes, but the evidence to support this contention is not present. Privatization means that we no longer believe that education is a public good—something to be provided by government. Commodification of education will necessarily mean that educational opportunity will not be uniform—if the marketplace were uniform, then what point would there be in having a choice between alternatives? In fact, uniformity would imply that distinct alternatives do not exist—perhaps cost would be the only difference.

Our philosophy of government will dictate to some degree what we ask of government. It may not, however, produce what is best for us, individually or collectively. Whichever path we choose—public schools or a limited government free market approach—the evidence presented here indicates that *commitment* to schools as institutions is a critical part of determining our satisfaction with organizational outcomes. We must be committed to our choice with full understanding of the outcomes that choice produces.

Many individuals were responsible for the successful completion of this book. Nicholas P. Lovrich, John C. Pierce, David C. Nice, and Brent S. Steel read and commented on earlier drafts of the work, which led to significant improvements in my approach to the research question. The innumerable conversations with Dr. Lovrich were much appreciated as well as his insightful and detailed critical analysis of my writings. If it were not for all four of these individuals, it is doubtful that the manuscript would have been completed in its current form. They challenged me to think outside of my intellectual comfort zone.

Enrico Yap and his colleagues at the Office of Superintendent of Public Instruction, State of Washington, were of enormous assistance in the data collection process necessary for the completion of this book. Dr. Yap and I have worked together on research projects of various types for nearly six years, and I have learned a great deal from him about public schools in Washington State.

I am particularly indebted to my parents, Raffi G. and Susan M. Simon, for what has amounted to over a quarter of a century of formal and informal education. . .and the lessons continue. The daily philosophical debates over dinner have helped me to hone my arguments and to explain them in a coherent fashion. My late grandparents, Lee H. and Marie Terzian, played an important role in directing my interests towards political science, organizational theory, and education policy.

Dr. James Sabin of Greenwood Publishing Group offered several helpful suggestions regarding book revisions. I am indebted to Lynne Goetz for editing the final book manuscript. Finally, I would like to thank the Departments of Political Science at Washington State University and the University of Nevada, Reno for their financial support through this research adventure. Discussing my thoughts and findings with colleagues and students was invaluable.

Chapter 1

Introduction

At various times throughout the last century and a half, American public schools have been alternately lauded and lambasted (Dougherty and Sostre 1992). A consistent and seemingly never-ending stream of education policy reform strategies have shaped and continue to shape our public elementary and secondary education system. Despite the well-intentioned efforts of politicians, concerned citizens and parents, teachers' unions, policy analysts, and university researchers, in most instances our attempts to improve the performance of the public school system have not resulted in the level of success that was expected. Americans often appear to be thoroughly disappointed in their public schools—dissatisfied with the level of student achievement, the subject matter included in the school curriculum, the quality of instruction, and the cost of administering the school organizations.

A partial explanation for the perennial malaise hanging pall-like over our public schools is related to the fluid nature of social values and changing patterns of social interaction in contemporary society. The expectations placed on public schools have changed and expanded tremendously since the public school system was first established in early 19th century Massachusetts. Traditional approaches to education might have been more efficient and possibly more effective in shaping student performance, but are no longer workable in today's social and political setting. For better or worse, the social values and political climate of American society have changed, particularly in the post-Second World War era. Different social values frequently shape individual and community priorities, which in turn affect the curriculum introduced to students and the methods by which they are instructed.

In the 1960's education policy theorists such as Ralph Linton (1969) and Urie Brofenbrenner (1961) solemnly reflected upon the challenges likely to face future generations of American public school teachers and administrators as public schools prepared to educate the Baby Boomer generation. One of the central issues addressed by these education theorists was youth-adult interaction in social settings, and its likely impact on the ability of public schools to maintain an orderly operational environment. 'Youth culture' was viewed as a new and serious socially based impediment to effective goal accomplishment and student academic achievement.

Linton and Brofenbrenner found that the Baby Boomer generation was substantially less deferential to authority figures, due to a couple of important social changes. Patterns of family interaction were changing dramatically. The urbanization and suburbanization of American life produced significant changes in the social and economic role of adolescents. Unlike agricultural or extraction-based economies, families in urban and suburban America often did not work in a *collective* manner to earn a family income. In the post-Second World War era, a large percentage of working adults earned incomes as industrial wage-laborers or salaried white-collar office workers. While their parents earned incomes through the selling of their labor, skills, and abilities, school-aged children spent the majority of their day separated from their families, attending public elementary and secondary schools.

In addition to increased urbanization, post-Second World War America experienced tremendous economic growth. Society became more itinerate, due to revolutionary changes in the nation's mass transportation infrastructure, and fueled in part by the growth in individual disposable incomes. Combined, these economic and technological advances presented new opportunities for American youth to act independently of their parents or guardians. These social and economic changes accommodated the development of a distinct 'youth culture,' through which adolescents increasingly began to learn social values and patterns of interaction from their peers, rather than from their families and established community institutions.

Brofenbrenner and Linton predicted that the long-term impact of these dramatic social changes on public school organizations and the education process would likely act to impede teachers and administrators in their efforts to shape student academic achievement. Waning social control over school-aged children resulted in declining patterns of deference on the part of adolescents for local school authorities. The authors expected that the teacher-student relationship would become increasingly onerous, due to changing patterns of communication and a new social dynamic surrounding the giving of orders by teachers to their young charges. Students would no longer simply accept instruction without question, but were more apt to speak their minds, questioning both the curriculum and pedagogical techniques. The issue of what was being taught to the students and what values that curriculum might represent was not a central concern to either Linton or Brofenbrenner. Rather, it was their contention that the jobs of the teacher and school administrator would be more onerous and possibly less effective due to the increased complications produced by the changing society in which they were forced to operate.

Linton and Brofenbrenner were describing the loss of what is commonly referred to in the social-psychology literature as *family social capital*, which has repeatedly been demonstrated to be a critical non-school-related factor in explaining the likelihood of post-secondary educational attainment, long-term economic success, and social advancement. In the evolving American social and economic landscape, school-aged children frequently were not encouraged to develop long-term goals to the same degree as had been the case at an earlier period in time. In 19th-century agrarian communities, long-term goals may have been more easily established for—rather than by—young people: women were encouraged to marry, and men were often directed to take over their family enterprises. Formal education was a method of legitimizing socially defined expectations while providing the necessary tools to reach them.

Families frequently operated in unison to achieve social and economic success, and parental expectations of children were often clearly communicated, understood, and followed. Moral education and guidance was provided to individual families by community social, educational, and religious institutions. Despite the fact that parental educational attainment expectations of their children may have been substantially lower in an earlier era, it is likely that these expectations were more clearly communicated and reinforced in families that were more tightly bound together than perhaps they are today. Career expectations have expanded tremendously, particularly since the Second World War. Unquestionably, young adults are freer today to decide their own paths in life, but it appears that important elements of family and social life have been lost in the process of change.

The same forces that in a sense 'liberated' American youth from a fairly rigid social structure may have resulted in the unintentional loss of family and generational interconnectedness. The decline in family social capital means that an increasing proportion of America's children arrive at school with very little in the way of educational guidance. Teachers can and do instruct students about important facts, and within the limits imposed by the law, they even offer students the logic skills necessary to interpret important facts and assign meaning—i.e., the process through which information is transformed into knowledge. Nevertheless, the legitimacy of the school, its curriculum, and most importantly, the value of actively engaging in the learning process cannot be effectively imbued by the schools themselves. Parents or legal guardians of school children, and the larger civic community in which schools operate, act as the critical 'legitimizers,' by encouraging children to develop long-term education and career goals, providing role models, and reinforcing subject matter by structuring an environment conducive for students to complete their homework studies. Tragically, the family and community social capital may not be uniform across student populations, thereby weakening our efforts to establish *de facto* equality of educational opportunity. The age-old issue of poverty and its impact on education appears to be inextricably tied to the loss of social capital.

In addition to value shifts in American society, social equity became a central education goal in the 1960's and 1970's. In 1954, the Supreme Court case *Brown v. Board of Education of Topeka, Kansas* firmly established an entirely new set of long overdue priorities for American public education. Racial integration of public schools became a paramount concern for education policy makers and school administrators at the federal, state and local levels, requiring extraordinary and administrative commitments often not readily available to school districts. The process of eradicating a terrible and long-standing pattern of social, political, and economic injustice has required substantial intergovernmental efforts. National, state, and local policymakers and administrators worked together to achieve the massive reengineering of educational goals and the methods of achieving those goals. The rebuilding process that was first started with the *Brown* decision and made tremendous strides during the Great Society has realistically not yet achieved its goal of a truly equal and fair educational process with positive outcomes for students of all economic and social backgrounds.

The intergovernmental partnership has the potential to produce both positive and negative outcomes for public schools. The administrative efforts necessary to coordinate the policy objectives of three different levels of government have led to enlarged public school district and unit administrative costs. The proportion of school resources garnered from the local level has declined substantially, making schools increasingly administratively accountable to state and federal agencies, while local citizens are often left wondering about their role in their children's education.

Additionally, the Cold War played an important role in shaping education policy. In 1957, the Soviet Union launched the first man-made satellite, Sputnik. The Eisenhower administration was not tremendously concerned about the Russian space program and remained fairly certain that the United States was at that time well ahead of its international foe (Greenstein 1994). Nevertheless, the American public was extremely concerned about the successful launch of the Soviet space vehicle and what this historic achievement represented. Taking advantage of the policy window provided, Congress successfully passed and Eisenhower signed into law the National Defense Education Act (NDEA) of 1958. In the increasingly high technology world, military and political leaders on both sides were acutely aware that the need for a well-educated populace was an important factor in determining the long-term outcome of the Cold War—well-educated citizens were seen as a critical weapon. Training in science and mathematics education was particularly important, and federal resources were used to encourage increased elementary and secondary school emphasis in these two areas of study. Citizens employed in the sciences and engineering fields would likely be involved in the creation of the next generation of military weapons, as well as in the production of the civilian goods necessary to build and maintain a strong domestic economy.

The changing goals of American society were reflected in the curriculum, the pedagogy, and ultimately the performance of the public school system. Facing a multitude of often conflicting demands, public schools were being pulled in a number of directions at once, making it exceedingly difficult to maintain a stable set of organizational goals that schools and teachers could reasonably meet, let alone exceed. School administrators were being forced to adapt organizational goals to meet the demands of parents, concerned local citizens, school board members, policymakers from the federal and state levels of government, and a fairly activist court system, all of whom were intent on placing their priorities at the top of the public education policy agenda.

Adaptation to an ever-changing set of priorities is difficult for any organization, and schools are certainly no exception. Elementary and secondary education is a twelve- or thirteen-year process in the United States, requiring a long-term commitment on the part of parents, children, teachers, and administrators. It is expected that a well-educated young adult capable of attaining further educational goals or gainful employment will emerge from the formal educational setting. Many things can change over a period of dozen years or so, and such change often catches school organizations and their pupils in "midstream." To illustrate this point, consider that first graders matriculating in 1957—the year of the Sputnik launch—were graduated from high school in 1969—the height of the Vietnam War. Better still, consider the time period between 1974 and 1986. In 1974, there was widespread public cynicism produced by Watergate and the ability of our public institutions to reflect the values of the nation. The Vietnam War appeared to be a tragic foreign policy failure that had consumed the better part of a generation and in which American families lost thousands of their loved ones. By 1986, however, America's faith in the nation's political, social, and economic institutions and the ability to achieve its foreign policy objectives was somewhat renewed. The clarion trumpet of victory was beginning to herald the conclusion of a long and bitter Cold War. How much changed for elementary and secondary school students between 1974 and 1986? Without delving into the complexities, the answer most simply is "a great deal." For in addition to the pressures associated with social and political changes, the public schools were being forced to make major modifications in their goals and processes of education, and frequently these changes occurred right in the middle of many students' elementary or secondary training.

How do organizations—in this instance, public schools—react to changing environmental demands and culture shifts originating primarily from *outside* of school organizational boundaries? To respond effectively to these external pressures would require that the organization somehow meet the expectations or limit the influence of these external forces (e.g., parents, state and federal agencies, social change, etc.) while simultaneously accomplishing the core goals of the education process (i.e., academic excellence). It would logically follow that an ineffective organization would not be able to deal with the external demands and changes, and would lose sight of its central purpose. The likely result would be a decline in performance and, for the public organization, a subsequent loss of legitimacy.

If standardized examinations are any indication of the public schools' ability to deal with the multitude of demands placed upon it, then there is fairly clear evidence that many public schools have been unable to meet the demands placed upon them and simultaneously concentrate on their core organizational goals. Student performance on the SAT and ACT declined significantly in the 1960's and 1970's, a decline from which student populations have been unable to completely recover on a sustainable basis. What went wrong with American education? Where does the fault for declining student performance lie? In 1983, the National Commission on Excellence in Education identified public education policy and the institutions which executed that policy as the chief culprits. The commission concluded that American public schools were in a serious crisis. Schools needed to refocus their curriculum, placing greater emphasis on instruction in basic skills. Following on the heels of this damning study was the 1988 report of the President's Commission on Privatization, which recommended the large-scale commodification of public education, along with a number of government functions (Linowes 1988).

The 1980's proved to be a period of deep introspection within the education policy arena. The evidence indicated that nearly three decades of public education policy and administration had led to widespread failure of public schools as institutions. The pursuit of academic excellence had not produced the desired outcomes—poverty and *de facto* discrimination continued to plague the public schools. According to Charles Murray in his critical public policy and social analysis *Losing Ground* (1983), the pursuit of equality of opportunity through education policy has had a deleterious effect on the social and economic opportunities for minority populations and the underclass. Perhaps even more to the point, academic studies of public schools began to question the legitimacy of the public school enterprise and the ability of public school administration to produce any sustainable positive impact on student performance.

Conversely, more recent studies challenge the notion that public schools are failing America's youth. In *The Way We Were?*, Richard Rothstein (1998) argues that it is nearly impossible to compare student performance across time. The content and style of examinations have changed tremendously. Examinations reflect factual information that is important to a particular era and are often time-bound because examination designers cannot predict what information will be "important" in the future. Additionally, the ability to control for changes in student economic and social characteristics poses a significant challenge to accurate analyses.

James Coleman (1990) and others have conducted important research relating student performance to social capital and economic disparity; there is much work to be done in this area of study. The unavailability of complete and accurate student population demographic data and the comparability issues involving examination score trend analyses seriously undermines the arguments of critics who adamantly claim that the quality of instruction has seriously—and possibly irretrievably—declined in America's public elementary and secondary schools.

Nevertheless, the critics' charges stand at the center of the education policy debate, contributing to an elevated interest in public school reform and alternative approaches to education such as government-sponsored private school voucher plans, charter schools, and home schooling options. Teacher testing schemes designed to monitor instructional quality and the meteoric rise in standardized testing to measure student academic achievement are clear and disheartening signs that both the general public and political leaders are growing increasingly pessimistic about the capacity of public schools to produce high quality and equitable educational outcomes. Whether or not public schools have lost ground in their endeavors to rectify past inequalities in educational opportunity and/or improve student academic performance, a loss of faith in a vital public institution's ability to grow out of the current perceived crisis and once again achieve its goals is perhaps even more troubling. The declining confidence in public schools signals a serious loss of organizational legitimacy, which must be recovered if future education reform is to have any real hope of success. Concurrently, there must be greater awareness of the growing organizational constraints with which public schools are faced as well as the critical need for consistent parental and community support if the public is to regain their confidence in public schools.

It is my contention that public schools operate in a manner consistent with the constraints or demands with which they are faced. School administrators attempt to maintain educational goals, establish stable resource bases, and deal with a whole host of factors that often limit school organizations' ability to concentrate on their primary functions. Public schools, as will be addressed in Chapter 2, are "open-systems" organizations—organizations whose performance is a function of the political, social, and economic environment in which they must operate. Schools are particularly vulnerable to organizational environmental circumstances that ultimately shape their organizational output (i.e., student achievement). Before discussing schools from an organizational perspective, it would be instructive to discuss briefly the evolutionary development of American public education. A clearer understanding of how educational systems operated in the past will likely provide important clues as to how we might improve our public schools in the future. Additionally, a brief discussion of the central arguments regarding public school organizational capacity and performance is imperative, so that the reader can clearly understand the nature of the current education policy debate. Conclusions drawn about public schools' capacity to produce a high quality and desirable outcome are frequently shaped by researchers' conception of the school organization, its legitimacy, and its capacity to operate effectively.

EDUCATION POLICY IN THE UNITED STATES

Theorists have often viewed education as the critical intergenerational link through which social values, traditions, skills, lessons, theories, and practices are conveyed from one generation to the next. Modern society relies increasingly on formal, professionalized educational systems as the primary source for education (Dewey 1944). American education policy has witnessed a persistent increase in support for enhanced access to purposive education provided via formal and professionalized educational organizations. Since the rise of the Progressive Era, the evolution of public education policy toward professionalization has been paralleled by an increase in both the number and variety of demands placed upon public educational institutions (Spring 1986).

During the colonial era, education policy was neither national nor state (colony) controlled. In Puritan New England, the colony's religious leaders controlled formal education. Villages within the colonies operated community schools, and the local minister most often taught classes. The Middle Colonies were a religious polyglot, and conflicts between Catholics and Protestant religious sects were quite prevalent. Generally, each religious group created schools for the children of their adherents. The Southern Colonies primarily consisted of Anglican adherents. Given their close religious and cultural ties with the mother country, they followed the English custom of that time and did not assign the responsibility of education to their colonial governments (Elazar 1994: 104-136). Wealthy families often hired private tutors for their children, while the poor were obliged by colonial law to become apprentices in a trade (Cubberley 1919: 21-22).

In New England and the Middle Colonies, the primary purpose of education was to provide instruction in the rudimentary skills of reading, writing, and arithmetic. Reading was especially important from the standpoint of religious practice as it was requisite for moral instruction via the Bible and other doctrinal writings. Consequently, the course of study was relatively simple, and the illumination of curriculum—through biblical readings—was directly related to moral education, seen to be one of the primary purposes of education.

In the periods immediately prior to and following the Revolutionary War, public school districts began to appear in New England and in the Middle Colonies. The increased flow of immigrants from Northern Europe occasioned the decline of the parochial school model of education. In some places, education was funded by local taxes beginning as early as 1750 (Spring 1986). The movement towards the secularization of education appeared to be well-tailored for the post-Revolutionary War period. Education was increasingly accepted as fundamental to the preservation of participatory democracy in a religiously tolerant yet secular nation.

Generally, boys were given priority in the provision of this basic level of education for at least two reasons. First, it was assumed that men would bring the household into contact with the marketplace. Second, religious traditions placed considerable emphasis on the family as a patriarchy. As women were often expected to be subservient to men in most matters of social import, educational equality was seen as undesirable from the standpoint of the omnipresent need to reinforce male dominance (Manley 1990; Sochen 1974: 73). The patriarch was partially responsible for preserving a moral code within the context of the household, thus necessitating that boys and men develop a stronger sense of morality through education than women (Pulliam 1993).

For the most part, private school options remained the sanctuary of the wealthy in the period following the Revolutionary War. The large-scale implementation of public education options was generally rejected; however, it became increasingly recognized that education potentially served both national and elite interests (Spring 1986). In the post-Revolutionary War period, educational institutions helped to instill a sense of nationalism within students. Education also appeared to serve as a method of political and social control in a traditional society—for men in relation to women, and for economic and political elites in relation to the American bourgeoisie, the proletariat, and the indigent.   With respect to the increasingly prominent nascent immigrant population, purposive education was the primary vehicle for cultural assimilation into the American way of life.

The advent of increased population migration into the Northwest Territories opened a significant policy window for education policy innovation at the national level.   The first large-scale national government-supported elementary education effort came to fruition with the passage of the Northwest Ordinance of 1787, a statute that established federal land grants for the creation of grammar schools in the territories adjacent to the Great Lakes.   While a noteworthy event for public support of education, the legislation was not the harbinger of large-scale state-sponsored public education throughout the United States.   Local movements, such as the charity schools, were more identifiable examples of the evolving role of education in American society.

The charity school movement advanced the notion that education was a public responsibility that should be formalized at the local policymaking level. While private schools had existed prior to the charity school movement, the former schools were often populated by children from middle- and upper-class families. Proponents of charity schools argued that there was a need to provide formal education to youth both for the purposes of the state *and* for the benefits derived by individuals.   Lower class children were seen as potentially falling prey to idleness, and thereby constituting a significant threat to public order— particularly in the nation's burgeoning cities. A formal education offered these children an opportunity to become disciplined, healthy, responsible, and productive members of society.

The establishment of charity schools in the early eighteenth century served at least two general purposes. First, by removing the responsibility for the education of children from the household and immediate community, education as a public responsibility may have gained further legitimacy in the eyes of both government officials and the general citizenry.   The paucity of affordable formal education was viewed as the source of increasingly serious social ills. The broader availability of education was considered to be a function of State power and purpose. Second, by legitimizing a public role in education, State values and goals—as represented by the elite—might be advanced, possibly at the expense of some household values and goals. The evolutionary trends in public policy following in the wake of the charity school and the Academy movements provide evidence that tends to support these conclusions.

While the charity school movement served as a foundation for free and universal public education, the Society for the Promotion of a Rational System of Education, which was established in 1814, is recognized as the groundbreaking effort to establish free schools in urban areas (Cubberley 1919: 89). Education policy historians generally conclude that one of the greatest impediments to the establishment of free schools was the associated cost of providing a universal education. The New York free school movement was successful largely because it claimed to produce, in an economically efficient manner, an educated populace through the use of the Lancasterian system of instruction (in essence, a production-line approach focusing on rote memorization and recitation of lessons).

For the many non-English-speaking denizens of American cities the charity schools and the free schools movement represented further attempts to transmogrify their traditional socialization processes through public education. In the pre-Revolutionary period, a few well-organized cultural groups, such as the Dutch and the Germans who dwelt in Pennsylvania, resisted cultural assimilation through education; nonetheless, the charity school and Academy movements persisted. The Anglicization of many immigrant populations in the United States remained an acceptable goal of public education until the 1960's (Spring 1986: 12; Spring 1976), and remains a central feature in contemporary debates over bilingual education.

The use of education as a tool of forced assimilation was paralleled by efforts to create a more unified education system within the states that extended the goals of the charity school and Academy movements. Dr. Benjamin Rush, for instance, was a leading advocate for the establishment of a unified educational system in the state of Pennsylvania. Unlike the decentralized charity schools and academies, Rush envisioned a hierarchical educational system controlled by the state, with a uniform and highly nationalistic curriculum (Pulliam 1993).

Two general goals emerged from Rush's educational philosophy. First, education was to be recognized as the responsibility of the state as opposed to that of the family. In fact, Rush argued that a uniform curriculum would promote the development of strong, unified communities by inculcating students with a particular conceptualization of good government. Second, the purposes of education were to be expanded substantially beyond the goal of creating cultural uniformity. One of the primary goals of education was to legitimize government at the national and state levels (Pulliam 1984).

Noah Webster is also credited with advancing a nationalistic approach to education. Through lessons printed in his long-popular grammar school speller, Webster sought to reinforce American nationalism, largely through creating and reinforcing American heroes and myths. The values of the American state were studied in near-catechismal form, designed for ease of memorization. Patriotic songs and stories were given great emphasis in the Webster spellers in order to advance further the ideals of national identity.

With the rise of industrialization in the late nineteenth and early twentieth centuries, the goals of moral instruction and the cultivation of civic-minded individuals gradually disappeared from the public school curriculum per se (Cubberly 1919: 45). Greater emphasis was directed toward the development of skills-related curricula and a strong current of utilitarian pragmatism characterized the evolution of American public education during the twentieth century (Spring 1986). Formal public education was increasingly viewed as the palliative for the pains of social change and socioeconomic disparity, while other important "incidental" sources of education (e.g., religious organizations, civic organizations, volunteer organizations, libraries, the elderly, and extended family) were shoved aside or simply ignored (Cremin 1976: 4). The informal relationships established through civic engagement are likely to be the crucial link between the lessons, traditions, myths, values, and beliefs of the past and the maintenance of the strong corral societies of the present and the future (Putnam 1993: 161-162). Nevertheless, society's ability to educate future generations has been diminished by both the celerity of technological advancement and the apparent failure of formal and informal educational processes to remain resolute when confronted with rapid social change. While progress often occurs as a result of technological advancements and the expansion of information, societal advancement is dependent on the successful transmission of theories, values, and traditions to the next generation. These theories, values, and traditions can serve as a social compass with which society—and the individuals within society—can maintain a steady course towards the good society or the good life. Societal advancement, therefore, is the combined product of strong formal *and* informal education systems. The ability to cope with the forces of dynamic change remains one of the central dilemmas facing public education organizations (Lindblom 1991).

ESTABLISHMENT OF CURRICULUM AND PEDAGOGY

Much to the chagrin of "great books" advocates such as Allan Bloom, American public schools have not known the establishment of a uniform traditional curriculum and teaching method. The difficulty in establishing educational uniformity is related to a multitude of factors. The so-called back-to-basics approach to education has not become a dominant force in the educational curriculum. Early curricula were largely the product of limited resources and limited demands upon educational systems. Since the advent of the Pestalozzian theories on education and those of other reformers, namely Hebert and Froebel who were prominent pedagogical theorists in the middle and late nineteenth century, public education curricula have expanded significantly (Cubberley 1919). This initial expansion was partially the result of new theories of how learning occurs and the delineation of new goals for education, many of which first emerged from Rousseau's *Èmile*. The Progressive Era reforms also resulted in curriculum expansion to include the development of urban technical high schools (polytechnics) (Spring 1986).

In *Traditions of American Education* (1976), Lawrence Cremin argues that the Progressive Era view of education—which continues to influence the current education policy debate—is perhaps best characterized by the principles laid out in John Dewey's *Democracy and Education* (1944). Dewey's primary assumption is that education can be divided into two different types: incidental and purposive. Incidental education is best characterized as the informal learning processes that occur in informal education settings, such as work, social organizations, and political parties. Dewey implicitly concludes that each of these settings of incidental education contains an educative function, but the primary purpose of the setting is not education. Purposive education, however, is that which occurs in the formal educational setting of the school. Dewey believed that society should direct its primary focus towards purposive education. Purposive education via public education is more likely to be responsive to public policymaking innovations than is incidental education. Cremin takes issue with Dewey, arguing that education must be studied in a holistic manner.

Cremin's inclusive education approach represents an important crossroads for education theory. Given that the education literature of the last century largely emerges from the Deweyan approach, goal enlargement in formal education is quite possibly the logical result of identifying schools as the primary locale for purposive education. Conversely, Cremin's decidedly multi-dimensional definition of education serves to reduce the expectations placed on formal educators and increase expectations of community institutions.

Given an awareness of the multiplicity of institutions that educate, one soon perceives the tendency of such institutions at particular times and places to relate to one another in what might be called configurations. Each of the institutions interacts with the others and with the larger society and that is in turn affected by it. (Cremin 1976: 30)

In the latter approach to education theory it would be necessary to study the strengths of numerous "educational" institutions in a given school district in order to determine the strengths and weaknesses of purposive educational organizations. A commitment to formal education would likely be reflected in a commitment to community organizations within the school district, and vice versa.

The foundation of Cremin's (1976: 37) argument lies in the role of education organizations as social adaptation or "coping" organizations, regularly responding to the ever-changing community social and economic needs through adaptable curricula and pedagogy. In the eighteenth and nineteenth centuries, Americans were more likely to turn to their families or to the church as coping organizations. Cremin argues that in the nineteenth and twentieth centuries, Americans have increasingly turned to the public school as an important coping organization within their communities. This shift might reflect the increasing complexity of our modern high technology world and the close relationship between formal training and social and economic security. Cremin approaches education policy as neither a sophist nor as a Jeffersonian. Rather, his intention is to simply redefine education so as to delineate fairly strict limits for the expectations placed upon formal public education agencies and organizations.

The argument that education organizations serve an important adaptation or "coping" function in the communities in which they are located is consistent with arguments made by organizational theorists as well. Michael Katz's *Class, Bureaucracy, and Schools* (1975) follows a similar line of argument in developing an *ecological approach* to education. His findings suggest that variations in curriculum and pedagogy do not appear to offer a complete explanation for educational outcomes. Rather, the conditions surrounding the formal educational institution and the structure of that institution are significant determinants of institutional performance.

THE COMMON SCHOOL MOVEMENT

The Common School movement represents the most important public policy innovation in the development of the contemporary public school system. The philosophical arguments of the advocates of the charity school and Academy movements and the poignant contributions of Benjamin Rush constituted a firm foundation for the Common School movement in the United States. The work of Horace Mann, generally recognized as the founder of the Common School movement, however, went several steps beyond the work of his erstwhile predecessors. While it could be argued that the Common School movement is an example of the incremental evolution of education policy, there are many principles which emanate from Mann's efforts that could be viewed as rather revolutionary for the time period in which his policy proposals emerged.

According to Joel Spring (1986), there were three key elements of Mann's thought that gave shape to the Common School movement. First, Mann envisioned a public school system in which children of all levels of society would be educated in a common schoolhouse. This principle was rather progressive for the 1830's, when "public" schools were generally charity schools for the lower classes, and families of means sent their children to private schools. The Common School was seen as representing an appropriate effort towards social equality and the creation of cross-class ties and affections. Second, the Common School was to serve as a powerful tool of socialization for the State, allowing it to promote its policy goals and objectives (e.g., national identity, training in civic affairs, inculcation of the work ethic, etc.) through education. Third, local schools were to be created and controlled by state agencies. While local schools would have some element of self-governance, state regulations would take precedence in most curricular and pedagogical matters in order to ensure a considerable degree of commonality in curriculum and educational practices.

Apologists for the Common School movement often point to the interpretation of the post-Civil War working-class view of the public school system. The Common School system offered a basic education to all non-minority children regardless of their families' socioeconomic condition. For many individuals (e.g., sons of the working class and many women of all classes), the public education system which emerged from the Common School movement led to greater political, social, and economic efficacy for many Americans who lacked the means to attend private schools.

The provision of state-sponsored education may have been partially responsible for the advancement of working-class issues during the period between the post-Civil War era and the Progressive era. Increased literacy rates and the declining cost of print media gave the working class greater access to timely political, economic, and social information. The development of unions further advanced working class political efficacy. Spring (1986) argues that spokesmen for the working class were well aware of the critical role state-sponsored education was playing in their efforts to improve the political, social, and economic status of workers in the American free enterprise system.

PROGRESSIVE ERA CONTRIBUTIONS

Spring (1986) argues that education policy during the Progressive Era reflected the desire to use the power of the state to moderate the inequities that stem from unfettered capitalism. Social scientific research on social stratification generally indicates that educational opportunity for the individual is a solid predictor of future socioeconomic success, especially within the context of high economic and technological specialization symptomatic of the modern world. While historians of education would generally agree that public education continued, with varying degrees of success, to fulfill its role as a primary means of cultural indoctrination, pedagogy increasingly came to reflect the training needs of the specialized nature of increasingly bureaucratized private and public sector employers of labor. A cardinal belief of reformers such as John Dewey (1944) was that educational opportunity would result in greater economic and social equity for the sons and daughters of the working class, sustaining a critically important sense that societal fairness would prevail (the "level of opportunity") over the evident social and economic inequities of the day over the long run.

One of the methods employed during this period to improve public school performance was the importation of business management strategies into the public sector for purposes of achieving efficiency, accountability, and morality. Frederick Winslow Taylor's (1911) testimony before Congress on the principles of scientific management was indicative of the belief that the routinization of human activity in the realm of work (and schools) would lead to greater efficiency in the public sector and hence the more cost-effective and successful implementation of public policy. The movement towards greater professionalization in public service was introduced at the national, state, and local level with varying degrees of success. Nevertheless, the promotion of professionalization was motivated to a considerable degree by an attempt to foster ethical behavior on the part of individual public servants and to further advance the ideals of bureaucracy and the promise of effective governance of public school organizations.

Education policy during the Progressive Era (c.1896-c.1920) was largely shaped by political elites who envisioned universal public education as the key to maintaining the extant capitalist system, the existing power structure, and the established social structure of the nation in the face of rapid demographic and technological change. In that regard, the further professionalization of school administration through the development of a relatively immutable hierarchy was adopted by many school districts. As a closed system of organization, one of the intended effects of such a hierarchy is to maintain the status quo, or at least to provide for only limited top-down reforms within organizations (Weber 1946; Thompson 1961).

The professionalization of American teachers was a long overdue educational reform. For most of the nineteenth century primary and secondary educators possessed only minimal levels of education. Educators were seldom paid salaries sufficient to encourage the development of a sense of professionalism, hence the field tended to attract primarily academically minded males who had failed to succeed in the private sector and young women seeking employment outside of the home. Education policy innovations at the secondary level and at the collegiate level—partially accomplished through the establishment of teachers' colleges—in the late-nineteenth and early-twentieth centuries resulted in the greater professionalization of teachers and of the teaching profession generally.

THE COLD WAR ERA

Primarily political and economic forces drove the education reform efforts of the 1950's and early 1960's. The launching of Sputnik I gave greater currency to the belief that the Cold War was both a political and a technological struggle. The National Defense Education Act (NDEA) of 1958 served as clear affirmation that a high technology world would demand a highly educated populace. The Cold War era education policies were grounded in the argument that education was part of a strategically guided and empirically measurable social, economic, and political weapon (Spring 1976). The reforms of this period were generally characterized by top-down, rigidly uniform approaches to increasing student achievement, with particular emphasis being placed on improved student performance in the areas of mathematics and science.

The late 1960's and the 1970's witnessed an elevated recognition of the plethora of pressures that have come to bear on American education. Standardized test scores, which had initially risen following the passage and implementation of the NDEA in 1958, began to decline. Many academics, education policymakers, school administrators, and teachers increasingly questioned the wisdom and desirability of further top-down efforts to improve student performance.

In addition to this concern, the education reform efforts following the *Brown* decision in 1954 were not delivering on the promise that desegregated schools would provide equal educational opportunities for historically disenfranchised minority groups. The political atmosphere surrounding efforts at desegregation was highly charged, in many cases acting as an obstacle to effective policymaking. American education went through a substantial period of self-doubt and seemingly fruitless, repeated problem identification efforts (Spring 1976; Wynn and Wynn 1991).

The Ford Foundation study (Meade 1972) and the National Commission on Excellence in Education Report, *A Nation at Risk* (1983), arguably provide the primary bases of the two general streams of the "second wave" reform efforts that developed in the 1980's (Wynn and Wynn 1991). The Ford Foundation study concluded that education problems could not be solved simply through efforts directed at internal school reform. The report, a culmination of a twenty-year effort to experiment with innovative school reform, concluded that there was a need to recognize the heterogeneous nature of both social problems and cultural diversity which students bring with them to school from their family and their community. The foundation's conclusion was that schools were best looked upon as just one element of broader societal problems, and student achievement was affected more by the health of our families and communities than by the character of school programs being offered.

PRIVATIZATION ALTERNATIVES: THE 1980's TO THE PRESENT

Advocates of market-based reform often employ the work of Milton Friedman (1955), who argued that the virtual monopoly position of public schools unwisely and unnecessarily limited individual freedom. Instead of promoting equality, the system encouraged inequality inasmuch as only wealthier individuals could freely exercise their freedom to exit the public school system by attending private schools. While Friedman recognized that government should require a minimum level of education for the purpose of preserving an understanding of regime norms and values, he argued that educational requirements beyond that goal hampered individual spirit and initiative. Friedman insisted that a free market approach would enlarge the scope of individual choice and promote freedom, equity, and efficient service delivery in virtually every area of economic life, particularly education.

A Nation at Risk (1983) provided the basis for a renewed emphasis on alternative methods of dealing with declining educational achievement in America. While the report concluded that there was a need for more stringent educational requirements and a return to some of the top-down themes of an earlier time period, a great deal of reflection and criticism of education reforms during the previous twenty years was featured in the study. While the report did not emphasize the privatization movement cultivated by Friedman (1955), it is quite possible that it generated a sense of urgency within the education policy arena, thereby rekindling discussion of privatization as a legitimate and acceptable policy innovation.

The Reagan administration, generally supportive of a devolution of power to the states and local governments, went a step further with education policy by recommending a school voucher method of finance (Linowes 1988). President Reagan believed that by leaving educational choice up to parents, local efforts to address poor school performance would lead to the proliferation of educational options for parents to consider. The Report of the President's Commission on Privatization, entitled *Privatization: Toward More Effective Government* (Linowes 1988), emphasized the need to form contracts with private sector industries for the provision of particular government services (e.g., prison construction and management) while still retaining a large degree of power over the contractees. In the case of education, however, this oversight function was not discussed, nor was the notion of the semi-privatization of ancillary services.

Different motivations for advocating school choice tend to reflect different expected outcomes resulting from choice. Some observers have argued that these reforms might lead to confusion and disappointment for those individuals viewing choice as a panacea for the perceived ills of the public school system (Honig 1994; Dougherty and Sostre 1992). Without entering into a full discussion of the various manifestations of privatization in education, it is important to mention a few of the most prominent alternatives proffered.

The voucher system is possibly the most revolutionary approach to market-based reform of the public education system. In its ideal form, parents would be able to use a state-provided education *voucher* to send their children to any public or private school of their choice. *Charter schools* operate under more restricted conditions, with stipulations in their state charter regarding expected educational outcomes. Finally, *magnet schools* are public schools that operate on a semi-competitive basis with other public schools; they are given greater flexibility in their curricula, operations and teaching methods than conventional schools.

THE CONTEMPORARY EDUCATION POLICY DEBATE: DO PUBLIC SCHOOLS WORK EFFECTIVELY?

Private School Advocates: Public Schools Don't Work

The philosophical grounding upon which privatization proponents toil was meticulously prepared nearly three decades earlier by economist Milton Friedman. Attaining the Nobel Prize in Economics for his work in *Capitalism and Freedom* (1955), Friedman's work is related to the ideas of the twentieth century European economists Ludwig von Mises and Friedrich Hayek. Based on their first-hand observations of European socialism and totalitarianism, von Mises and Hayek warned that the enlarged role of the state in social and economic planning would lead to the erosion of personal freedom and the destruction of liberal democratic institutions. In his now classic 1955 treatise *Capitalism and Freedom*, Friedman meticulously delineated an economic argument that stood solidly against the perpetuation of the public school education monopoly and proposed the need for greater educational choice made possible through privatization. Parents and students would be able to pursue their individual benefit through the selection of a curriculum best suited to meet their needs, at a price that would be determined by supply and demand.

While James Q. Wilson (1989) arrives at a conclusion similar to Chubb and Moe (1990), the foundation of his argument rests to a large degree on the organizational nature of public schools. His central argument is that "organization matters" in the assessment of public policy processes and outcomes. "Organization matters, even in government agencies. The key difference between more and less successful bureaucracies...has less to do with finances, client populations, or legal arrangements than with organizational systems" (Wilson 1989: 23).

Wilson is interested in determining how different types of public organizations cope with the environmental forces that may shape organizational performance and outputs. Additionally, Wilson argues that a successful public organization possesses the ability to coordinate its internal activities and focus individual and subgroup efforts on a central goal. Wilson concludes that the success of a public organization can largely be contributed to its ability to deal effectively with three central organizational concerns:

First, each had to decide how to perform its *critical task*. . .not goals. . . . The second challenge overcome by these organizations was agreement about and widespread (if not enthusiastic) endorsement of the way the critical task was defined. When that definition is widely accepted and endorsed, we say that the organization has a sense of *mission*. . . . The third problem that each organization had to solve was to acquire freedom of action and external political support (or at least nonopposition) to permit it to redefine its tasks as it saw best to infuse that definition with a sense of mission. Each organization managed to acquire a reasonable degree of *autonomy*. (Wilson 1989: 25-26)

Wilson believes that the effective organization requires a stable power base and a sense of mission if it is to operate effectively. At least two hypotheses emerge from these conclusions. First, Wilson hypothesizes that effective public schools require a supportive community whose education goals are relatively homogeneous. A second hypothesis that emerges is that effective public schools require strong internal leadership to craft a coherent sense of mission from internally and externally generated goals. Wilson argues that public schools often do not have a strong sense of mission because they operate in environments in which goals are often inchoate and conflicting. "Government executives must spend so much time coping with their agencies' external environment that they have relatively little time to shape its internal life" (Wilson 1989: 32). Wilson hypothesizes that in organizations that lack a strong sense of mission, "circumstances become important" (Wilson 1989: 36).

According to Wilson, changing circumstances set up an entirely different organizational dynamic. Unpredictable circumstances appear to be anathema to the development of strong and consistent organizational goals and shared sense of mission. For those organizations whose operations are heavily dependent on circumstances, vague and ad hoc "tasks" replace goals as the basis of organizational activity (Wilson 1989: 33). Wilson is critical of public organizations that operate on the basis of vague tasks, which may not be consistent with the goals defined by the organization or with the objectives established by elected officials to which the public organization is legally accountable. Organizational activity may become circumstance-sensitive, and as a consequence difficult to assess in a uniform manner. Public schools fall into his category of organizations that are not likely to be held accountable for their activities.

A government agency . . . is usually a monopoly provider of some service and is supported by a legislative appropriation that is paid for by taxes extracted from citizens who may or may not benefit from that agency. The tasks of operators in private organizations with vague goals become defined through a process by trial and error and internal negotiation that is then tested by competitive natural selection. Some organizations prosper, others merely survive, still others fail. The tasks of operators in government agencies with vague goals are probably set in much the same way, but without a regular test of the fitness of the solution. (Wilson 1989: 33)

A central argument which emerges from this passage in relation to public organizations operating with vague goals (e.g., public schools) is that they are not held accountable effectively because they are not subject to the competitive forces of the marketplace. This argument could be tested by exploring the effect of the presence of private schools on their public school counterparts. Do public schools respond to the competition afforded by private schools within public school districts? One way of exploring this question would be through an analysis of public school student achievement at the school district level, controlling for private school enrollment within the district. Alternative methods of exploring the extent of accountability of public schools would be to study the level of support of voters for public school districts on support levies or on ballot initiatives favoring the privatization of elementary and secondary education.

Schools are unique because the "products" of this type of organization are the individuals who attend; these matriculated students are not simply inanimate widgets, but rather are complexly motivated social actors. Arguably, students may be viewed as part of the school organization. They are subject to many of the same standards as the classified employees in schools: entrance to particular grades—similar to organizational sub-units—is subject to examination, and promotion is made on the basis of merit. Disciplinary activity is subject to a hearing process. Additionally, if learning is viewed as an active process, students play an integral role in determining the organizational outputs. Because students are viewed as organizational members, their expectations of the school may play an integral part in organizational output.

While the philosophical ideals underlying the conservative argument were provided by the work of prominent twentieth-century economists, the empirical evidence has been most prominently provided by two well-known political scientists. In *Politics, Markets, and America's Schools* (1990), John Chubb and Terry Moe argue that "all schools are shaped in overt and subtle ways by their institutional settings, and that the kinds of organizations they become and how effectively they perform are largely functions of the institutional contexts in which they operate" (2). The authors contend that prior to the Progressive Era reforms, public school districts were relatively autonomous. The schools within these school districts were largely shaped by the communities in which they operated. Education was a partnership between the school organization and the parents of the school children. The result was a well-coordinated educational process that responded well to individual needs (Chubb and Moe 1990: 3).

The Progressive Era reforms forever altered the relationship between the school and the community. Public schools no longer operated within the context of majoritarian politics, and responded far less effectively and directly to the needs of the local community. Public schools became much more the product of elite politics, at that time a largely white Anglo-Saxon Protestant elite that sought to eliminate what it saw as the nefarious influences of the uneducated mass public and to secure education policy in the hands of a few enlightened professional educators and administrators (Chubb and Moe 1990: 4). The presumed "principles" of scientific management served as the basis of both curriculum and pedagogical development, and a rigid bureaucracy was placed atop the school district hierarchy and the state offices of public education to limit the threat of political influence.

Chubb and Moe observe that state and federal education bureaucracies continue to maintain what they perceive to be an ossified and ineffective public education monopoly that limits the ability of the nation's schools to respond to the needs of local communities. The authors indicate that a public education elite—namely, teachers' unions, private businesses, and public bureaucrats— continues to dictate what constitutes locally delivered public education. The result of this trend has been an arguably bloated education bureaucracy; a curriculum and pedagogy that sharply deviate from community desires; and declining performance as judged from student test scores. In short, Chubb and Moe argue that public schools act to simply maintain their control over the educational experiences of the vast majority of America's youth and have lost sight of their primary purpose—namely, promoting academic achievement.

The elite control of public education was not effectively challenged until American business leaders began in large numbers to support education reform as an important solution to their decline in economic competitiveness. The report of the National Commission on Excellence in Education released during the Reagan presidency in 1983, which had the support of many American business leaders, concluded that public education was largely failing to produce desired academic outcomes. Often referred to as the Coleman Report, the study commission's members concluded that academic excellence was largely explained by parental education rather than by how schools did the job of educating. The purpose of the schools was to maintain order in the education process and establish high standards for student achievement in traditional subject areas such as reading and mathematics. Public schools would have to refocus their organizational goals, placing order as a top priority.

Chubb and Moe (1990) argue that public schools are not likely to respond effectively to this need for institutional change. They argue that schools should be open systems that respond to the needs of the community in which they operate. Public school bureaucracy in the Progressive Era paradigm of expertise-determined policy is not designed to encourage schools to consider their environments as primary factors in curricular and pedagogical practice decisions; the bureaucracy was intended by-and-large to displace public opinion from the education policy process (Bryk et al. 1997).

Chubb and Moe (1990) conclude that the optimum solution to the problems facing American education is to be found in market-based policies. The competition of the marketplace would likely ensure that schools would become responsive to their clientele—namely, parents and their school-aged children. The widespread privatization of education is also believed to produce the outcome of eliminating what Chubb and Moe (1990) see as an entrenched public education bureaucracy, properly returning education policymaking to individual citizens and their communities.

Chubb and Moe (1990: 35-38) contend that private school administration would not pursue bureaucratization as a method of producing efficient education. They hypothesize that greater teacher autonomy would produce improved student achievement, and that bureaucracy would only serve to impede teacher autonomy. Second, private schools would have to respond to parental input if they were to retain their students. The authors argue that the development of bureaucratic structures would likely undermine the critical parent-school relationship.

Conversely, public schools are designed to restrict parental input and promote a uniform curriculum and an established pedagogy. Public school bureaucracy serves to diminish the effects of public input on school operations. Bureaucracy also serves to limit the effects of federal and state government education policy. The authors conclude that school district bureaucracy is too often self-serving, defining its own survival as the paramount goal of collective action rather than serving their clientele (Chubb and Moe 1990: 38-41).

While they argue that public schools are bureaucracies seeking to preserve their organizational power and autonomy, Chubb and Moe (1990: 48-53) indicate that school administrators have limited ability to control their personnel. Union efforts to formalize personnel administration have contributed to larger school administration and have detracted from the goal of promoting academic excellence. School administrators and teachers do not function as a unified "team" (Chubb and Moe 1990: 51). The authors conclude that there is very little organizational incentive to develop strong leadership in public schools; organizational goals are commonly defined by powerful unions and public policymakers, and large central administrative organizations too often limit individual administrator and teacher autonomy (Chubb and Moe 1990: 53-60).

When public schools are faced with intense external pressure to respond to a perceived social ill, they will often formalize the issue by creating a new bureaucratic unit to deal with the problem. Chubb and Moe (1990: 63) argue that the formalization inspired by external pressures is often a form of organizational rent-seeking behavior, which is consistent with public choice critiques of public administration (e.g., William Niskanen).

Chubb and Moe hypothesize that the bureaucratization of schools is related to the nature and magnitude of the "problems" (e.g., poverty, limited English proficiency, and student drug use) with which they must deal. They argue that urban schools are much more likely to experience problems than are suburban or rural school districts. With limited bureaucratization, the authors argue that suburban and rural schools are more likely to be "effective school organizations" (Chubb and Moe 1990: 65).

Public School Apologists: Public Schools Can and Do Work

In their polemic, *The Case Against School Choice: Politics, Markets, and Fools* (1995), Kevin Smith and Kenneth Meier conduct a quite exhaustive critique of Chubb and Moe (1990). The authors argue that while school choice advocates claim market-based approaches to elementary and secondary education, school choice is actually a generic term for a plethora of reform alternatives. There is no clear evidence that any or all of these approaches will lead to improved student achievement. Smith and Meier are, consequently, skeptical of the claims of school choice proposals outlined by Chubb and Moe (Smith and Meier 1995: 12-13).

Taking a macro-level approach to analyzing public school organizations, Smith and Meier (1995: 47-61) find that competition between public and private schools results in a creaming effect. In other words, socioeconomic status will act to constrain the school choices of individual students. Poor students will generally remain in free public schools, while students from wealthier families will be more likely to attend private schools. This phenomenon has the effect of producing educational inequities for many minority students, who hail disproportionately from families with lower socioeconomic status.

Smith and Meier found that public school reforms in the 1980's— reforms made in the wake of the Coleman Report—appear to have had a positive influence on student achievement. Teacher certification, curriculum mandates and graduation tests are positively related to improved student achievement. "Contrary to the claims of school choice advocates, the controlling institutions of education seem to be making successful attempts to improve performance. The gains are not dramatic, and they certainly stop short of being a cure-all. Nonetheless, the reforms appear to be working" (Smith and Meier 1995: 91). The authors conclude that Chubb and Moe are likely to have been incorrect in concluding that: a) "bureaucratization" has had a deleterious effect upon student performance; and b) competition will have a positive effect on student achievement. The privatization advocates fail to account for the creaming effect in their analyses.

CONCLUSION

The current education policy debate focuses squarely on the issue of privatization alternatives, such as school vouchers and charter schools. The commodification of elementary and secondary education is gaining in popularity, which can be interpreted as a sign that public schools are losing their legitimacy in the minds of policymakers and the general public. Public schools are being judged primarily on the basis of outputs without a thorough understanding of the process-related issues involved. The primary goal of this book is to discuss in macro-organizational terms the organizational processes associated with public school districts. It is my contention that contingency theory—a variant of general open systems theory—provides a solid foundation upon which to model public school organizational behavior. I will employ four general categories of quantitative data in the analysis: financial data, personnel data, organization environmental characteristics data, and standardized examination score data.   It is my contention that at the macro level, organizational goals and processes can best be understood in terms of the prioritization of money and personnel, given various theoretically relevant constraints on the organization.

WORKS CITED

Brofenbrenner, U. 1961. "The Changing American Child—A Speculative Analysis," *Journal of Social Issues*. 17(1): 6-17.

Bryk, A., Easton, J., Rollow, S., and Sabring, P. 1997. *Charting School Reform in Chicago: Democracy as a Lever for Change*.   Boulder, CO: Westview Press.

Chubb, J. and Moe, T.   1990.   *Politics, Markets, and America's Schools*. Washington, DC: The Brookings Institution.

Coleman, J. 1990.   *Equality and Educational Opportunity*.   Boulder, CO: Westview Press.

Cremin, L. 1976. *Traditions of American Education*. New York: Basic Books.

Cubberley, E. 1919.   *Public Education in the United States: A Study and Interpretation of American Educational History*.   Boston, MA: Houghton Mifflin.

Dewey, J. 1944. *Democracy and Education*, Second Edition. New York: Free Press.

Dougherty, K. and Sostre, L.1992. "Minerva and the Market: The Sources for the Movement for School Choice," in P. Cookson (ed.), *The Choice Controversy*. Newbury Park, CA: Corwin Press, 24-45.

Elazar, D. 1994. *The American Mosaic: The Impact of Space, Time, and Culture on American Politics*. Boulder, CO: Westview Press.

Friedman, M. 1955. *Capitalism and Freedom*.   Chicago, IL: University of Chicago Press.

Greenstein, F. 1994. *The Hidden Hand Presidency: Eisenhower as President*. Baltimore, MD: Johns Hopkins University Press.

Hayek, F. 1944. *The Road to Serfdom: A Classic Warning Against the Dangers to Freedom Inherent in Social Planning*. Chicago, IL: University of Chicago Press.

Honig, B. 1994. *Last Chance for Our Children*. New York: St. Martin's Press.

Katz, M. 1975. *Class, Bureaucracy, and Schools*. New York: Praeger.

Lindblom, C. 1991.   *Inquiry and Change: The Troubled Attempts to Understand and Shape Society*. New Haven, CT: Yale University Press.

Linowes, D. 1988.   *Privatization: Toward More Effective Government*. Washington, DC: President's Commission on Privatization.

Linton, R. 1969. "Society, Culture and the Individual," in J. Johnson, H. Collins, V. DuPuis, and J. Johanson (eds.), *Foundations of American Education*. Boston, MA: Allyn & Bacon, 9-19.

Manley, J. 1990. "American Liberalism and the Democratic Dream: Transcending the American Dream," *Policy Studies Review*. 10(1): 89-102.

Meade, E. 1972. *A Foundation Goes to School: The Ford Foundation Comprehensive School Improvement Program 1960-1970*. New York: Ford Foundation.

Murray, C. 1983. *Losing Ground: American Social Policy 1950-1980*. New York: Basic Books.

National Commission on Excellence in Education. 1983. *A Nation at Risk*. Washington, DC: U.S. Government Printing Office.

Pulliam, R. 1993. *History of Education in America*, Third Edition. Columbus, OH: Charles E. Merrill.

Putnam, R. 1993. *Making Democracy Work: Civic Traditions in Modern Italy*. Princeton, NJ: Princeton University Press.

Rothstein, R. 1998. *The Way We Were? The Myths and Realities of America's Student Achievement*. New York: Century Foundation Press.

Smith, K. and Meier, K. 1995. *The Case Against School Choice: Politics, Markets, and Fools*. Armonk: M. E. Sharpe.

Sochen, J. 1974. *Her Story*. New York, NY: Alfred Press.

Spring, J. 1976. *The Sorting Machine: National Education Policy Since 1945*. New York: David McKay, Co.

———— 1986. *The American School: 1642-1985*. New York: Longman.

Taylor, F. 1911. *The Principles of Scientific Management*. New York: Harper.

Thompson, V. 1961. *Modern Organizations*. New York: Alfred Knopf.

Von Mises, L. 1981. *Socialism*, Second Edition. Indianapolis, IN: Liberty Fund.

Weber, M. 1946. "Bureaucracy," in H. Gerth and C. Mills (eds.), *From Max Weber: Essays in Sociology*. New York: Oxford University Press, 196-244.

Wilson, J. 1989. *Bureaucracy: What Government Agencies Do and Why They Do It*. New York: Basic Books.

Wynn, R. and Wynn, J. 1991. *American Education*, Ninth Edition. New York: Harper & Row.

Chapter 2

Organization Theory and Public School District Organization

INTRODUCTION

One dilemma that faces scholars interested in studying public school district organization is the task of choosing a theoretical lens through which to analyze organizational behavior and outcomes (Meehan 1994; Forester 1993; Stone 1988). Dwight Waldo (1948) argued that the apparent success or failure of nearly any public enterprise will vary in accordance with the theoretical expectations defined by the researcher. In studying public school districts, the choice of theoretical lenses often involves either the adoption or the casting aside of much normative baggage attached to a particular theory.

James Q. Wilson (1989) and John Chubb and Terry Moe (1990) ground much of their respective analyses of public school organizations in classical, modern, and public choice theories of public organizations. The assumptions in which those theoretical traditions are grounded appear to have had a significant effect on the conclusions drawn by these respected scholars. Wilson concludes that the bureaucratic model is the ideal organizational design for public organizations, limiting external influences and concentrating organizational energies on maintaining internal order and goal accomplishment. Chubb and Moe argue that public school organizations are rent-seeking organizations captured by powerful interests, whose primary functions are to react and adapt to the ephemeral and oftentimes unmanageable demands placed upon them. If the bureaucratic model is the ideal organizational model for public organizations, and public schools are largely incapable of operating under such a model, privatization is the preferred alternative for these public choice theorists.

Kevin Smith and Kenneth Meier (1994, 1995) adopt a different approach to public school district organization. These scholars ground their work in open systems theories of public organization. While consistent with Wilson's (1989) 'coping' organization model, Smith and Meier find that public schools have been largely successful in their efforts to react to the demands emerging from their organizational environment. Interests and circumstances have not weakened public school district organizations' ability to serve their clientele; rather, they have enhanced schools' ability to act in a rational manner and fulfill their prescribed goals and tasks.

As noted earlier, these disparate approaches to theories of public school district organization are to some degree grounded in normative arguments based upon different assumptions of the duties of the state in relation to the citizenry. Theorists such as James Q. Wilson, and to some degree John Chubb and Terry Moe, argue that the central purpose of the government is to establish and maintain an orderly society. They conclude that order is a regulative goal generally accepted by all rational members of society. As such, institutions promoting order can with some ease adopt and maintain a bureaucratic organizational design. Alternatively, public education policies can be alternately described as distributive or redistributive and are less amenable to bureaucratic organizational design due to the ephemeral pluralistic forces shaping organizational behavior and goals (Lowi 1969). The public choice theorists conclude that public education policy is anathema to the development of their notion of the good society, and is rightly handled by the private sector on the basis of free exchange of fees for services.

Smith and Meier (1994, 1995) take the role of public school apologists, whose findings support their underlying normative conclusions. Unlike Chubb and Moe (1990), the authors do not find that pluralism has resulted in nonrational public education policy. Instead, they argue that the input of interests—such as teachers' unions and the inclusion of disabled students—has resulted in improved public education. Smith and Meier (1995) stand vehemently opposed to the possibly nonegalitarian outcomes of school choice, implicitly accepting public schools as legitimate mechanisms of economic and social redistributive policy. Their acceptance of public schools as legitimate open systems organizations quite possibly reflects their normative foundation as much as their confidence in their empirical studies.

At least four possibilities can be deduced from this particular situation entailing competing theoretical approaches and sharply conflicting claims. First, it is possible that the public choice scholars are correct in their analyses of public school districts. A second possibility is that public school apologists are correct in describing public school districts as open systems. A third possibility is that both theoretical approaches have merit. Finally, it might be the case that both approaches are incorrect and it is necessary to search for alternative models of public school district organizations to understand their behavior, account for their performance, and offer appropriate prescriptions.

At this point, it is necessary to discuss the theoretical grounding of the two approaches outlined above. It will be argued that historical developments in public education policy reflect both theoretical approaches to a considerable degree. Second, alternative organization models that might be pertinent to our analyses will be discussed. Generally, public school district organizations can be described through a combination of organization models.

ORGANIZATION DEFINED

The presence of different approaches to the study of public school district organizations is partially a product of the availability of different definitions of organizations in the social science literature. Those who take a *rational design* view of organizations define the organization largely in terms of the goals that have been defined for any particular organization. W. Richard Scott (1981: 20) identifies two major characteristics of rational design organizations. First, such organizations are oriented toward "specific goals" and are highly "formalized." With well-defined goals, the rational design organization is capable of creating a formal organization that can best accomplish these goals. While definitions of rational design organizations generally recognize the existence of individuals within the organization, they are inclined to assume that the individual's goals do not play a particularly noteworthy active role in organizational behavior. A rational organization is "a collectivity oriented to the pursuit of relatively specific goals and exhibiting a relatively highly formalized social structure" (Scott 1981: 21).

Not all definitions of organization assume that the organization is capable of maintaining clearly defined goals accomplished through formal structures. *Natural systems* approaches to organization reflect the assumption that individuals within organizations and the informal patterns of behavior which they adopt shape organizational goals and outcomes to a substantial degree. A natural systems definition of organization is "a collectivity whose participants arc little affcctcd by thc formal structure or official goals but who share a common interest in the survival of the system and who engage in collective activities informally structured, to secure this end" (Scott 1981: 22).

A third definition outlined by Scott is the *open systems* definition of organization. Open systems models of organization reflect the belief that organizational goals are generally not uniform and stable. Open systems models of organizational goals are largely derived from demands emerging from interests existing within the organizational environment and from organizational personnel. According to Scott (1981: 22-23) an open systems definition of organization holds that an organization can be thought of as "a coalition of shifting interest groups that develop goals by negotiation; the structure of the coalition, its activities, and its outcomes are strongly influenced by environmental factors."

In his book *Organizations: Structure and Process* (1977), Richard H. Hall offers two definitions of organization. One definition is grounded in the rational Weberian approach to organization. From Weber, Hall (1977: 18-19) deduces that the rational organization is both "corporate" and "associative." In other words, rational organizations are formalistic and feature goals that "transcend the lives of their members" (Hall 1977: 19). The second definition of organization emerges from Chester I. Barnard's *Functions of the Executive* (1938). Barnard sees organizations as systems made up of individuals whose diverse interests and goals must be taken into consideration by the organization. As Hall (1977: 19-20) concludes, this second approach conceptualizes organizations as cooperative bodies, instead of "associative" entities, whose membership is assumed to adopt organizational goals willingly.

Hall's approach to defining organization is divided along the lines of rational formalistic approaches and human relations approaches. The author's approach is slightly different than Scott's (1981), and introduces a slightly different perspective on the nature of open systems. Scott places a great deal of emphasis on the role of the environment in the formation of organizational goals. Hall considers the nature of the employee/employer relationship and the nature of informal organizations that exist within formal organizations. This latter point is important to our later discussion of schools as loosely coupled systems because it relates to the ability (or lack thereof) of a formal organizational authority to evoke a desired response from subordinates. Barnard's approach implies that formal authority has relatively little to do with the ability to evoke a particular response, and that informal norms and bargaining play a much more significant role in explaining organizational behavior in many organizational settings.

Hall's definition of organization incorporates elements of both the Weberian and Barnardian schools. Most organizations are semi-formal structures, but they are not rationally designed closed systems.

An organization is a collectivity with a relatively identifiable boundary, a normative order, ranks of authority, communication systems and membership-coordinating systems; this collectivity exists on a relatively continuous basis in an environment and engages in activities that are usually related to a goal or a set of goals. (Hall 1977: 23)

Hall's definition represents a synthesis of the definitions of organization presented thus far. The definition implies that organizations exist on a continuum between entirely closed systems and entirely open systems. Organizations will, on their own accord, move along this continuum given the state of their environment and the inherent characteristics of informal organizations. In other words, Hall considers organizations to be dynamic, and believes that they must be defined and studied with this assumption in mind.

Scott and Hall offer us two distinct approaches to the study of organizations. Scott's three distinct definitions of organization accommodate an analysis of the two different approaches to analyzing public school district organization and outputs presented in the first chapter of this book. Such analysis is important if we wish to determine the strengths and weaknesses of the two approaches and make judgments regarding their relative conclusions. Alternatively, Hall's synthesized definition—while clearly leaning toward the open system approach—provides us with the ability to study the variation of public school organizations and see schools as dynamic organizations seeking to both maintain their formal structure and simultaneously to respond to the demands emerging from their environment and indigenous informal organizations. Hall's definition is consistent with that of Bacharach (1981), who argues that analysis of public school district organizations must consider the formal organizational structure *and* the influence of the organizational environment on organizational outputs analyzed in public school research.

To a large extent, the variation in these three definitions is due to different arguments regarding: (a) the relationship between an organization and its environments; (b) the ability of an organization to rationalize its goals or mission; and (c) the power relationship between those positions or individuals vested with organizational authority and those individuals who serve below them in the formal organizational structure.   Given the different expectations of organizations inherent in these three different definitions, it could be argued that the strengths and deficiencies of each would become evident when transposed with particular cases.

An analysis of particular organizational models based upon these definitions is necessary to gain further appreciation for the disparate arguments currently shaping the education policy debate.   The analysis to follow will be divided between rational approaches and open systems approaches to organization.   While theoretically insightful, the natural systems approach will not be the focus of this analysis, largely due to data limitations.

RATIONAL APPROACHES TO ORGANIZATION: THE BUREAUCRATIC MODEL

Max Weber's (1946) "Bureaucracy" clearly delineates many of the elements of the classical model of organization.   Weber melds into an ideal type formulation the sociological principles surrounding the division of labor and utilitarian theories regarding human rationality.   'Bureaucracy' is primarily concerned with organizational developments surrounding the division of labor in 'rational' organizations.   Such organizations process a clear and often economically driven set of organizational goals, and feature coordinated task roles that reflect an efficient method or technology necessary for accomplishing those goals.

Weber outlines six major elements of the ideal bureaucratic organization, which can be divided into two general types—namely, aspects of personnel management and features of general organizational characteristics. First, a bureaucracy must have "fixed jurisdictional areas."   Official responsibilities must be clearly defined and maintained; the authority of each official within the organization must be commensurate with the scope of the responsibilities associated with the organizational position filled.   Entrance into the organization and into various positions would be based upon predetermined requisite qualifications and examination.   Second, modern organization "requires full-time employees."   Finally, the bureaucratic organization demands that employees are engaged as full-time "professionals" whose security needs are met through a guarantee of tenure of office on condition of adequate performance. The maintenance of expertise would require continuous organizational training programs.   According to Weber, the ideal bureaucratic organizational structure is monocephalic and hierarchical.   The positions lower in the hierarchy are more specialized than those occupied by individuals at the top of the hierarchy.   The breadth of responsibility is directly related to scope of authority.

In order to preserve rational decision-making processes, the bureaucratic organization would maintain an exhaustive system of files. The efficient filing of information would preserve organizational memory and greatly limit the possibility of arbitrariness in decision making. Organizational consistency would also be advanced by a system of stable and more or less exhaustive rules.

Bureaucracy was a critical element in education policy in the nineteenth and twentieth centuries. In order to provide public education via the Common School system, Horace Mann sought to institute more efficient and effective curricula and teaching methods. State common school systems were bound by strict guidelines and clear lines of authority for the maintenance of command and control. A well-defined administrative hierarchy was granted the legal authority to create a curriculum and to devise a system for hiring qualified instructors to effectively produce an educated populace (Cubberley 1919; Cremin 1965).

Scientific Management

The theory of scientific management is, for the most part, consistent with the assumptions of classical organizational theory. Scientific management sought to alleviate organizational problems associated with inefficient employee behavior that would effectively limit organizational and employee economic maximization. Whereas Henry Towne (1886) recommended that engineers pursue the science of organizational efficiency, Frederick Winslow Taylor arguably remains the most prominent advocate of scientific management.

In testimony before the United States Congress in 1912, Taylor outlined the use of time-motion studies in managerial enterprises, with the expectation that the routinization of human labor would maximize organizational efficiency. His theory was grounded in the assumption that the goal of both the organization and the individual employees was to maximize economic benefit. Taylor outlined four general principles of scientific management. First, knowledge and experience that had once been gathered over the lifetime of the craftsman would be systematically collected and reduced to a set of processes and rules. Second, optimum organizational personnel would be scientifically selected—only those individuals with the correct "character, nature, and performance" would be retained by the organization. Third, the worker and the newly established system of knowledge would be brought together. Finally, the equal division of workplace responsibilities between management and the workers would be established. The responsibility of the manager was to aid the worker in achieving his maximum level of efficiency, an outcome which was beneficial to both the worker and to the organization. The manager, therefore, played the key role of coordinator.

The principles of scientific management began to appear in public education many decades before Taylor's landmark work. The Pestalozzian method of classroom instruction relied on a highly regimented classroom structure and the use of rote memorization techniques with the goal of maximizing the limited educational exposure of the students. Students were treated in a manner similar to the workers in a factory, with teachers operating as classroom managers. Teaching colleges established in the latter half of the nineteenth century were intended both to select and to train those individuals most capable of becoming effective educators. Administrative hierarchies within schools and school districts sought to manage pedagogy with a limited degree of success—the circumstantial nature of educating is not easily held to a predetermined set of rules. The products of education—educated students—are not comparable to the inanimate objects created on the factory assembly line envisioned in Taylor's model of scientific management.

Elements of classical organization theory are still seen in the formal structure of the nation's public school districts. School districts fulfill many of the requirements outlined in Weber's model of bureaucracy. A chain of command exists, with district superintendents sitting atop the hierarchy, principals serving as middle management, and teachers serving as the "street level" bureaucrats. Power is primarily a function of formal authority in this ideological setting.

Progressive Era reformers employed classical organizational theory when devising many of their proposals for improved education. The goals of theorists such as John Dewey were largely grounded in the ideals of theorists such as Èmile Durkheim (1933). Society could be perfected through well-regulated modern organizations. The division of labor would produce organizations made up of specialists who would be trained to deal with the issues associated with their respective organizational positions. In the case of public education, this meant that a professional teaching staff, supervised by a cadre of scientifically selected and specially trained administrators, would effectively and efficiently provide basic education to the nation's youth. Effective outcomes were assumed to emerge from rationally organized, publicly governed educational institutions following dictates on curriculum and pedagogy proscribed by a state-level office of public education.

PROPONENTS OF MODERN ORGANIZATIONAL APPROACHES

Critics of formal organization models often claim that such organizational designs are neither efficient nor effective in terms of their organizational output. Herbert Simon's (1946) critique of Gulick (1937) and of associated formal organizational theorists (e.g., Brownlow et al. 1937; Fayol 1929), is the basis of much criticism of formal organizations and their ability to produce efficient and/or effective outcomes. Simon argued that the task of simply outlining a formal organizational structure did not in itself justify claims of efficiency and effectiveness. By way of illustration, Simon pointed to a number of inconsistent elements in Gulick's principles of good organization. Simon would later argue in *Administrative Behavior: A Study of Decision-Making Processes in Administrative Organization* (1976) and with J. March in *Organizations* (1958), that organizational behavior was shaped primarily by informal organizations made up of employees seeking to develop rational decisions in a world of bounded rationality. Formal organizational structure was generally relied upon when informal organizations failed in their search process. As a consequence of these considerations, Simon maintained that the manifest aspects of formal organization often had limited explanatory value in the analysis of organizational outputs.

Another criticism leveled at formalistic approaches to organizational theory emerges from the human relations tradition in the organizational theory literature. In a term coined by Graham Astley and Andrew Van de Ven in their article "Central Perspectives and Debates in Organizational Theory" (1983), human relations theorists view organizational life as being primarily "voluntaristic" in nature. In other words, most employees in formal organizations are not capable of divorcing themselves from their individual conditions, needs, and desires. Rational formal organizational theories too readily assume that individuals are capable of adopting organizational goals, needs, and desires as their own while at work, with scientific management advocates—such as Taylor (1911)—going so far as to claim that individuals will view such behavior as rational in terms of their own self-interest as time passes.

Mary Parker Follett (1992) was among the first theorists in the American organizational theory tradition to question the assumption that individuals will easily replace their own needs with those of the organization. She argued that the relationship between the employee and the employer was profoundly cooperative rather than unilateral. Employees did have interests and influence of their own, and did not simply defer to superiors seeking to fulfill organizational goals without some careful thought. Organizational leaders and employees engaged in both formal and informal bargaining and negotiations in order to accomplish both organizational and individual goals and in the organization.

Robert K. Merton (1957) was openly critical of the rational organizational models and their effects on employees. Employees stripped of their personal needs and goals, engaging in organizational behavior as amoral cogs in the organizational apparatus, would suffer psychological dysfunctions. Merton argued that rational closed-system models of organization were dangerous to the individual (in cultures where individualism runs strong) and were not likely to produce efficient and effective outputs over the long run.

In *The Bureaucratic Experience* (1987), Ralph Hummel offers further support for critiques of classical Weberian approaches to organization. Hummel's findings support many of Merton's hypotheses predicting that employees in highly rationalized organizations would in time engage in highly dysfunctional behavior. His evidence demonstrates that closed-system models of organization tend to inspire paranoia, depression, amoral activities, and a general sense of malaise among employees. Hummel claims that the ultimate result is psychological impairment of employees and sub optimum organizational performance.

The critiques of rational closed-system models of organization would indicate that Weber, Taylor, Fayol, and Gulick—to name but four of the most well-recognized scholars in the classical organizational tradition—do not present feasible alternative models of organization. The alternatives proposed by critics include neo-Weberian approaches, human relations approaches, and open-systems approaches (please note that these categories are not mutually exclusive). Generally, it is argued here that these approaches alternately: (a) are more realistic descriptions of organizations; (b) promote healthier organization-employee relations; and (c) result in improved organizational output.

PERSISTENT CLAIMS OF CLOSED-SYSTEM THEORISTS

In defining 'organization,' Richard Hall (1977) addresses an important point often ignored by the critics of rational closed-system organizations. Hall pays homage to the concept of formal organization in his definition, while simultaneously seeking to incorporate important elements of open-systems approaches and human relations approaches into his conception of organization. He accomplishes this largely through his discussion of the closed-open system continuum, arguing that the organizational environment and the nature of informal organizations within a formal setting will determine the degree to which a rational closed-system approach can reasonably be adopted. Implicit in his definition is a recognition of bounded rationality and the limitation it imposes on an organization's ability to become truly rational. To the extent that an organization's environment and mission are stable, variants of closed-system approaches to organization are viable methods of organizing a purposive activity.

Hall's argument echoes the contentions of many theorists who find continuing value in variations of classical theories of organization. While recognizing the criticisms leveled at classical models of organization, structural organization theorists argue that certain basic elements of the bureaucratic model and scientific management remain the foundations of well-designed organizations. They conclude that classical models of organization remain viable in many settings, as evidenced by the fact that these models still constitute the foundation of many contemporary organizations.

In *The Management of Innovation* (1961), Tom Burns and G. M. Stalker argue that "mechanistic" or rational closed-system models of organization remain viable theories for practice. The authors do not entirely deny the arguments of the critics of closed-system models. They argue, however, that closed-system models are best applied in situations in which the organizational environment is stable and the goals of the organization are clearly defined and generally accepted. Additionally, informal organization must not be a necessary component of task completion. Rather, each employee must know his or her job and complete it independently from other employees, communicating primarily with his or her superior. Organizational leaders must possess panoramic vision and establish and preserve employee loyalty to organizational goals. Organizations whose environments and methods do not meet the standards outlined in the Weberian model of bureaucracy must adopt organizational strategies best suited for their needs. In other words, there is a best way to organize, but this "best" way is relative to the conditions under which a given organization necessarily operates.

DEALING WITH THE ORGANIZATIONAL ENVIRONMENT

One point often ignored by contemporary advocates of rational closed-system approaches is the dynamic nature of many organizational environments, particularly those of public agencies. Paul Lawrence and Jay Lorsch (1967) note the problems of maintaining organizational stability when operating in a dynamic environment, and conclude that organizations faced with complex environments must respond by developing appropriate environmental *interfaces*. Such interfaces will generally involve the development of complex organizational subunits specifically designed to deal with particular high-priority problems. The capacity for the development of such organizational complexity, however, is premised on the assumption that resources for such growth will be available and that changes in formal organizational structure will necessarily lead to a more stable organizational environment. Neither of these two requirements for organizational adaptation to the environment are necessarily present in any particular case, of course.

On the question of adapting to changing environments, Norton Long (1949) hypothesized that public organizations would be highly vulnerable to political pressures, and that these influences could distort organizational goals from their original direction. Confronted with this hypothesis, organizational theorists have developed and continue to fine tune approaches to deal with the chaotic organizational environments present in the public sector in a manner that will promote organizational responsiveness while also maintaining organizational goals and processes. Two general approaches to dealing with such conditions, while succeeding in maintaining organizational integrity, are referred to as cooptation and selective adaptation.

Philip Selznick's 1949 classic *TVA and the Grassroots* is the landmark analysis of organizational cooptation as a practical solution to the problem of an unstable and highly charged public agency organizational environment. The Tennessee Valley Authority (TVA) was surrounded by a largely hostile clientele comprised of state and local officials wary of federal influence. These officials were, however, eagerly anticipating the prospect of federal monetary resources entering their respective jurisdictions. The TVA was also faced with a skeptical public, eager to garner the benefits of cheap power and water resources but displeased with the displacement of property owners whose lands would become an integral part of the massive hydroelectric system being developed with federal resources. The TVA clientele could have dramatically altered the organization's goals and redirected the means by which it was accomplished.

Selznick (1949) argues that cooptation, or "the process of absorbing new elements into the leadership or policy determining structure of an organization as a means of averting threats to its stability or existence" best describes the TVA's response to these external forces. "Cooptation reflects a state of tension between formal authority and social power" (Selznick 1949: 219). Cooptation can take at least two different forms, these being formal and informal. Formal cooptation is often an administrative tool to gather or disseminate information to the organization's clientele, or to establish the legitimacy of the organization's goals and processes. Informal cooptation is a process of responding to select groups or individuals in the organizational environment in a manner which maintains organizational integrity while simultaneously promoting environmental stability.

Selznick warns that the cooptative mechanism does not necessarily guarantee organizational integrity. In the process of selective interaction with and incorporation of particular elements of the organizational environment, organizational goals and processes can be altered substantially. Cooptation, therefore, does not necessarily ensure the stable environment needed to maintain a "mechanistic" organizational system of management (Burns and Stalker 1961: 207). Nevertheless, cooptation is one method for an organization to maintain its goals and processes while simultaneously legitimating its authority, mission, and processes.

Selective adaptation, which traces its roots to systems theory, is a second method organizations may employ when interacting with the organizational environment. Systems theory—first delineated in Political Science by David Easton in 1965—contends that organizations continually influence and are influenced by their respective environments. In terms of organizational theory, the systems approach builds on Simon's (1946, 1976) critique of rational-comprehensive models of organization and his advocacy of the application of a behaviorial science approach to the study of organizations.

Adopting systems theory for the study of organizations, Daniel Katz and Robert Kahn argue that organizations possess many of the same characteristics as living organisms. In their classic study, *The Social Psychology of Organizations* (1966), Katz and Kahn argue that closed-system models of organization are applicable when the organizational environment is stable, but that traditional bureaucratic structures are not workable in most modern dynamic organizational environments.

Systems theory is basically concerned with problems of relationships, of structure, and of interdependence rather than with the constant attributes of objects. In general approach it resembles field theory except that its dynamics deal with temporal as well as spatial patterns. Older formulations of system constructs dealt with the closed systems of the physical sciences, in which relatively self-contained structures could be treated successfully as if they were independent of external forces. But living systems, whether biological organisms or social organizations, are acutely dependent upon their external environment and so must be conceived of as open systems. (Katz and Kahn 1966: 16)

Katz and Kahn (1966) outline nine characteristics of open systems, which are closely related to cell theory in the biological sciences.

Organizational survival is often heavily dependent upon energy availability in the environment. Consistent with Long (1949), Katz and Kahn argue that organizations—particularly public administrative organizations— must *import some of their power from their environment*. This energy must then be converted—the *"through-put"*—in a manner that will be readily usable by the organization. Drawing upon their energy sources, open systems "export some product into the environment"—the *output* (Katz and Kahn 1966: 18). Unlike the closed-system model, the open systems approach views this process as *cyclical* rather than linear.

Katz and Kahn argue that input can also exist in the form of *information* or *feedback*. Information from the environment can guide an organization's future actions, avoiding those activities which have a tendency to generate negative feedback from the environment. Organizations seek to develop a steady state—*homeostasis*—a condition under which energy importation and organizational production remain stable, with no net loss of energy for the organization. Organizations often seek conditions in which there is net gain of energy, so as to store energy for purposes of growth or long-term survival under unknown conditions—a condition which is referred to as *negative entropy*.

Katz and Kahn argue that intraorganizational relationships in open systems change over time. Relatively young organizations are often best characterized as dynamic systems. Organizational outputs are reached by a number of different paths and under a variety of conditions—a process labeled *equifinality*. Organizational subunits do not have uniform and regular methods of interaction and may openly compete for power and resources. Over time, the organizational subunits begin to *differentiate* themselves from one another and begin to develop regular patterns of interaction. Standard methods of operation begin to appear and equifinality declines. While this movement towards standardization may lead to greater efficiency of organizational operation in the short run, it may also lead to organizational ossification and the potential for declining adaptiveness in the event that the organization's environment changes.

Katz and Kahn incorporate many theoretical arguments addressed previously in the organizational theory literature. The theoretical developments discussed are clearly grounded in the behaviorial school of thought, thus reflecting much of the work published by Herbert Simon. Katz and Kahn argue that organizations operate in a world of bounded rationality, but seek to rationalize their environment and internal operations so as to perpetuate their continued existence and provide for future growth. Organizational response to external stimuli is partially a function of the organization, its structure, processes, and goals.

The work of Katz and Kahn also grows out of the tradition established by Long (1949). They argue that organizations are largely dependent upon their environment for the resources (e.g., power, information, money) necessary for survival and growth. Open-system organizations operate in a dynamic environment, and they must respond to this environment in a manner that will promote organizational homeostasis and possibly permit growth. Conversely, classical models of organization assume that power is an intrinsic part of organizations, and resources are by-and-large in continuous supply. Long's theories regarding power and resources serve as the underlying foundation for the open-system model of public agencies.

Internal operations of the open-system organization are consistent with Barnard (1938), Simon (1976), and March and Simon (1958). Earlier theorists argued that intraorganizational behavior is defined to a lesser degree by the formal structure of organizations, and to a greater extent by the informal organizations that develop within formal structures. Katz and Kahn's principles of equifinality and differentiation are consistent with the concept of informal organization.

While the work of Katz and Kahn is insightful in many respects, it does fail to address the notion of organizational integrity, and it does not identify methods by which organizations can maintain such integrity. In other words, the authors fail to address clearly how organizations will avoid problems of interest group capture and goal redefinition that can occur when an organization maintains a close relationship with or demonstrates sensitivity to environmental forces. The concept of through-put does address this concern to some degree. Nevertheless, the maintenance of organizational integrity remains a central dilemma in organizational theory. In terms of public organizations, theorists find it difficult to establish a balance between the maintenance of organizational integrity and the promotion of democratic policymaking and governance.

James D. Thompson's *Organizations in Action* (1967) attempts to address this dilemma, seeking to identify rational organizational responses to the need of the organization to place limits on environmental influences so as to maintain the necessary input functions while simultaneously protecting the integrity of organizational goals and operations. While in some respects similar to the cooptative method in ultimate intent, contingency theory is more closely aligned with the open-systems approaches to organization than were Selznick's theories, and approach the issue of environment-organizational interface in a potentially less divisive manner.

CONTINGENCY THEORY: THE ORGANIZATIONAL THEORY MIDDLE-GROUND

Contingency theory approaches emerge from the organizational behavior tradition established by Herbert Simon, James March, and Richard Cyert (Thompson 1967: 9). Beginning with Simon's classic article "The Proverbs of Administration" (1946), the tradition established by these three authors radically altered the study of public sector organizational theory, which has ever since retreated from highly formalistic models of public organization. Writing from an administrative perspective (Cyert and March 1963: 17), these three prominent theorists argue that organizations operate under conditions of bounded rationality (Simon 1976; March and Simon 1958); within these limits, however, organizations employ various search mechanisms (emerging from both formal and informal organization and processes) in order to make satisfactory or adequate decisions (Cyert and March 1963). Contingency theory is deeply grounded in the behaviorial tradition in organizational theory.

Herbert Simon's *Administrative Behavior: A Study of Decision-Making Processes in Administrative Organization* (1976) grew out of the work of Chester I. Barnard (1938), as did the open-systems tradition (Thompson 1967: 7). Unlike the open-systems theorists, however, Simon sees organizational goals as the product of compromise among organizational participants (e.g., administrative entrepreneurs, agency employees, organizational consumers) and are ultimately shaped by constraints (Simon 1976: 277) that emerge from bounded rationality, the search for Pareto optimal solutions, and the scope of organizational purpose as defined by statute, custom, and organizational authorities.

Open system theorists tend to argue that organizational goals are *the* product of demands emerging from the organizational environment. Simon argues that goals are—to some significant degree—a product of compromise; however, in discussing organizational equilibrium he notes that organizational goals are often shaped by senior organization leaders more than by stakeholders in the organizational environment: "This group [top administrators] may be strongly imbued with the organizational objectives, with conservation aims, or both" (Simon 1976: 121). Simon argues that oftentimes the stakeholders in the organizational environment play a passive role unless they see direct benefits (e.g., monetary, social, etc.); they are rational in their act of leaving organizational goal definition, within limits, up to the organizations' administrative leaders.

Simon argues that organizational efficiency is the primary criterion upon which organizations are to be judged (Simon 1976: 122). Through the use of standard operating procedures, decision rules generated by information processing systems, and administrative decisionmaking, which is to some degree the product of compromise between various organizational stakeholders, organizations must pursue efficiency in order to maintain their goals, structure, and processes. Consequently, the overarching purpose of organizations is to maintain those conditions necessary for survival. Simon argues that organizational survival is largely dependent on the avoidance of uncertainty, which he implicitly argues is most likely to emerge from the organizational environment.

Cyert and March (1963) define "organization" in a manner similar to the open-systems theorists:

Let us view the organization as a coalition. It is a coalition of individuals, some of them organized into subcoalitions.... In the governmental organization the members include administrators, workers, appointive officials, elective officials, legislators, judges, clientele, interest group leaders, etc. Drawing the boundaries of an organization once and for all is impossible. Instead, we simplify the conception by focusing on the participants. (Cyert and March 1963: 78)

Organizational goals are shaped by demands placed upon the system from the various stakeholders in the organization, given the formal constraints that exist. Cyert, March, and Simon are open-systems theorists; but open-systems theory is bifurcated between those theorists taking the rational choice approach and those scholars taking the collaborative approach to organizational governance. In this case, these aforementioned theorists are tracked to the rational choice approach. While operating within the confines of bounded rationality, organizations will seek to develop standard operating procedures (Cyert and March 1963: 101-102). The successful organization is one that makes satisfactory decisions and limits the need to instigate a search process to produce those decisions.

Organizations avoid uncertainty: (1) They avoid the requirement that they correctly anticipate events in the distant future by using decision rules emphasizing short-run reaction to short-run feedback rather than develop long-run strategies. (2) They avoid the requirement that they anticipate future reactions of other parts of their environment by arranging a negotiated environment. They impose plans, standard operating procedures, industry tradition, and uncertainty-absorbing contacts on that environment. In short, they achieve a reasonably manageable decision situation by avoiding planning where plans depend on predictions of uncertain future events and by emphasizing where plans can be made self-confirming through some control device. (Cyert and March 1963: 119)

The work of these pioneers of the behaviorial theory of organization provides the foundation of the contingency theory approach. Contingency theory further refines organizational approaches to avoiding uncertainty. Contingency theory posits that organizational function will shape organizational administrative control and institutional autonomy.

James D. Thompson's *Organizations in Action* (1967) is a foundational work in contingency theory. Thompson argues that one of the central methods of dealing with uncertainty in complex organizations is to protect the core tasks of the organization by "creating certain parts [suborganizations] to deal with it [uncertainty]" (Thompson 1967: 13). The primary goal of his work is to discuss the role of the specialized parts whose purpose is to help maintain or foster organizational certainty.

Thompson argues that there are three primary components of organizational rationality: "(1) input activities, (2) technological activities, and (3) output activities" (Thompson 1967: 19). He argues that input and output activities involve the organizational-environment interface. Technological activities are interrelated with this interface. In order to establish and maintain certainty, organizations develop standard operating procedures and specialization.

Thompson outlines three types of organizational "technologies," or technical functions, which shape organizational processes and ultimately the organizational relationship with the environment: 1) long-linked technology, 2) mediating technology, and 3) intensive technology. Long-linked technology describes production-line organizations: "it approaches instrumental perfection when it produces a single kind of standard product, repetitively and at a constant rate" (Thompson 1967: 16). Organizational certainty in an organization defined by mediating technology is largely determined by its ability to *coordinate* the activities of its various suborganizations. "Standardization makes possible the operation of the mediating technology over time and through space by assuring each segment of the organization that the other segments are operating in compatible ways. It is in such situations that the bureaucratic techniques of categorization and impersonal application of rules have been most beneficial..." (Thompson 1967: 17). Organizations that operate under conditions of intensive technology, however, are the most likely to suffer from problems associated with uncertainty. Thompson argues that technology-intensive organizations—such as public schools—operate under dynamic conditions and rely heavily on feedback from their environment on how well the technology is serving its intended purposes.

Pursuant of their goal of limiting operational and environmental uncertainty, organizations seek to define those variables that are central to the effective performance of their core technologies. "Under norms of rationality, organizations seek to seal off their core technologies from environmental influences" (Thompson 1967: 19). By limiting "exogenous" variables, the organization is more likely to establish a causal relationship between organizational actions and particular organization outputs. If organizational efficiency is central to "good" organizations, as Simon (1976) argues, then either controlling or effectively predicting environmental influences shaping organizational output is essential to the efficient accomplishment of organizational goals.

Thompson (1967) argues that one common method of maintaining stable core technologies (or technical cores) is to establish buffers between the technical core and the environment. "Under norms of rationality, organizations seek to buffer environmental influences by surrounding their technical cores with input and output components" (Thompson 1967: 20). The establishment of suborganizations that are specifically intended to maintain the organizational-environmental interface would limit direct contact between the environment and the technical core, while attempting to "smooth" or predict fluctuating demands and respond to such changes. Thompson (1967: 21) hypothesizes that organizations that are not able to develop or maintain technical rationality at their core by effective buffering mechanisms will become dysfunctional.

Thompson (1967) argues that organizations seek to develop stable clientele and resource bases. In an atmosphere of competition, organizations may seek to coopt, contract, or form coalitions with competitors. If resource providers are "concentrated," the organization might be vulnerable to the price demands of a fairly restricted group of resource providers and may attempt to adopt strategies similar to those addressed above. In the case of public school districts, resource providers typically are widely dispersed and the threat of competition from private school options is fairly limited; with respect to concerns regarding resources, the exercise of influence, and clientele support, they all appear to be in fairly limited supply for most school districts studied in this book.

It should be noted, however, that the introduction of large-scale private school options into the education policy debate has sparked some discussion of an enlarged role for public schools in the area of social welfare policy via such policy innovations as "21st Century Schools" (Zigler and Gilman 1994; Anderson, et al. 1995). Policy shifts of this nature could represent confirmation of Thompson's propositions regarding the defense of organizational domain:

The more sectors in which the organization subject to rationality norms is constrained, the more power the organization will seek over remaining sectors of its task environment . . . . The organization facing many constraints and unable to achieve power in other sectors of its task environment will seek to enlarge the task environment. (Thompson 1967: 36-37)

In addition to input and output factors, Thompson (1967: 64) argues that organizations seeking to develop or maintain technical rationality must develop internal coordination amongst their various core functions. In part this task requires the development of a hierarchical structure. The more complex the organizational tasks, however, the greater the need for coordination and specialization of task. Additionally, the greater the number and the wider the variety of contingencies that an organization has to consider the greater the need for boundary-spanning activities (Thompson 1967: 61).

Contingency theory assumes that organizations seek out and are generally capable of developing technical rationality. Assessments of the level of rationality, however, may be inappropriate for organizations in which the validity and reliability of efficiency analysis is questionable (Wilson 1989).

TECHNICAL RATIONALITY AND SCHOOL DISTRICTS: EVIDENCE IN THE LITERATURE

Herbert Simon (1976) argues that organizations seek to develop a level of rationality necessary to pursue the goal of organizational efficiency. James March and Richard Cyert, contemporaries of Simon and advocates of his theoretical approach to the study of organizations, support this conclusion and attempt to outline a series of empirically testable arguments derived from Simon's work. James Thompson has advanced Simon's theories by delineating a series of propositions related to the organizational pursuit of technical rationality.

The analysis of public school districts in terms of organizational theory proves to be quite challenging. If Lindblom's (1959) theory of incrementalism is accurate to any appreciable degree, public school district organization behavior and performance should be best described by the historical changes that have occurred over the past 170 years, with the caveat that major policy innovations appear to parallel elite-defined goals. Based upon the evidence presented here, this certainly appears to be the case. The result, however, is that public schools are *both* public administrative organizations and units of local government.

Under these conditions, the varying demands of organized interests, different levels of government, voters, and students from communities within the school district may shape organizational behavior and ultimately affect the technical core of the school district organization. Based on the propositions outlined in Thompson (1967), such sources of external influence may contribute to the development of boundary-spanning sub-organizations in public school districts and/or an enlarged scope of responsibilities of public school districts. The size and structure of bureaucracy in public school district organizations may to a substantial extent be a reflection of conditions in the organizational environment.

For most of the twentieth century, education policy research generally ignored environmental influences on public school district organizations. Harry F. Wolcott's classic study, *The Man in the Principal's Office* (1973), recognized the influence of the organizational environment on public schools. Wolcott argued that school districts, particularly school boards, were comprised of people with diverse interests and strategies in school governance. Wolcott recognized that public school administrators played an important role along the organization-environmental interface. The recognition of the school board and the larger community as a source of significant environmental influences represented a significant movement away from closed-system approaches to school district governance generated during the nineteenth century and during the Progressive Era in the twentieth century (Lutz and Iannaccone 1978: 3; Davies 1981).

Mark Hanson (1981), in "Organizational Control in Educational Systems: A Case Study of Governance in Schools," argues that there are three distinct models used to conceptualize public school districts. First, the bureaucratic model is often employed, as schools possess many of the characteristics of bureaucracy. The Common School model and the Progressive Era public education reforms, which remain a prominent component of public school district structure and processes, have produced highly formalistic public school organizations. Second, the social system model is based in the argument that "issues of decision making are complicated by the fact that the informal social systems have their own sets of norms" (1981: 247). In other words, the technical core of public school districts is often coopted by the organizational environment, resulting in a high level of organizational uncertainty, limiting the ability of the organization to produce efficient outcomes. Third, Hanson argues that contingency theory is applicable to the study of public school organizations, which "are supported by and in turn must support the social, political, and cultural demands of the community" (Hanson 1981: 247). He goes on to observe that "the contingency theory perspective stresses that the school requires variability in organizational response capabilities to cope with changing environmental needs and demands" (Hanson 1981: 248).

Hanson hypothesizes that contingency theory is perhaps the most applicable approach to the study of schools: "school governance . . . is certainly not the product of hierarchy" (Hanson 1981: 272). Additionally, he argues that many public school districts are "loosely coupled" organizations (1981: 252). In such organizations, power and authority are dispersed due to a high degree of professionalism and specialization among organizational elements. Additionally, resources are highly concentrated, resulting in interorganizational contracting. The relationship between teachers' union officials and public school district administrators is an example of concentrated resources and the need for contracting. "Loosely coupled" organizations have limited ability to integrate their efforts to cope with their environments.

Hanson (1981) concludes that March and Olsen (1976) were correct when they labeled public school districts "loosely coupled" organizations, and such organizations will find it difficult to rationalize their environments and protect their technical core. Conversely, tightly coupled organizations are perhaps more capable of integrating the subsystem efforts to anticipate the demands from their environment and protect their core goals and processes.

Hanson (1981) argues that tightly coupled organizations are more likely to be successful in adopting contingency theoretical approaches to public organization management than loosely coupled organizations.

Hanson's argument is supported by earlier findings in the contingency theory literature. Jeffrey Pfeffer's (1978: 30) consonance hypothesis proposes that "those organizations that deviate less from the optimal structure will be more effective." According to Hanson's (1981) evidence, public school districts are often incapable of reaching an "optimal" structure given their "loosely coupled" state. Thus, Pfeffer's (1978: 31) "managerial adaptation" does not appear to be a plausible method of "obtain[ing] higher levels of organizational performance." John W. Meyer and Brian Rowan (1978) conclude that managerial activities in public school district organizations are largely symbolic, focusing primarily on the legitimization of the contract relationship between resource providers (i.e., teachers' unions) and the public school district organization.

From the viewpoint of an administrator, maintaining the credulity of his or her school and the validity of its ritual classifications is crucial to the school's success. With the confidence of the state bureaucracy, the federal government, the community, the profession, the pupils, and their families, and the teachers themselves, the legitimacy of the school as a social reality can be maintained. However, if the groups decide that a school's ritual classifications are a 'fraud,' everything comes apart. (Meyer and Rowan 1978: 98-99)

Administrative activity, therefore, is more likely to be reactive than proactive, attempting to limit what Hanson (1981) refers to as the "contested" zone, in this case the conflict between administration and teachers. In addition to maintaining stable core technologies, therefore, public school district organizations seek to develop stable relationships with their environments through the maintenance of an image of organizational legitimacy. Thus, public schools are inclined to use two different techniques to protect their technical core: they establish contract relationships with their suppliers, and they attempt to co-opt extra-organizational stakeholders through the maintenance of symbolic legitimization.

Martin Burlingame (1981), in "Superintendent Power Retention," discusses the processes by which administrators engage in symbolic legitimization techniques. To a large degree, school district administrators seek to fulfill public needs through the use of symbolic activities and policies, while at the same time shielding teachers in their specialized instructional roles. As Wolcott (1973) argues, administrators serve as the primary organizational representatives along the organizational-environmental interface. Thus, administrators act to fulfill symbolic needs so as to protect the school district organization's core technologies. Burlingame (1981) argues that much of this administrative behavior resembles what Victor Thompson refers to as "dramaturgy," a form of showmanship engaged in by senior organizational administrators, particularly in organizations that feature high levels of professionalism among the workers.

CONCLUSION

There are two organizational theory-based approaches to analyzing public schools outlined here. Wilson (1989) argues that the bureaucratic model is the most appropriate model for analyzing governmental institutions. His findings would support the contention that public schools fail to maintain the strong sense of mission and highly formalized structure necessary to maintain the principles delineated in the bureaucratic model. Contingency theory, a variant of open-systems theory, appears to represent public schools accurately, and may prove to be a useful theoretical tool for the development of a more refined and insightful understanding of public school districts studied from an organizational perspective.

This book adopts the contingency theory conceptualization of public school organizations. The evidence discussed here would tend to indicate that contingency theory offers significant explanatory power in terms of the organizational behavior of public school districts. School districts possess many of the characteristics discussed in Thompson (1967). The bureaucratic model, while the historically identified model of public schools, appears to have limited explanatory power in relation to public school district behavior, as evidenced in this literature review. The model does not adequately address the organizational environment of public schools. Wilson (1989) implicitly argues that public school districts (or any public administrative organization, for that matter) should be consistent with the bureaucratic model if they are to operate in an efficient and democratically accountable manner. The contingency theory model, however, deals with the issue of democratic accountability and the maintenance of efficiency, while consciously considering the dynamic nature of organizational environments. For this reason, public school organizations will be conceptualized as open-systems organizations, quite possibly operating in a manner consistent with contingency theories of public organization.

WORKS CITED

Anderson, K., Battles, M., and Billings, J. 1995. *Final Report to the Legislature on the Schools for the 21st Century Program (Chapter 525, Laws of 1987)*. Olympia: Washington State Board of Education.

Astley, G. and Van de Ven, A. 1983. "Central Perspectives and Debates in Organizational Theory," *Administrative Science Quarterly*. 28: 245-273.

Bacharach, S. 1981. "Organizational and Political Dimensions for Research on School District Governance and Administration," in S. Bacharach (ed.), *Organizational Behavior in Schools and School Districts*. New York: Praeger, 3-43.

Barnard, C. 1938. *Functions of the Executive*. Cambridge, MA: Harvard University Press.

Brownlow, L., Merriam, C., and Gulick, L. 1937. *President's Committee on Administrative Management in the Government of the United States*. Washington, DC: U.S. Government Printing Office.

Burlingame, M. 1981. "Superintendent Power Retention," in S. Bacharach (cd.), *Organizational Behavior in Schools and School Districts.* New York: Praeger, 429-465.

Burns, T. and Stalker, G. 1961. *The Management of Innovation.* London: Tavistock Publications.

Chubb, J. and Moe, T. 1990. *Politics, Markets, and America's Schools.* Washington, DC: The Brookings Institution.

Cremin, L. 1965. *The Genius of American Education.* New York: Vintage Books.

Cubberley, E. 1919. *Public Education in the United States: A Study and Interpretation of American Educational History.* Boston, MA: Houghton Mifflin.

Cyert, R. and March, J. 1963. *A Behavioral Theory of the Firm.* Englewood Cliffs, NJ: Prentice-Hall.

Davies, D. (ed.) 1981. *Communities and Their Schools.* New York: McGraw-Hill.

Durkheim, E. 1933. *The Division of Labor in Society.* New York: Free Press.

Easton, D. 1965. *A Framework for Political Analysis.* Englewood Cliffs, NJ: Prentice-Hall.

Fayol, H. 1929. *General and Industrial Management.* Trans. J. Conbrough Geneva: International Management Institute.

Follett, M. 1992. "The Giving of Orders [1918]," in J. Shafritz and A. Hyde (eds.), *Classics of Public Administration.* Pacific Grove, CA: Brooks/Cole, 66-74.

Forester, J. 1993. *Critical Theory, Public Policy, and Planning Practice: Toward a Critical Pragmatism.* Albany: State University of New York Press.

Gulick, L. 1937. "Notes on the Theory of Organization," in L. Gulick and L. Urwick (eds.), *Papers on the Science of Administration.* New York: Institute of Public Administration, 3-13.

Hall, R. 1977. *Organizations: Structure and Process,* Second Edition. Englewood Cliffs, NJ: Prentice-Hall.

Hanson, M. 1981. "Organizational Control in Educational Systems: A Case Study of Governance in Schools," in S. Bacharach (ed.), *Organizational Behavior in Schools and School Districts.* New York: Praeger, 245-276.

Hummel, R. 1987. *The Bureaucratic Experience,* Second Edition. New York: St. Martin's Press.

Katz, D. and Kahn, R. 1966. *The Social Psychology of Organizations.* New York: John Wiley & Sons.

Lawrence, P. and Lorsch, J. 1967. *Organizations and Environment: Managing Differentiation and Integration.* Boston, MA: Graduate School of Business Administration, Harvard University.

Lindblom, C. 1959. "The Science of Muddling Through," *Public Administration Review.* 19(2): 79-88.

Long, N. 1949. "Power and Administration," *Public Administration Review*. 9(4): 257-264.

Lowi, T. 1969. *The End of Liberalism*. New York: W.W. Norton.

Lutz, F. and Iannaccone, L. 1978. *Public Participation in Local School Districts: The Dissatisfaction Theory of Democracy*. Lexington, MA: Lexington Books.

March, J. and Olsen, J. 1976. *Ambiguity and Choice in Organizations*. Bergen, Norway: Universitetsforlaget.

March, J. and Simon, H. 1958. *Organizations*. New York: John Wiley.

Meehan, E. 1994. *Social Inquiry: Needs, Possibilities, Limits*. Chatham, NJ: Chatham Publishers.

Merton, R. 1957. *Social Theory and Social Structure*. New York: Free Press.

Meyer, J. and Rowan, B. 1978. "The Structure of Educational Organizations," in M. Meyer (ed.), *Environments and Organizations*. San Francisco, CA: Jossey-Bass, 78-109.

Pfeffer, J. 1978. "The Micropolitics of Organizations," in M. Meyer (ed.), *Environments and Organizations*. San Francisco, CA: Jossey-Bass, 29-50.

Scott, W. 1981. *Organizations: Rational, Natural, and Open Systems*. Englewood Cliffs, NJ: Prentice-Hall.

Selznick, P. 1949. *TVA and the Grassroots*. Berkeley: University of California Press.

Simon, H. 1946. "The Proverbs of Administration," *Public Administration Review*. 6(1): 53-67.

_____. 1976. *Administrative Behavior: A Study of Decision-Making Processes in Administrative Organization*. New York: Free Press.

Smith, K. and Meier, K. 1994. "Politics, Bureaucrats, and Schools," *Public Administration Review*. 54(6): 551-558.

_____. 1995. *The Case Against School Choice: Politics, Markets, and America's Fools*. Armonk, NY: M. E. Sharpe.

Stone, D. 1988. *Policy, Paradox, and Political Reason*. New York: HarperCollins.

Taylor, F. 1911. *The Principles of Scientific Management*. New York: Harper.

Thompson, J. 1967. *Organizations in Action: Social Science Bases of Administrative Theory*. New York: McGraw-Hill.

Thompson, V. 1961. *Modern Organization*. New York: Knopf.

Towne, H. 1886. "The Engineer as an Economist," *Transactions of The American Society of Mechanical Engineers*. 7: 428-432,

Waldo, D. 1948. *The Administrative State: A Study of the Political Theory of American Public Administration*. New York: The Ronald Press.

Weber, M. 1946. "Bureaucracy," in H. Gerth and C. Mills (eds.), *From Max Weber: Essays in Sociology*. New York: Oxford University Press, 196-244.

Wilson, J. 1989. *Bureaucracy: What Government Agencies Do and Why They Do It*. New York: Basic Books.

Wolcott, H. 1973. *The Man in the Principal's Office*. New York: Simon & Schuster.

Zigler, E. and Gilman, E. 1994. "What's a School to Do? Meeting Educational and Family Needs," in R. Berne and L. Picus (eds.), *Outcome Equity in Education*. Thousand Oaks, CA: Corwin Press, 71-86.

Chapter 3

Organizational Environment

In the previous chapter, contingency theory was identified as the most applicable theoretical approach when analyzing public school organizations. Unlike classical organizational theories, contingency theory takes into consideration the dynamic qualities of public organization. Change that occurs within or outside an organization can have a tremendous impact on the ability of an organization to achieve its objectives. The theories discussed in Chapter 2 are of great value to educational administrators as they respond to environmental constraints. For instance, from a classical bureaucratic perspective, school district administrators must ensure that school priorities accurately reflect the priorities of elected officials (e.g., national and state legislatures, and school boards) and education departments at the state and national level. Additionally, the school district superintendent and his or her subordinate staff should focus the bulk of their attention on the efficient and politically neutral implementation of education policy. In this sense, public schools are largely driven by expectations—in the form of statutes, rules, regulations, and court decisions—emanating from institutions superior to them and to whom school administrators are responsible, rather than the demands of citizens.

Conversely, open-systems theory in general and contingency theory more specifically emphasize the role of the environment and resources in explaining organizational 'outputs.' In order to achieve their goals, administrative actors operating in public school districts, for instance, must remain fully cognizant of the social, political, and economic conditions present in communities outside of the district's formal boundaries which are likely to constrain the desired accomplishments of public school educators. The organizational environment comprises more than just the characteristics of communities surrounding local school districts. The political dynamics of education policy extend far beyond the school district. School policy and organization are regularly influenced by state and national level political and legal bodies and administrative organizations. The aforementioned scholarly efforts of Chubb and Moe, Smith and Meier, and James Q. Wilson should make it abundantly clear that erudite debates in academic circles also influence the policy agenda and actively shape the policy preferences of attentive citizens and political leaders. Wilson's book *Bureaucracy: What Government Agencies Do and Why They Do It* (1989) was on the national bestseller list. In order to form their opinions and attitudes, community leaders and members gather information through the media and through contemporary issues literature. What they hear and see often has a profound impact on the future and the direction of public agencies such as schools.

The preparation of academic tomes frequently requires some foreknowledge of earlier academic literature upon which arguments and conclusions are often grounded. Thus, these pedantic studies are frequently not as accessible to laypersons as are national and regional newspaper articles and popular periodical literature. An analysis of popular media sources, therefore, will help explain the general atmosphere surrounding public schools. The policy preferences of voters, state elected officials, public school personnel, and teachers' unions often become abundantly clear through content analysis of this type.

Archival analysis is valuable, but the political and social environment of public schools can only be understood in very general terms using this approach to analysis. Statewide newspaper articles can be found on electronic databases, but small circulation community newspapers are not consistently available either electronically or in printed form. The result is that while one can get a general sense of state-level education policy issues, the subtle variations across Washington's 296 school districts are difficult to observe.

The environment of a public school district is far-ranging, largely due to the funding arrangements of elementary and secondary education. While the state treasury provides an average of nearly 70 percent of school district finances statewide, a little more than one tenth of school district finances on average are collected from local taxpayers in the form of property taxes and other incidental tax and nontax sources (e.g., user fees). Additionally, voter-approved supplemental property tax levies help to defray the costs associated with unexpected district budget shortfalls. Voters' support or rejection of these supplemental levies is another important measure of school district environment. Are voters willing to shoulder an additional tax burden for public schools, and, more specifically, does the level of voter support tell us anything about the level of support extant in the community for an important public institution? Supplemental levy support is a terrific way in which to measure the relationship between schools and voters, providing some indication of the level of community institutional confidence and trust in the public schools. A lack of voter support for public school finance would indicate that as an organization, the public schools are operating in a hostile environment, perhaps one that requires greater citizen-administrator interaction to further legitimize the public school goals and explain how and why these goals either are or are not being effectively accomplished.

Socioeconomic conditions represent another important environmental constraint on public school districts and on their ability to meet critical organizational goals. At an earlier time, particularly in the 19th and early 20th centuries, public school organizations were designed and operated in a manner consistent with the principles of classical organizational theory.   School curriculum and pedagogy were fairly uniform, and the administrative control over public schools was hierarchical with most decision-making power concentrated in the hands of principals and district superintendents. The primary purpose of the schools was to instill a particular set of values and clearly defined set of facts in the minds of students, who were often viewed—particularly in larger urban schools—as little more than products. Minor consideration was given to the conditions under which pupils dwelled or how those conditions might influence academic performance. It was not until the 1960's that serious consideration was given to the expected impact of *human capital*—such as poverty, parental educational attainment, and limited English proficiency—on student academic performance.   Work conducted independently by the Ford Foundation (Meade 1972), James Coleman (1988), and Christopher Jencks and colleagues (1972) provides fairly clear evidence that education does not occur in a vacuum. School administration, curriculum, and pedagogy are by no means the primary influences on student learning. Dewey's exhortations on purposive education do not adequately account for variations in pupil characteristics and the effect those differences are likely to have on student learning. Education, as we now know, is not easily separated from the family and community conditions under which students exist on a daily basis.   Parental educational expectations of their children, the enforcement and monitoring of consistent study habits at home, and the development of long-term educational goals comprise what is often referred to as *family social capital*, which contributes greatly to student academic and life achievement.   Family social capital, however, originates within the private realm of the home, and is largely outside of the grasp of public policymakers, administrators, and teachers.

When considering the successes and/or failures of any particular public school, we all too often search for an organization-related factor to explain student performance outcomes. Organizational successes are often attributed to an outstanding teacher or administrator, whose charismatic qualities electrify the school or classroom, motivating teachers and pupils to achieve what they might otherwise never have succeeded in accomplishing. A clearer understanding of how schools are organized and how these complex organizations react to their changing environment is critical if long-term improvements to elementary and secondary education are to be achieved. Certainly, there are wonderful teachers and administrators in our public schools, but we should focus less attention on the unsung heroes (many of whom are accomplishing the educational equivalent of the Labors of Hercules, but with much more limited resources) and greater attention on the capacity of public schools to meet our demands. Often invoking the "cult of the great leader and teacher" myth, we tend to ignore the context in which student learning occurs—the larger structure and processes surrounding public education. Unlike the success stories, failing schools tend to invite a much more holistic analysis of the school organization, with calls for systematic reform and greater accountability. Rather than wait until a school 'fails,' it would be wiser to consider the school organization and the constraints facing it in a consistent manner. Only then will policymakers and citizens be able to understand if public schools are operating at their optimum capacity, and if so what other factors, either external or internal to the school organization, that shape student achievement must be remedied via public policy or private choices and behavior so as to achieve higher levels of student performance.

SALIENT EDUCATIONAL ISSUES IN WASHINGTON STATE, 1990-1999

The education policy issues and priorities in the State of Washington were fairly clear and consistent in the 1990's, which is vitally important to public schools as organizations. A rapidly changing and unpredictable policy environment necessitates the expenditure of greater organizational energies to minimize the impact of environmental influences hampering the ability of the school organization to identify clear goals and to prioritize and accomplish its objectives. Nevertheless, it would be misleading to report that the consistency of citizen policy priorities over that decade can be equated with environmental tranquility. The nature of policy priorities does not mean that schools are able to meet demands placed upon them by concerned parents, attentive local citizens, interest groups, and politicians. The relative uniformity of general priorities simply means that school districts in Washington were operating in a fairly stable policy environment for a decade, and if the past is any guide to the future, there did not appear to be any tremendous surprises that would have made it exceedingly difficult for public schools to adequately and rapidly respond.

Education policy objectives in the State of Washington are not noticeably different from the priorities in school districts nationwide. Washingtonians, however, are particularly passionate about the quality of education—perhaps more so than about other major policy concerns such as the conservation of natural resources and crime control. In a public opinion poll of over 500 Washington voters conducted in 1996, the quality of public elementary and secondary education was the number one concern in the minds of voters. Almost 90 percent of voters felt that education was a very important issue in the 1996 general election. Appoximately 60 percent of voters responding to the poll felt that public schools had witnessed a significant decline in student performance and that the issue was best remedied by increased funding for education (Turner and Callahan 1996).

Voter concern for education was on average greater than concern for budgetary control. The state of Washington has a spending cap to prevent budget deficits, but survey results indicate that voters were willing to spend beyond the state budget constraints in order to ensure that public elementary and secondary schools were well-funded. Voter beneficence, however, did not extend to the state university system—voters were not interested in substantially raising the higher education budget (Paulson 1996). Washington voters appear to be highly loyal to their public school system. Voters openly express their concern for the quality and performance of public schools. In the 1996 polling data, they did not appear to have lost any significant level of confidence in the public schools as *institutions*. It is critical that any effort to improve student performance have the full support of parents and community residents. A hostile or uncommitted school environment would make it difficult for schools to legitimize their goals and methods, hamper efforts to obtain necessary funding, and likely result in increased pressure on schools to solve the student achievement problem without parents' and community members' actively reinforcing the importance of education to school-aged children.

While the state voters are generally very supportive of public schools, there are a few intradistrict school choice movements afoot (Beason 1996), and advocates continue to press their issue in the state legislature and local newspapers (*News Tribune* 1998). This is perhaps best exemplified by the low level of voter support for two educational reform initiatives on the 1996 state ballot. If successfully passed by voters, Initiative #173 would have established a statewide public school voucher program. Gradually implemented from the elementary schools and then up through the high school grades, the $3,400 scholarship vouchers for basic education would have provided parents and school-aged children with the ability to choose schools most consistent with their personal academic standards. Initiative #177 proposed the creation of charter schools throughout the state. Charter schools would have resulted in the privatization of school administration, and freed schools from much of the state-level regulation of local school districts. Charter school administrators and instructional personnel would report pupil performance to the Office of Superintendent for Public Instruction. Theoretically, superior school performance would be rewarded with the renewal of a school's charter and the continued public financing of school operations (*Seattle Times* 1996).

The assumption underlying both of these ballot initiatives is that public education administrators and instructional staff are bogged down by state-level bureaucracy. Education privatization plans would free both schools and parents from the yoke of government regulation. School administrators would become more dynamic organizational managers, and teachers would be able to focus their energies on student mastery of basic subjects. Accountability would be measured in monetary terms. The charter or private voucher-school would survive and grow *if* its clientele (state education officials and parents of school-aged children) remained satisfied with the school's ability to promote academic excellence. Conversely, organizational death or funding termination would signal a severe loss of confidence in a public school. Organizational loyalty and a commitment on the part of communities to preserve and reform sometimes troubled public institutions would decline tremendously if commodified approaches to public education grew significantly in number, size, and popularity. In November 1996, however, Washington voters soundly rejected both ballot initiatives, demonstrating their commitment to the current public school system (Holt 1996).

Despite their support for public schools, voters have been equally clear as to what they expect from public schools. In a public opinion survey conducted in 1997 (Cafazzo 1997), voters strongly supported a renewed emphasis on a core curriculum focusing primarily on the three "R's." Nearly half of the respondents indicated support for greater emphasis on reading, arithmetic, and writing. Additionally the respondents indicated that in order to be effective, schools must direct greater energies toward providing safe and orderly school environments. For the most part, Washingtonians are highly enthusiastic about public schools and are willing to offer even greater financial support, but that they are currently dissatisfied with school performance and student achievement.

Public schools have attempted to coopt those parents who have lost faith and chosen to enroll their children in private schools or who have opted for home schooling. It is difficult to bring the parents and children attending private schools to renew their ties to the public school system. In most cases, parents of private school students have higher socioeconomic status. Contemporary private schools offer students extracurricular cultural, religious, and sports programs as well as advanced educational opportunities. Given their higher socioeconomic status, parents of private school students can often afford to purchase additional education opportunities that often are not available through private or public schools. From an organizational theory perspective, private school students and their parents are less likely to be supportive of public schools and public school finance. Pure self-interest would indicate that private school students' parents are paying twice—once in the form of taxes and then again in the form of tuition—yet they directly benefit from their expenditures only once—at the school their children attend. The angst that develops under this circumstance is often exhibited in support for voucher programs, allowing parents of private schoolers the option to take their tax dollars to the school of their choice. From the public school perspective, the proliferation of private schools—whether or not the voucher system were implemented—would spell disaster. Public schools would lack the support necessary for adequate funding, and community members would likely be less interested in legitimizing public school goals and methods of accomplishing those goals. Rather, individuals dissatisfied with public schools would simply 'exit,' sending their children elsewhere. Commodification would mean less community commitment to the public school organization.

Homeschooled students, however, are more easily targeted by public schools attempting to establish some form of educational partnership between the school and the homeschooled students and their parents. Parents of homeschoolers are paying once (through their taxes), but benefiting as a result of their own efforts. Usually, one parent must stay home to instruct the children, which severely limits family earnings for two-parent families—not to mention the financial burden on a single-parent household. Public schools have begun to form partnerships with homeschoolers' parents, offering some courses and extracurricular programs to these nontraditional students. In this way, parents are freed up to earn a living, and are able to cover subject areas in which they are unable to adequately instruct their children. Additionally, learning centers are being established where homeschooler parents can cooperatively educate their children, in addition to providing both parents and children the opportunity to share ideas and build socialization skills.   Homeschoolers working in cooperation with the public schools are able to see some benefit in the maintenance of strong and effective public schools. Unlike individuals choosing the private school approach and opting out of public schools entirely, homeschoolers' education is often directly tied to the goals and methods of the public schools.

In addition to the cooperative efforts between public schools and homeschoolers, tax reductions for the parents of homeschoolers and private school students were proposed in the 1999 legislative session. "The bill offered a reimbursement of costs for parents that file a 'Freedom of Conscience' statement with their county treasurer and provide a receipt for the . . . home school expenses." In addition, taxpayers could divert to private schools the amount of their tax bill that would have gone to public schools (Shapley 1999). Despite its ultimate failure, the populist spirit behind the measure is potentially damaging to public schools, eroding community support for schools and increasing the level of resource uncertainty. Contingency theory would predict that such environmental conditions would reduce organizational effectiveness and increase administrative boundary-spanning efforts. School officials would have to redouble their efforts to preserve the organization's ability to maintain a stable resource base. In addition, public schools would have to expend precious time and resources maintaining public support for the value of democratic education on which the public school system is grounded, and legitimize the process by which schools educate students.

Student achievement on standardized examinations has clearly been disappointing to parents, concerned citizens, elected representatives, school administrators, and teachers alike. The disappointment, however, has focused on different issues surrounding testing as well as outcomes. Teachers and their unions are often concerned about the rapid increase in standardized testing because they claim that the examinations do not represent all aspects of the learning experience.   Simply teaching to the exam, which is how student performance is often gauged, would either omit or appreciably diminish time spent on subject areas not directly related to the 'basics.' Teachers argue that students need a diverse curriculum if they are to master the subject matter they will need in the future. Standardized tests, however, have come to "run the school system," dictate the curriculum, and shape pedagogy. In short, schools have moved away from their role as centers of education and have begun to resemble exam preparation training centers (Roeder 1999). Schools and parents have indicated that students become obsessed with the examination process, too. Students in the fourth grade, who assiduously prepare for the state examination, fear failure and become extremely demoralized if they fail to achieve state standards.

Standards are shaped by the governor, state legislature, and the Office of the Superintendent of Public Instruction, and have been toughened significantly since the state legislature passed the Education Reform Act in 1993. It is assumed that tougher standards will force both teachers and students to become more goal-directed in the educational process. The results, however, have been mixed. After the standardized examination expectations were toughened, elementary school students failed the test in overwhelming numbers; nearly half of the students did not achieve the new requirements. The effect on school districts has been a noticeable increase in political pressure to match curriculum to the examination in order to meet the expected educational outcomes.

For public school districts, the dynamic and increasingly toughened standards have meant that principals and teachers are under intense scrutiny from lawmakers and citizens eager to improve student achievement. Failure to meet those standards is not viewed with much sympathy. In many school districts nationwide, school administrators have been fired for not achieving the state- or district-mandated standardized examination benchmarks. Additionally, teachers whose students are not able to "produce" are occasionally reassigned to other schools. When Washington State schools were given a "C" by a study conducted by the Washington Schools Project, some concerns were raised as to whether public schools in the state would be able to be improved.

Nevertheless, not all is bleak. Scores on the SAT have begun to improve in Seattle, the state's largest school district. Fourth grade test scores, which slipped below the national average in the mid-1990's, have now begun to inch up once again. There are indications that pupils are beginning to demonstrate improved performance on the Washington Assessment of Student Learning, now that the teachers and administrators are becoming more familiar with the more rigorous student achievement expectations.

The expectations of public schools have not changed dramatically in Washington in the 1990's, but calls for school reform, accountability, and improved student performance are becoming consistently more evident. Citizens are still quite loyal to the public school system, and they are willing to pay the costs associated with improvement—but they are quite clear in their message that they want to see results. The expenditures for public education must produce tangible outcomes or they will likely begin to "exit," eventually transferring their children and their tax dollars to private school options. For public schools, therefore, it is clearly a fork in the road. The crisis of legitimacy has not yet been fully heralded. There is time still to produce education outcomes that parents and citizens have been increasingly demanding.

The current social and economic climate is acutely unforgiving of failure to meet expectations. The world has become highly commodified. Consumers search for companies that produce products that are reliable and available at a low cost. When products fail to meet individual quality standards or the costs rise above self-defined budget constraints, consumers are less likely to be loyal to a particular company, and more likely to simply search for another producer that has higher product quality at a lower price. In this environment, public schools must become entrepreneurial.   School administrators must actively develop partnerships with other schools and with the private sector in order to maintain steady resources and to search for methods of improving student achievement (i.e., the product). Simply following the classical model of organization, which assumes that goals and resource provision remain constant, is often a formula for failure, primarily because organizations—particularly schools—operate in a dynamic environment.

Schools in the State of Washington have been very active in becoming more entrepreneurial and consumer-driven.   With the help of federal grant money, eight Washington school districts and several individual schools across the state participated in the Schools for the 21st Century Program. Based on a generic model proposed at the national level, the Washington State variation relaxed state-level regulations on public school management and curriculum, giving administrators and teachers greater flexibility to experiment with new education tools and pedagogy. Public-private partnerships between schools and local businesses were developed to help students become more aware of the long-term economic value of their education and occupation options. Parents were encouraged to become more active in the educational process, with particular attention paid to the special needs of low income families. Schools were given extra in-service days every year so that administrators and teachers could develop cooperative relationships and coordinate the implementation of new and highly innovative educational programs.

The Schools for the 21st Century program was a clear attempt to recognize the demands being made on schools. Rather than build boundaries around public school organizations and fend off environmental constraints, public schools were actually recognizing the needs extant in school environments and attempting to meet those needs. In the end, however, the program's success was analyzed largely along one dimension: test score improvements, which for the most part remained quite low. The disappointing results were perhaps not a very big surprise. The program was pilot tested in some of the most disadvantaged school districts in the state, where poverty rates among students were staggering and the challenges associated with limited English proficiency abundant.   The entrepreneurial spirit of school administrators—while certainly not encouraged by this "if it works in the toughest cases, then it will work anywhere" approach—has survived.

In the midst of this effort to build more dynamic schools, the state legislature passed the Education Reform Act of 1993, which makes it very clear what is expected of schools in the way of performance. State-level policymakers clearly defined, via standardized examination, what 'academic excellence' (or at least 'acceptable performance') currently means. In other words, schools are being provided with the benchmark that must be met or exceeded—the central goal of the school is being more clearly defined and the flexibility necessary to meet these goals is being increasingly provided to public schools.

Adopting   a   'reinventing   government'   schema,   school   district superintendents and principals are able to identify and correct specific problems with school operations and goal-setting.   With increased authority come increased opportunities to exhibit the strong leadership needed to reinvigorate schools and reinforce organizational goals. Hands-on approaches to administration encourage policy experimentation. Parents, teachers, and administrators in school districts nationwide increasingly develop collaborative approaches when both identifying problems and attempting to resolve them. Cooperative efforts are more likely to succeed because the complexities surrounding many highly customer-driven public policies are frequently identified by the consumers of public goods and services, who are experts in their own right. Additionally, shared leadership often means shared responsibility. By collectively deciding on strategies and identifying reasonable policy goals, citizen-stakeholders are less likely to become frustrated with outcomes and simply choose to exit the public school system.

Increased local control, however, does face many problems that must be more widely recognized and solved in a timely manner. Frequently, a lack of community 'ownership' that should accompany any movement towards local control spells personal disaster for local school administrators. State-level demands for higher test scores often mean that local administrators and teaching staff find themselves faced with a task incommensurate with the level of increased local authority. Evidence from the organizational social psychology literature indicates that work-related stress can become unbearable under such conditions. When outcomes are agreeable and students meet or exceed the mandated benchmarks on standardized examinations, political leaders, parents of school-aged children, and other community members are satisfied. Unmet expectations, however, are frequently greeted with hostility and demands for accountability, which may mean the termination of administrative staff and the wholesale transfer of 'ineffective' teaching staff to other schools.

Not only are teachers and administrators made to suffer, but public schools as organizations can be severely weakened when resources and environmental constraints fluctuate as a result of client anomie. School administrators and teachers must have the resources necessary to respond to new student cohorts. In some instances, particular student cohorts face far greater educational challenges than previous or later cohorts. A particular curriculum and pedagogy that produced outstanding student achievement in a particular year might produce underachievers when employed with student cohorts with more limited educational abilities. An organizational reward/punishment system that focuses on standardized test performance, with 'punishment' in the form of resource curtailment for underperforming schools, would likely have a chain reaction. Underperforming schools are likely to face the greatest educational challenges and require steady resources if improved performance is to be achieved. As an educator speaking to other educators, this author would likely receive some affirmation from fellow pedagogists: there is abundant anecdotal evidence to be found in every teachers' lounge and departmental meeting rooms to indicate that, controlling for instructional methods and curriculum, some students are easier to educate than others. The more challenging cases require more instructional resources and time, but are frequently highly rewarding. Performance may or may not meet preordained standards, but is frequently higher than if extra time and resources had not been committed to the education of these students.

In this regard, merit pay plans have been promoted in Washington, with the intent of rewarding individual teachers who have produced demonstrable education results in their classrooms.   Teachers' unions, however, have openly rejected the merit pay plans.   Unions are concerned with merit pay for a number of reasons.   Merit pay works against the general goals of teachers' unions, which is to promote the *collective* interests of education workers in the state.   Unions work for the rights and interests of educators by representing workers in interaction with management (e.g., school boards, administrators, state legislatures, and superintendents of public instruction).   Part of a union's power is a function of the effective representation of its members.   Merit pay, however, has the effect of weakening the representative power of teachers' unions.

Pay-for-performance (i.e., merit pay) is a function of a direct relationship between supervisors (i.e., management) and teachers (i.e., labor).   In this relationship, teachers and their supervisors negotiate performance standards with the expectation that superior performance will produce merit rewards.   The negotiated standards and rewards are likely be curriculum- and grade-specific and thus will vary from teacher to teacher and across school districts. Additionally, it is likely that outcomes will be judged differently, and the size of merit pay rewards are partially a function of resource availability.

Unions reject merit pay schemes because they have a tendency to erode the strength of their representative function, giving educational management greater power over teachers.   Additionally, union leaders complain that variations in the process by which merit pay is rewarded and the size of the reward promote pay inequity, and will ultimately have a negative impact on student achievement.   Teachers will be attracted to districts that offer greater financial compensation and merit pay plans, exiting districts that are underfunded and have a greater proportion of challenging student-learners.   The result will be an ever-widening gulf in educational achievement, contributing to the destruction of the public school system.

The Washington State Teachers' Association successfully redirected the teacher pay debate towards the issue of across-the-board salary increases. Union representatives argued that inflationary trends reflected in the Consumer Price Index in the early 1990's had resulted in lost income for the state's educators, which was not equitably adjusted given changing economic conditions.   As a result, teachers were not adequately compensated for the vast majority of the decade.   In 1999, the state teachers' association called for a 15.5 percent raise to compensate teachers for lost wages.   Additionally, the union pushed for the pegging of increases in teacher compensation to the CPI index so as to ensure equitable salaries (Turner and Burns 1999).   The state legislature balked at the union proposal, proposing a variable salary increase—dependent largely upon teacher rank and grade—of approximately 6 percent.   The union threatened to strike, but in the end the 6 percent raise went into effect (Gavin and Harrell 1999).

As addressed earlier, resource allocation reflects the priorities of school organizations. In large measure, resource priorities are mandated by political leaders and state education bureaucracies. Teachers' compensation has become a larger portion of school district budgets in Washington, which is evidence frequently cited by critics of public schools. The growing portion of the budget dedicated to instructional compensation is a reflection of increased interest on the part of policymakers to shrink classroom sizes. Smaller teacher-pupil ratios necessitate the employment of more teachers. Hence, a distinct policy priority is reflected in the budgets of Washington school districts. In viewing a thirty-year trend, teachers' salaries nationwide have remained relatively flat when adjusted for inflation. In adjusted dollars, the average teacher salary nationwide rose just $500 during the period 1977-1998. Budget commitments to teachers' salaries demonstrated marked increases in the 1990's. Teachers' salaries in Washington State—in constant 1995 dollars—rose from an average of $38,467 in 1996 to $42,235 in 1998—an increase of approximately 7 percent. The commitment to teachers and classroom size is growing, reflecting public concern with the quality of public elementary and secondary education and outcomes on standardized student achievement examinations.

SCHOOL VIOLENCE AND DISRUPTIVE BEHAVIOR AS AN ENVIRONMENTAL CONSTRAINT

Education quality focuses not only on issues of pedagogy, curriculum, and achievement, but is also related to school safety. Public school shootings such as the tragic events occurring in Washington, Oregon, and Colorado and elsewhere in recent years are a grave indication that public school safety is of growing concern. The highly traumatic images of slain and injured students, and weapon-toting students on campus and in communities are a reminder of the potential for future violence with possibly deadly consequences.

In their historical analysis of school violence *The Evolution of School Disturbance in America: Colonial Times to Modern Day*, Gordon Crews and M. Reid Counts (1997) study the theoretical explanations for adolescent violence, evolving institutional responses to the deviant behavior of school-aged children, and the sociocultural changes frequently attributed to both the changing nature of adolescent misbehavior and society's responses to it. The evidence indicates that adolescent violence and crime is not a new phenomenon brought about by less stringent social standards, the disappearance of the "traditional" family, or illegal drug use among youth; nevertheless, these factors either contribute to or are causally related to individual adolescent criminal activity. In order to reduce adolescent crime and violence, policymakers must develop a greater understanding of the needs of their student population as individuals as opposed to amorphous "students" (i.e., education products).

The concept of adolescence is a fairly recent development in human history. In the Middle Ages, for instance, children engaged in what are commonly considered to be adult behaviors from a very young age, to include sexual behavior, alcohol consumption, and the use of coarse language. In many societies, adolescents were not held accountable for their youthful behaviors. The educational expectations of young people were relatively low. Most occupations were not technical and children often labored from a very young age alongside adult workers (Crews and Counts 1997: 4-5). As society modernized, urbanized, and became increasingly affluent, the concept of 'childhood' became more widely recognized. As 'children,' adolescents were viewed as having a very high potential for irresponsibility, thus requiring strong discipline to maintain social control. It is possible that the maintenance of this stereotypical view of adolescence contributes to youth-related behavioral problems in contemporary society.

There are a variety of theoretical explanations for criminal and violent behavior, ranging from free will and social anomie to gang theory and biological perspectives. Behavior is often explained using socioeconomic factors, group association factors, and even school-related factors. Children living in poverty may suffer to a greater extent from the psychological stresses associated with adolescence. Patterns of social interaction and general behavior within families may be linked to youth violence. Children raised in discordant or violent families are likely to adopt similar patterns of behavior. Children who are neglected by their parents may develop nihilistic attitudes towards life, demonstrating little concern for their own social and economic future (Lawrence 1998: 59). Student absenteeism, academic failure, and delinquency only serve to compound problems and contribute to frustration. These individuals are often labeled 'losers' by high-achieving students or as 'problem students' by administrators and teachers. Gang membership may serve as a surrogate family of many delinquent students and reinforces the role of violence and crime as gang norms. Under such conditions, violent and destructive behavior on the part of such students becomes more common as those forms of behavior become the individuals' only 'successful' efforts, frequently rewarded through positive recognition from peer groups (Lawrence 1998; Crews and Counts 1997).

Group membership at school offers another interesting explanation for youth behavior problems in schools. Behavioral expectations are defined in part by group membership—a phenomenon that is frequently emphasized in popular movies and television programs directed at teenagers.   School-aged children and young adults within particular school social groups tend to enforce group norms, reinforcing the behavior of other group members either through positive or negative recognition depending upon whether actions taken by individuals associated with the group are consonant with recognized patterns of behavior (Devine 1996).

The organization of schools and the policies pertaining to the preservation of order may further inform our understanding of the factors related to school violence. American elementary and secondary education, for instance, has historically placed tremendous emphasis on the prevention of social disorder. The educational process served as a first step for youth socialization into society and its norms. As such, the schools have a system of uniform rules and regulations to be obeyed by students, regardless of age or maturity. Individuals who act independently or in a manner that is not consistent with school organizational expectations are punished in some manner in order to discourage aberrant behavior. Punishments were much more severe in the 18th and 19th centuries than during the Progressive Era in American education. Crews and Counts (1997: 45-46) provide a schoolmaster's list of punishments that he had administered over the course of a fifty-year career. The punishments included nearly 1 million blows with a cane, over 20 thousand blows with a ruler, and approximately 1.1 million raps on the head.

Social order within the school was a salient concern to common school administrators and teachers in the early part of 20th century. Youth rebellions in the 1920's were perceived as evidence of the need to maintain strong social control over children and young adults through the education process—either in the common system of education or through reformatory schools. Changes in youth culture brought on initially by increased mobility and individual freedom—paralleling increased adolescent access to the automobile in the 1950's, combined with a significant culture shift in the 1960's—correlated with a decline in social disorder in public schools (Crews and Counts 1997).

For the most part, the most visible signs of school disorder are physical attacks/fights without weapons, vandalism, and theft. Data collected in 1998 by the National Center for Educational Statistics, U.S. Department of Education, indicate that physical attacks/fights were the most common crime reported to the police, occurring at a rate of 0.08 percent. The rate was higher among middle school children—8.7 incidents reported to the police for every 1,000 students. Reported thefts occurred at a rate of 5.6 incidents per 1,000 students and 3.7 incidents per 1,000 students, while reported cases of vandalism occurred at a rate of 3.4 and 2.8 incidents per 1,000 students in high schools and middle schools respectively. In viewing national data, physical attacks/fights with weapons, robberies, and rapes/sexual assaults occurred a much lower rate—in all instances at a rate less than 0.5 cases per 1,000 students (Kaufman et al. 1998: 17).

Student victimization rates remained fairly stable between 1976 and 1996. The percentage of 12th graders who reported having something stolen from them remained at approximately 40 percent. The percentage of 12th graders who reported either being injured by someone at school or being threatened with physical violence remained stable during the same twenty-year time period. In 1996, 13 percent of all twelfth graders reported that they had been threatened with a weapon, and 22 percent reported having been threatened without a weapon. The prevalence of 12th graders threatened with injury was higher for male students than for female students. Urban schools are much more prone to disruptive behavior than is the case in suburban and rural schools (Kaufman et al. 1998: 8).

In *Maximum Security: The Culture of Violence in Inner-City Schools*, John Devine (1996) observes that many present-day attempts at establishing order in public schools have not been highly effective. The introduction of security guards, metal detectors, and video-monitoring devices has changed the role of both teachers and administrators. Historically, school principals, deans of students, and teachers were responsible for maintaining order on the school campus and within the classroom. The introduction of security teams and technology, however, has meant that school safety specialists are now in charge of maintaining order, while administrators serve as school administrative representatives in punishment review hearings held at district administrative meetings or in the courts. Teachers are still faced with threatening and violent students, but are largely helpless to discipline students. Public schools' response to school violence and disruption does little to replace the image in the minds of students (particularly male students) that as a group they are viewed as potentially dangerous individuals expected to behave in a disruptive manner.

Reactive approaches, such as security guards and surveillance, serve to limit the introduction of many dangerous weapons into the school building, but do not actively prevent violence and disruption. Devine (1996) documents many examples of student fights and nonweapon assaults on teachers, that were nonetheless violent and disruptive. In many instances, security guards simply document incidences, fearing civil court actions if they become too involved in breaking up the disturbances. Principals, in turn, are frequently frustrated with their inability to effectively punish or even fire lax security personnel. Beyond this, the introduction of security guards has paradoxically led to the introduction of new social and sometimes criminal problems. Familiarity between guards and students has occasionally led to consensual or forced intimacy leading to student pregnancies and rape. Students often view school guards as authority figures who care about student safety, but occasionally witness security officer activities that are anathema to the idealized image.

Youth criminality, school violence, and social disorder beginning in the mid-1960's and continuing to the present day have provided ammunition for the critics of public schools, who frequently call for stronger controls on student behavior and more severe punishments for those youthful miscreants. Prior to the 1960's, school-related problems were most commonly vandalism, truancy, and disrespectful acts towards teachers and administrators. Since the 1970's, student violence involving murder, physical assault of teachers and other students, and forcible rape became more common. Paralleling the rise in school violence has been an increase in the identification of chronic social dilemmas among students. Teen pregnancy, child abuse, and the spread of sexually transmitted diseases, for instance, are serious issues increasingly addressed by school teachers, administrators, and counseling staff. Additionally, school violence and social problems are spreading beyond urban areas into suburban and rural school districts. Crews and Counts (1997) report that gang activity, which was more commonly found in urban school districts, is all too easily exported to nonurban school districts through student transfers from urban areas and the emulation of gang-like behavior depicted in the popular media.

There appears to be a strong correlation between social problems and school violence, which would indicate that factors commonly originating in the environment surrounding schools often force school districts to redirect organizational resources and reshape goals and priorities. School size and structure are also related to school violence. In larger schools, a smaller percentage of students become actively engaged in school-related activities, such as intramural athletics, drama clubs, and bands, which has a negative impact on students' social interconnectedness within the education process.   In larger schools, administrators and teachers often find it more difficult to identify and track delinquents, thus increasing the probability of student violence (Lawrence 1998: 227-228).

At a time when schools are being asked to place greater emphasis on student achievement, they are simultaneously forced to battle school disorder. Ironically, one of the solutions to the disorder problem—namely, strong student commitment to the learning process critical to the test score improvement agenda—often falls victim to environmental constraints. Strong and consistent conduct guidelines combined with consistently administered rewards and punishments represent one path to orderly schools and improved learning (Lawrence 1998: 229), but administrative decisions regarding the most severe punishments—suspension or expulsion—are subject to appeal in the court system. Students appear to be aware of the limitations of school administrators in their efforts to uphold student conduct regulations and to offer punishment for deviations from the rules of conduct. The powerful constraints on public school administrators' and teachers' ability to maintain control in the educational setting lead scholars to place even greater emphasis on the role of family and community in arriving at solutions to student delinquency and school violence.

In *Gangs in Schools: Signs, Symbols, and Solutions* (1998), Arnold Goldstein and Donald Kodluboy advocate multi-dimensional approaches to dealing with school violence, gang encroachment, and student drug use. The first step in establishing or reestablishing an orderly school environment begins with the hiring process.   It is essential that high quality instructional and administrative staff are recruited and retained. Applicants with close ties to youth gangs, for instance, have proven to be ineffective counselors and school safety officers due to their allegiance to their gang.

In *Creating Safe Schools: What Principals Can Do* (1994), Marie and Frank Hill argue that school social order requires the organizational skills and leadership of prescient and vigilant building administrators. The authors provide a checklist for principals in order to gauge school safety and order. The primary role of the principal is not to attempt to solve the problem alone, but to actively engage teachers, students, parents, and the larger community in attempting to prevent school violence and disruptive behavior.   Principals should pursue contingency plans designed to reduce the impact of student social problems (e.g., psychological difficulties, behavioral problems, drug use) on the larger school community.   Administrative leadership should actively facilitate the development of a curriculum and pedagogy that will be proactive in curbing school disorder.   Leadership that fosters a greater sense of personal responsibility among all stakeholders in the educational process is likely to be highly effective.

A strong commitment to school organizational goals must be cultivated within each teacher and administrator.   The optimum method of achieving organizational unity is through collaborative consensus-building in the establishment of school policies. Administratively derived solutions to school disorder and student violence are not sufficient because they ignore the input of "street level bureaucrats" (Lipsky 1980)—teachers and building-level administrators. Teachers often use the first few days of a course to establish some sense of community within the classroom. Students are encouraged to develop an understanding of the broader goals for the course and its relevance. Additionally, an informal social network develops among students in the first few weeks of a course, whereby they learn about the diversity of interests and knowledge of their fellow classmates. Uniform administrative solutions to reduce school disorder and violence lack the more complete information that teachers are apt to enjoy due to their regular contact with students. Consensus among organizational members on the general goals and priorities regarding school disorder and violence, therefore, will foster greater organizational unity when threatened by violence or disorder within the school.

In addition to consensus-building, there is a need to clearly and regularly inform students of the organizational goals regarding school environment and education. Information campaigns via posters have proven to be an effective tool in reinforcing student conduct policies but, as a uni-dimensional strategy, are not sufficient. Conflict-resolution training is another method of limiting school disorder and violence. Informative campaigns that are targeted towards drug prevention and that discourage gang membership are valuable provided there is a substantial effort to use role playing and realistic skits to reinforce the knowledge gained due to program participation (Goldstein and Kodluboy 1998).

Finally, there is a need to establish a strong link between the school organization and the surrounding community. Vocational training centers, for example, serve to reinforce the value of education. Through practical experience, students are made more aware of the need to pursue knowledge if they wish to succeed in their chosen profession. Programs such as the Neutral Zone in Mount Terrace, Washington, have also proven to be effective community-school efforts to reduce youth violence. The Neutral Zone provides school-aged youth with a safe environment in which to interact socially as well as to gain access to counselors and other social services. An evaluation of the Neutral Zone has demonstrated the positive impact programs of this type can have on schools and communities (Thurman et al. 1996).

The resources available to limit the impact of disruptive student behavior on the core mission of public schools are somewhat limited, reducing the ability of the school to insulate its teaching staff, administrators, and student body from the school environment. Under the norms of rationality presented by contingency theorists, such as James Thompson (1967), organizations that are unable to effectively achieve their goals may choose to rely on other organizations for resources, solving problems collaboratively. The Juvenile Justice and Delinquency Prevention Act of 1974 is a good example of a cooperative effort on the part of national and state governments, and local school districts to control disorder in public schools. The act encourages the development of innovative grassroots delinquency prevention. Families, communities, and schools must be committed to reducing youth criminality.

Long-term educational innovations, such as the Perry Preschool in Ypsilanti, Michigan, encourage families and communities to become more closely connected to the formal educational process, while socializing children to view education in a broader context. Otherwise, juvenile delinquency programs are likely to fail to achieve their desired effects (Lawrence 1998: 225).

A few academic accounts of school violence run counter to the more common perceptions. In *School Crime and Juvenile Justice* (1998), Richard Lawrence argues that school violence has not increased dramatically. Studying national survey trends of student attitudes towards campus climates, Lawrence found that violent behavior remains relatively low, most commonly involving school vandalism or petty theft. For the most part, students are not victimized regularly by their fellow students. Teachers in junior high schools do report that student intimidation and cursing is quite common, particularly in urban school settings; but Lawrence argues that physical violence against teachers has remained fairly stable. "Contrary to media accounts of school crime, survey measures indicate that there is no strong evidence that serious crime in schools is an extensive problem or that the problem has increased significantly . . . . Many of the problems can be reduced through greater adult supervision and by providing students with skills to prevent conflicts and disputes from escalating into violence" (Lawrence 1998: 32).

One program that has sought to create peaceful and lasting solutions to school disruption and violence is the Resolving Conflicts Creatively Program. RCCP is a nationally recognized program designed to promote safer schools through a multi-dimensional approach to conflict resolution. Initially implemented in a handful of schools in New York City, the program has subsequently been introduced in several other states. Education and school safety are not viewed as separate organizational functions, but are considered to be equally important concerns to be addressed simultaneously. The innovative plan intends to build the social and conflict resolution skills of students so as to prevent violence and disruption *before* they occur. Students are made aware of the consequences of disruptive and violent behavior not only for themselves, but also for the victims in the school and the surrounding community. RCCP actively seeks to create an atmosphere in which teachers, parents, and students can collectively identify paths to conflict-free schools in which all parties are encouraged to be highly committed to the educational process (Lantieri and Patti 1996).

In schools that have adopted the RCCP approach, positive outcomes have been consistently recognized. Students take what they have learned in school about anger management and conflict resolution and apply their newly acquired skills to problems arising in nonschool settings. The exportation of such principles learned at school are an indication that RCCP is not just an effort to solve problems within the school environment, but a long-term effort to repair the social fabric in the communities in which students live.

In Washington State, Governor Gary Locke has promoted a no-tolerance policy regarding weapons carried by students either on campus or in the surrounding community. Students found in the possession of illegal weapons can be punished for violating school policy as well as be held criminally liable for their actions. The policy appears to be moving towards success. Handgun violations have decreased 68.4 percent on average in Washington school districts since 1993. The total number of handgun violations in 1998 was 154 compared to 488 violations in 1993. Knife and dagger violations, however, increased 3.24 percent during the same time period. There were 1,604 knife and dagger violations in 1993 and 1,656 violations in 1998. Overall, total weapons violations in Washington school districts decreased from 3,019 in 1993 to 2,624 in 1998—a decrease of approximately 13.1 percent.

Office of Superintendent of Public Instruction (OSPI) data for 1993-1996 indicates that weapons violations—on a per student basis—in Washington school districts peaked during the 1994-1995 school year at 1.84 weapons violations per 1,000 students. The average weapons violation rate in 1995-1996 was 1.52 violations per 1,000 students, which is slightly below the 1993-1994 weapons violations rate. The handgun violation rate has remained quite low in Washington school districts at *below* one violation per 2,000 students. In 1995-1996, there were on average 0.13 handgun violations per 1,000 students. Knife violations have steadily declined between 1993 and 1996. In the 1993-1994 school year, there were 1.55 knife violations per 1,000 students—in 1995-1996, that number had declined to 0.99 violations per 1,000 students.

It should be noted that these statistics do not provide a complete picture of school safety in Washington State school districts because *a large percentage of school districts had no reported weapons violations* between 1993-1996. In 1993-1994, 34 percent of the school districts in the state had no reported weapons violations, which nominally increased to 41 percent in 1995-1996. Approximately one in five school districts had no weapons violations during the entire three-year period. Perhaps even more encouraging is the evidence that the most unsafe school districts are making tremendous efforts to improve school safety. The thirty school districts with the greatest problems with weapons violations in 1993-1994 had more than halved the weapons violation rate in their districts. The mean weapons violation rate in 1993-1994 for these relatively 'unsafe' schools was approximately 6 weapons violations per 1,000 students; but that figure had declined to less than 3 weapons violations per 1,000 students by 1995-96. Contributing significantly to this decline was the marked decline in handgun violations—an astounding 87 percent decrease in violations during the three-year period Weapons violations rates for knives declined from 3.3 violations per 1,000 students to less than 1.7 violations per 1,000 students. The data suggest that on average, public schools in Washington are fairly safe and becoming even safer. School safety and order are critical to producing high quality learning environments and outstanding student achievement. School safety is even greater in the state's private schools, which witnessed less than twenty weapons violations per year during the same period; but the public school system in the state is making remarkable progress towards a weapons-free learning environment.

Weapons are but one form of disorderly behavior in school environments. To take the National Rifle Association motto slightly out of context for a moment, weapons themselves are not the cause of violence but rather the very deadly instruments used by irrational individuals intent on harming others. Clearly, there is no place for deadly weapons on a school campus for reasons that go beyond the fact that such weapons are outlawed from the school environment. Metal detectors and locker searches, which have become a much more visible part of the public school standard operating procedures, represent attempts to remove the instruments that advance violence, but perhaps do little to refocus the energies and behaviors of students who are intent on acting in a disruptive manner.

Metal detectors are mechanical devices that focus on a fact-based element of school organization—are students carrying weapons into the school? Such measures will not lead to improved student learning if students make the value-based decision to cut class or fail to show up at school on a regular basis. Irregular classroom attendance creates disorder in the school environment. Teachers must frequently spend extra time with students who have failed to master materials presented during their absence. Given that formal education occurs in a collective setting, teacher-time spent with students with attendance problems means that other students are made to suffer.

Drug and alcohol use among students distracts teachers and administrators from the core mission of public schools. Students who are under the influence of drugs or alcohol can disrupt the educational environment for their peers and instructors. Drugs can cause individuals to behave in an erratic fashion, leading to violence against school personnel and students. In order to reduce the impact of drug and alcohol use on the core mission of schools, administrators must create 'buffer units' designed to deal specifically with students' problems. School psychiatrists and counselors seek to help students overcome social and psychological problems frequently associated with drug or alcohol use. Vice principals or deans of students attempt to deter personally destructive or socially disruptive behaviors associated with drug and alcohol use. Information campaigns are often developed to discourage students from using illegal substances. In short, drug and alcohol use among students draws school resources away from the schools' core technologies and diverts attention from the core mission.

Finally, effective education requires that students respect the authority of their teachers and school administrators. Students with behavioral problems frequently show little respect for the authority of school personnel. When students challenge teachers' authority, the educational process is effectively put on hold. The primary goal of the teacher under these circumstances is to regain authority so that attention is directed at the instructor as an educator. So long as the teacher's authority is challenged, the core mission of the school is obscured or is at best only partially fulfilled.

The Office of Superintendent of Public Instruction annually surveys all 8th and 11th graders attending public schools in the State of Washington. The student survey data collected between 1991 and 1997 indicate that pupils' perceptions of school disorder are mixed (Billings 1991, 1992, 1993, 1994, 1995, 1996; Bergeson 1997). In many instances, the results offer a great deal of promise for the future, but there is a wide gulf separating middle school environments and high school environments with trends occasionally moving in opposite directions.

In 1991, greater than one in ten high school juniors indicated that student absenteeism was a serious problem at their high school, while approximately 5 percent of eighth graders reported that absenteeism was a serious problem at their middle school. Almost 70 percent of 11th graders and 29 percent of 8th graders thought that absenteeism was a moderate problem. Nearly 17 percent of 11th graders and approximately 9 percent of 8th graders felt that cutting class was a serious problem—60 percent of 11th graders and 21 percent of 8th graders viewed cutting class as a moderate problem at their schools. Alcohol and drug use was of particular concern to the high school juniors who completed the student survey. More than one in three respondents felt that alcohol use was a serious problem among their peers; and approximately 45 percent indicated that it was moderate problem. For the 8th grade survey respondents, the figures were 27.2 percent and 18.7 percent, respectively. Finally, student behavior was viewed as a serious to moderate problem by approximately 72.6 percent of 11th graders and 50.4 percent of 8th graders.

Based on student perceptions of school social order, it is fairly clear that in 1991, Washington's public schools were suffering from a fairly high level of potentially disruptive student behavior. With some exceptions, the numbers have not declined to any significant degree. In 1992, there was a fairly dramatic drop in the 11th graders' perception of absenteeism as a serious problem, but approximately 7 percent of high school juniors have consistently felt that it remains a serious problem in their schools. Among 8th graders, the perception that absenteeism is a serious problem has been steadily growing. There has been a nearly five percentage point drop in 11th graders' perception of cutting class as a serious problem, but among 8th graders there has been a marginal increase. Student perceptions of drug use as a problem at their schools have witnessed a sharp increase since 1991, but peaked in 1995 and have retreated slightly. Perceptions of alcohol use among 11th graders have declined somewhat, but have steadily increased among 8th graders.

The survey also asks students about their perceptions of the general school spirit. School spirit reflects student happiness with the general school climate as well as satisfaction with school policies, goals, and educational outcomes. On average, 35 percent of the students indicate that a lack of school spirit is a problem in their schools. Conversely 65 percent indicate that a lack of school spirit is a not a problem at their schools, which is 3.5 percent below the national average (Snyder and Hoffmann 1999: 154).

Students' perceptions of school spirit experienced a slight downward trend between 1991 and 1997. Eighth graders perception of the presence of real school spirit in middle schools declined 3.7 percent. In 1991, 13.1 percent of 8th graders thought that a lack of school spirit was a serious problem at their school, while roughly 15 percent were similarly concerned about school spirit in 1997. While there was a small dip between 1992 and 1996 in 11th graders' perceptions of school spirit, 1991-1997 survey results were fairly stable—on average 15 percent of 11th graders felt that a lack of school spirit was a serious problem. In 1991, 11th graders' concerns about the campus climate at their high schools was approximately 2 percent higher than 8th graders surveyed in the same year. By 1997, students' perceptions of school spirit were virtually identical.

Simple correlative analysis indicates that student academic performance is not significantly related to perceptions of school disorder or school spirit. Nevertheless, schools that have significantly higher aggregate student achievement on standardized examinations tend to report greater problems with school disorder than schools with lower standardized test scores. Weapons violations as a measure of school safety, however, indicate that the higher performing schools are actually safer. How does one explain the fact that students perceive that there are more serious problems at their school than appears to be the case?

One possible explanation is that students at higher performing schools are more *sensitive* to the conditions in their learning environments. When students are more committed to the learning process they are likely to be less tolerant of disruptive classmates. At schools in which physical violence, theft, and bullying, for instance, are more common, students may be desensitized to the conditions. Additionally, schools with a record of disruptive behavior frequently have metal detectors and enhanced security measures designed to limit the impact of disruptive students. Evidence in the extant literature indicates that disorderly schools are frequently plagued by other problems, such as poverty and lower levels of family social capital. Students from lower socioeconomic backgrounds are less likely to perceive that their formal education experience in public schools will translate into a brighter future. Disruptive behavior in the classroom would be less of a concern to students if they are not committed to the learning process. Worse still, for those students who live in conditions of low socioeconomic status but are committed to escaping the cycle of poverty, the disorderly conditions in their school environments may impede their progress.

The data on student perceptions of disorder indicate that despite the drop in weapons violations, public schools are still besieged by other pressing social problems. These social problems stand in the way of effective student learning, necessitating the diversion of resources away from student learning. Administrative subunits designed to deal with the effects of these problems continue to have their work cut out for them, and the probability that classroom time is being diverted from the education of the larger student group and towards the disruptive behavior of particular students remains a serious problem for educators.

HUMAN CAPITAL AND FAMILY SOCIAL CAPITAL

Since the early years of the Cold War federal and state funding has often surpassed local funding as the primary resource base for local schools. In the process, local citizen 'voice' in elementary and secondary education policy was greatly diminished. With the enactment of the National Defense Education Act of 1957, public education was increasingly viewed by lawmakers as a strategic weapon in a life-or-death struggle with an evil and relentless foe. Reflecting the dominant policy objectives of the era, education policy became substantially less responsive to community-based stakeholders than it had been historically.   Bureaucratically derived solutions were intended to produce a technologically   advanced   workforce   capable   of   scientific   inquiry   and engineering accomplishments superior to those of the U.S.S.R. and the Soviet bloc (Spring 1976).

In time, however, the travails of the nation as it dealt with the Civil Rights Movement, Vietnam protests, Watergate, environmentalism, and feminism gave rise to a plethora of cause groups and an explosion of advocacy across the political landscape; in many cases the target of change which was most immediate and accessible to local action by such groups was the public school system in their communities. Along with this renewed interest in local-level policy and practices came the realization that active parental engagement and community support played a marked role in shaping student performance (Hanushek 1994; Meade 1972). In more recent years the challenge of private and charter school competition has hastened the movement toward "site-based" management in the public school establishment, making the connection among schools, parents, and local communities even more critical for school performance.

In contradistinction to the Ford Foundation study (Meade 1972), contemporary researchers seeking to identify the correlates of school performance frequently distinguish between *socioeconomic constraints* and *community and family affirmation of organizational goals* when studying the school-environment interface.   Socioeconomic conditions within the school district are identified as dimensions of human capital. Human capital relates to individual   human   potential   extant   within   communities   or   families. Parenthetically,   while socioeconomic conditions have improved for many Americans in recent years, student performance and the quality of public school district organizational 'output' has remained largely unchanged at a clearly sub-optimal level.

Exogenous institutional abutments, the foundational elements of 'social capital,' are generally analyzed by contemporary researchers in terms of the interactions occurring between individuals and among civic, social, religious, and public organizations. The building and nurturing of the strong communities requisite for the maintenance of social capital necessitate high levels of interpersonal trust and active citizen engagement in social networks. Social networks are composed of "a variety of different entities," both "individual" and "corporate" (Coleman 1988: S98).

It is likely that public school district organizations benefit from strong social capital in a number of ways. The presence of healthy social networks and related generalized   social   trust   emanating   from   such   interactions   reduce organizational stress within school settings. The effort to promote the coproduction of education services via parental and community contributions to the educational efforts of teachers and school officials is likely met with greater success. Organizationally, parental and community support for school district programs and goals reduces the need for investment in boundary-spanning activities, thus enabling greater energy to be focused on core goals and tasks.

The existing public education policy literature tends to uphold the hypothesized relationship between social capital and public school performance (student achievement). Families with a consistent parental presence and expressing high academic expectations for children tend to produce superior performance by pupils. To some degree, family effects are independent of variation in socioeconomic human capital characteristics of families. Family social capital is preserved through "intergenerational closure" and "exchange" (Hogan et al. 1993) critical in establishing "a set of effective sanctions that can monitor and guide behavior" (Coleman 1988: S107).

Toby Parcel and Elizabeth Menaghan (1994) explore further relevant indicators describing family effects in relation to the promotion of early child intellectual and emotional development. They found that family stability had a significant impact on both the bounds of intellectual growth and the celerity with which it occurs. The "occupational complexity" of mothers had a positive impact on children, provided working hours were relatively stable and predictable.   "[The] emphasis on mother foregoing employment to prevent children's social maladjustment . . . does not receive strong support" (Parcel and Menaghan 1994: 1002). Inconsistent working conditions for fathers generally had a negative impact on child educational and social development. Single-parent households followed patterns similar to those households featuring a lack of paternal employment stability (Astone and McLanahan 1991).

Family setting appears to have a sustained impact on individuals, extending beyond their early childhood and pubescence. Educational aspirations extending beyond secondary education can be credited in large measure to patterns of behavior and attitudes established through nurturing. Controlling for social and economic conditions, Mark Smith et al. (1995) found than parental expectations and active involvement in the monitoring of children's school work during high school was positively related to the probability of a young adult's pursuit of higher education. Community stability was isolated as a significant ancillary influence in predicting educational goals.   In contradistinction to Parcel and Menaghan (1994), mothers' extradomiciliary work patterns were negatively related to student educational attainment.   While the research observations addressed here reflect somewhat inconsistent empirical findings, the substantial role of family setting in accounting for educational outcomes is clearly evidenced.

Beyond educational performance and aspirations, it is possible that social capital influences the choice of occupational status and work-related goals. Kevin Marjoribanks (1991: 238) found that twenty-year-old Australians' educational attainment and occupational aspirations could, to a significant degree, be explained by the levels of human capital and social engagement capital present in their families.   Family social capital was significantly and positively related to the educational attainment and occupational aspirations of survey respondents of both genders. The educational achievement of women was significantly influenced by family human capital; social capital explained 30 percent of the variance in the predictive model of occupational attainment.

The social capital literature related to student achievement pays only slight attention to the inclusiveness of a society. Civic communities often have an accepted set of standards and behaviors, a tendency which can result in the exclusion of particular individuals and groups. Ricardo Stanton-Salazar (1997) argues that strong social capital collectivities must seek to be inclusive, particularly in the elementary and secondary educational setting. Social networks would be enriched if 'community' was defined broadly.

Given strong findings of factors exogenous to schools reported in the social capital literature, researchers seeking to understand the determinants of school performance must actively consider the role of organizational environment when seeking to remedy apparent shortcomings in public schools and school districts. Community and family social capital has a significant impact on student aspirations, behavior, and achievements (Brooks-Gunn et al. 1993). The relative inclusiveness of community appears also to be an important consideration when pursuing improved school district organizational outputs (i.e., student academic achievement).

Family social capital can be measured through analyses of students' study habits, grade point average, and future educational aspirations. Theoretically, students with advanced educational goals will enroll in advanced high school courses and study harder. A dedication to learning frequently yields higher grade point averages.

In practice, however, grade point averages follow a path that deviates from changes in students' study habits. Grade point averages have steadily increased amongst high school students. In 1991, approximately 13 percent of high school juniors reported having a cumulative high school grade point average of 3.70 (i.e., an 'A' average) or better. The percentage of 'A' students increased to nearly 18 percent by 1997. There are at least three plausible explanations for this significant increase in the proportion of 'A' students. One possible reason might be grade inflation, which is the result of lowering the standards for the top letter grade, a problem which has been documented in the academic literature (Edwards 2000). A second explanation would be that students are becoming more dedicated to their school work and are performing significantly better. Finally, schools might be developing more orderly learning environments, thus making the precious hours in the formal classroom setting more amenable to effective education.

Perhaps the best method of analyzing the first explanation would be to study the evidence for the second and third explanations. Students are clearly not becoming more dedicated to their school work. In 1991, approximately one-half of the high school juniors surveyed indicated that they studied less than four hours per week, while only one out of every five students studied at least one hour per day. Homework time declined marginally between 1991 and 1997, which would likely eliminate study habits as an explanation for the significant increase in 'A' students.

The rise in grade point average parallels increased student optimism about college attendance and graduation. In 1991, only 13.1 percent of high school juniors in the State of Washington anticipated that they would attend college and graduate. In 1997, nearly 18.5 percent of high school juniors eagerly reported the desire to attend college and pursue either a four-year degree or graduate education, which represents a greater than 40 percent increase in college-bound high schoolers. A technologically advanced job market demands that high school students focus greater attention on earning a college degree in order to achieve economic success.

The time management of high school juniors is quite revealing when attempting to explain the commitment to attaining a four-year college degree. In 1991, nearly 42 percent of high school juniors reported watching more than two hours of television per weekday evening during the school year—at a minimum, ten hours of television viewing per week. The proportion of students watching two or more hours of television per night remained fairly stable but decreased marginally to 38.3 percent in 1997. Nearly half of the juniors indicated that they worked one or more hours per day during the school week.

The data indicate that students are generally more dedicated to fulfilling immediate gratification in the form of television than they are to their studies. It could be argued that students work in order to save money for college, but the argument has certain weaknesses—namely, the very small proportion of students who work twenty or more hours per week, which would indicate a more serious commitment to paying for further education. A much more likely explanation for high school student employment is that the funds generated help to finance the conspicuous consumption necessary to gain peer group acceptance.

Student goals, therefore, are frequently related to short-term social 'needs' rather than long-term goals. Despite their goals of college entrance and degree attainment, students tend to view education as a secondary demand on their time, which means that school administrators and teachers are likely to find the educational process challenging. Students tend not to see a direct short-term reward from a large time commitment to learning, implicitly demanding—either through disruptive behavior at school or through prioritization of their out-of-school time—that schools regularly legitimize goals and processes. Organizations facing chaotic and highly variable environmental pressures of this type are less likely to regularly produce predictable and desirable outputs.

Eighth grade students exhibit an even greater desire to pursue a college education. In 1991, nearly 70 percent of eighth graders in the State of Washington believed that they would attend college. By 1997, over 80 percent indicated that at the very least they would matriculate at a four-year college or university, and 20 percent believed that they would eventually earn an advanced degree. Between 1991 and 1997, less than 13 percent of eighth graders spent one hour of night on their homework during the school year, which would further reinforce the limited connection drawn between homework (as a display of commitment to the attainment of future educational goals), school achievement, and the attainment of future educational goals.

Students are increasingly focused on gaining college entrance, but they appear to be slightly less dedicated to their school work. Nevertheless, they are seemingly rewarded for their reduced commitment to education through grade inflation. These findings are worrisome for a number of reasons. First, it appears that student achievement is now to a lesser degree a function of dedication, and to a greater degree the result of relaxed grading standards. Second, students whose high school grades were achieved with little difficulty may become disillusioned after matriculating at a university. College classes frequently demand a greater time commitment on the part of students, and offer more detailed and complex homework assignments. A student who is not experienced in devoting large blocks of time to studying class material is likely to perform suboptimally. Finally, disillusioned college students are increasingly dropping out of school due to mediocre performances, poor advising, and an insufficient transition from high school. High school grade inflation—combined with the resource motivations of the full time equivalent-generated public university (i.e., student enrollment and retention)—means that college entrance is more assured for larger portions of high school students.

CONCLUSION

Environmental conditions play a significant role in explaining public school performance. In Washington State, voter support for public schools is best exemplified by the rejection of two large-scale privatization initiatives, which would have resulted in the weakening and potential elimination of a large portion of the public school system. Additionally, voters supported two candidates for public office (Governor Locke and Terry Bergeson) who called for the reform of public schools focusing on a two-pronged approach: encouraging innovation and increasing accountability. Neither Locke nor Bergeson called for the introduction of market-based competition, choosing instead to insulate the schools from this additional external influence and allowing the reform effort time to develop and produce results. Voters are very clear in their views—they want improved student performance and safer schools. The opinion polls indicate that voters are growing restless, often embracing market-based reforms and losing their confidence in public schools.

While the privatization movement is a significant environmental constraint facing public schools, other environmental constraints are more directly related to the issue of school performance and delegitimization of public schools. Socioeconomic conditions, school safety, and family social capital are serious perennial problems constraining the learning process. Disruptive behavior in schools results in a weakening of core technology (i.e., teachers). Instructional staff must spend greater time maintaining classroom order and legitimizing the learning process and curriculum to students. Socioeconomic disparities and weakened family social capital mean a lower probability that students will have a sense of hope for their future. Without a long-term educational outlook, students will be less likely to see the process of education as anything more than a mechanical exercise with little in the way of personal benefit.

Appendix 3.1
Median Weapons Violations in Washington State School Districts, 1993-1997

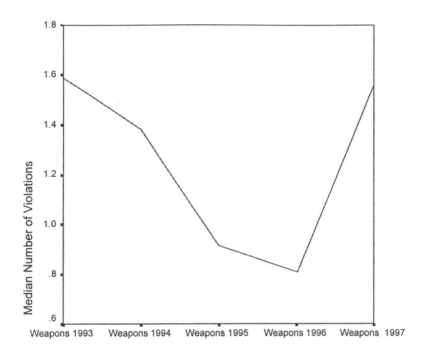

WORKS CITED

Astone, N. and McLanahan, S. 1991. Family Structure, Parental Practices, and High School Completion, *American Sociological Review*. 56(3): 309-320.

Beason, T. 1996. "Parents Push for 'Classic School': Issaquah Proposal to Let Citizens Do It." November 15. *The Seattle Times*, B1.

Bergeson, T. 1997. *Washington State Assessment Program: Student Questionnaire*. Olympia: Office of the Superintendent of Public Instruction.

Billings, J. 1991. *Washington State Assessment Program: Student Questionnaire*. Olympia: Office of the Superintendent of Public Instruction.

_____. 1992. *Washington State Assessment Program: Student Questionnaire*. Olympia: Office of the Superintendent of Public Instruction.

_____. 1993. *Washington State Assessment Program: Student Questionnaire*. Olympia: Office of the Superintendent of Public Instruction.

_____. 1994. *Washington State Assessment Program: Student Questionnaire*. Olympia: Office of the Superintendent of Public Instruction.

_____. 1995. *Washington State Assessment Program: Student Questionnaire*. Olympia: Office of the Superintendent of Public Instruction.

_____. 1996. *Washington State Assessment Program: Student Questionnaire*. Olympia: Office of the Superintendent of Public Instruction.

Brooks-Gunn, J., Duncan, G., Klebanov, P., and Sealand, N. 1993. "Do Neighborhoods Influence Child and Adolescent Development?" *American Journal of Sociology*. 99(2): 353-395.

Cafazzo, D. 1997. "A Call for the 3 R's and Discipline: Statewide Poll Shows Public Support for Schools—With a Definite Back-to-Basics Sentiment." January 17. *The News Tribune*, B1.

Coleman, J. 1988. "Social Capital in the Creation of Human Capital," *American Journal of Sociology*. 94(Supplement): S95-S120.

Crews, G. and Counts, M. 1997. *The Evolution of School Disturbance in America: Colonial Times to Modern Day*. Westport, CT: Praeger.

Devine, J. 1996. *Maximum Security: The Culture of Violence in Inner-City Schools*. Chicago, IL: The University of Chicago Press.

Editorial. 1996. "State Ballot Initiatives." November 1 *The Seattle Times*, H22.

Editorial. 1998. "School Vouchers May Be the Answer," January 5 *The News Tribune*, A6.

Edwards, C. 2000. "Grade Inflation: The Effects on Educational Quality and Personal Well-Being.," *Education*. 120(3): 538-46

Gavin, R. and Harrell, D. 1999. "Senate Plans Guarantees 6% Teacher Raise, but Educators Call Proposal an 'Insult,' Threaten Strikes" April 20 *Seattle Post-Intelligencer*, B1.

Goldstein, A. and Kodluboy, D. 1998. *Gangs in Schools: Signs, Symbols, Solutions*. Champaign, IL: Research Press.

Hanushek, E. 1994. *Making Schools Work: Improving Performance and Controlling Costs*. Washington, DC: Brookings Institution.

Hill, M. and Hill, F. 1994. *Creating Safe Schools: What Principals Can Do*. Thousand Oaks, CA: Corwin Press.

Hogan, D., Eggebeen, D., and Clogg, C. 1993. "The Structures of Intergenerational Exchanges in American Families," *American Journal of Sociology*. 98(6): 1428-1458.

Holt, G. 1996. "State Voters Reject Both Charter School and Voucher Initiatives." November 6 *Seattle Post-Intelligencer*, A15.

Kaufman, P., Chen, X., Choy, S., Chandler, K., Chapman, C., Rand, M., and Ringel, C. 1998. *Indicators of School Crime and Safety, 1998.* Washington, DC: U.S. Department of Educational Research and Improvement/U.S. Department of Justice, Office of Justice Programs.

Lantieri, L. and Patti, J. 1996. *Waging Peace in Our Schools.* Boston, MA: Beacon Press.

Lawrence, R. 1998. *School Crime and Juvenile Justice.* New York: Oxford University Press.

Lilly, Dick 1997. "Can All Seattle Schools Go Charter?: Stanford Explores Option if State Legislation Passes." April 16 *The Seattle Times*, B2.

Lipsky, M. 1980. *Street-Level Bureaucracy: Dilemmas of the Individual in the Public Services.* New York: Russell Sage Foundation.

Marjoribanks, K. 1991. "Family Human and Social Capital and Young Adults' Educational Attainment and Occupational Aspirations," *Psychological Reports.* 69: 237-238.

Meade, E. 1972. *A Foundation Goes to School: The Ford Foundation Comprehensive School Improvement Program (1960-1970).* New York: Ford Foundation.

Parcel, T. and Menaghan, E. 1994. "Early Parental Work, Family Social Capital, and Early Childhood Outcomes," *American Journal of Sociology.* 99(4): 972-1009.

Paulson, M. 1996. "Survey Finds Voter Support for Education: Most Would Lift State Limit on Public School Spending." October 28 *Seattle Post-Intelligencer*, A1.

Roeder, D. 1999. "Obsession With Testing Fails Students" May 26 *Chicago Sun-Times*, 49.

Shapley, T. 1999. "Bill Would Offer Parents Tax Relief for Home Schooling" February 9 *Seattle Post-Intelligencer*, B2.

Smith, M., Beaulieu, L., Seraphine, A. 1995. "Social Capital, Place of Residence, and College Attendance," *Rural Sociology.* 60(3): 363-380.

Snyder, T. and Hoffmann, C. 1999. *Digest of Education Statistics.* Washington, DC: National Center for Education Statistics.

Spring, J. 1976. *The Sorting Machine: National Education Policy Since 1945.* New York: David McKay, Co.

Stanton-Salazar, R. 1997. "A Social Capital Framework for Understanding the Socialization of Racial Minority Children and Youths," *Harvard Educational Review.* 67(1): 1-40.

Thompson, J. 1967. *Organizations in Action: Social Science Bases of Administrative Theory.* New York: McGraw-Hill.

Thurman, Q., Giacommazzi, A., Reisig, M., Muller, D. 1996. "Community-Based Gang Prevention and Intervention: An Evaluation of the Neutral Zone," *Crime & Delinquency.* 42(3): 279-295.

Turner, J. and Burns, S. 1999. "Washington State Teachers' Union Sticks to Pay-Increase Campaign" April 25 *The News Tribune* (Tacoma, WA*)*, A1.

Turner, J. and Callaghan, P. 1996. "Education Above All, Voters Say: A Survey of 556 Election-Year Voters Tested the 'Mood of Washington' and Found a Lot of the Hot-Button Issues Merely Lukewarm" May 20 *The News Tribune*, A1.

Wilson, J. 1989. *Bureaucracy: What Government Agencies Do and Why They Do It*. New York: Basic Books.

Chapter 4

School Finance Issues
and Organization

Organization and finance issues are inextricably linked in analyses of public schools. The vast majority of funding for Washington State's public elementary and secondary schools comes from state and federal sources. Generally, these funds are allocated on a per pupil basis. Larger schools receive more basic education funds than do smaller schools. Schools with a greater proportion of students who fall under special education guidelines are provided a larger portion of state and federal special fund revenues for the specific purpose of providing education to differently abled students than are other schools with fewer special education students.

Greater funding in particular areas, such as transportation or bilingual education, shapes the organization of a school and school district. A rural district with a widely dispersed student population living on family farms often miles from the school building will likely have a well-financed school bus system, a pool of qualified drivers, a "bus barn" staffed with mechanics, and a fuel budget that will fluctuate depending upon current market prices. School districts with students living in close proximity to the schools might have a very limited transportation budget, but might face other constraints that require greater resources to fulfill these school-related needs.

Beyond the fairly uniform positions of school district superintendent, school principal, and teacher, there is likely to be a great deal of heterogeneity in school district organization depending in large part on the socioeconomic and geographical conditions surrounding a school. Schools are 'intensive technology' organizations, and their structure is shaped to a significant degree by the conditions existing in the organizational environment. The finance of public schools, therefore, frequently reflects the variations in student need which exist between school districts; through resource allocations, the state and federal funding sources attempt to further advance the goal of equity in education.

School finance systems in Washington and in other states have not always been as demand-driven as is currently the case. Prior to largely court-driven policy reforms, school finances were generated primarily at the local level. In many respects, school funding reflected the willingness of local voters to pay for public elementary and secondary education. In theory, a system of predominantly local funding made the public schools highly accountable to local government, voters, and parents. In fact, local funding models that advance the accountability argument are partially accurate at best, for they assume that local taxpayers actually have available the resources needed to operate a successful school system, and that this resource potential holds the attention of school administrators and teachers. Additionally, the local funding model assumes that voters and local government representatives are united in their view of a successful school, which is probably not the case. Not all districts have a similar tax base nor do all registered voters turn out to support school financial measures for the same reasons. Therefore, a funding system that relies heavily on local taxpayers may produce highly variable levels of funding and divergent funding priorities that may or may not reflect student needs.

State courts began to explore more fully the need for equality of educational opportunity in the early 1970's. In the landmark cases of *Serrano v. Priest* (1971, 1976), the California Supreme Court explored the wide disparity in local property tax rates needed to adequately finance local schools. Districts with high property values could tax at a much lower rate and still achieve their resource goals than could districts with low property values. In the 1971 *Serrano* decision the court found that these fiscal inequities violated the Equal Protection Clause in both national and state constitutions. The 1976 *Serrano* decision, saw the courts pursue a remedy for funding inequities, requiring the state to finance local school districts at a level that would simultaneously produce equalization in local school district tax burden and in school resource provision. In *San Antonio Independent School District v. Rodriguez* (1973), the U.S. Supreme Court found that the Equal Protection Clause was not violated by the variations in the local financing of schools; it did not limit the power of state courts to explore remedies to funding disparities.

Low tax base districts are not necessarily poorer school districts, and high tax base districts are not necessarily wealthy school districts. Tax bases are to some degree a function of local economies present in a school district. Poorer school districts might have a high tax base due to commercial industry, whereas wealthier districts might reject industrial development and have a lower tax base. Variations in tax bases were found to be systematically related to socioeconomic disparity (Campbell and Fischel 1996). Assumptions made in the local finance literature regarding tax bases are at times inaccurate, but those inaccuracies have not led to a reversal of the courts' school financing agenda.

The courts have shaped and continue to shape educational funding formulae in an effort to promote equity. The legitimacy of their growing role in this area is questionable, due in large part to the conditions that led up to court involvement. Critics charge that the framers of state constitutions did not originally intend to finance schools through state-sponsored tax structures.

Elementary and secondary education was viewed as the primary responsibility of local government, which would be funded through local property taxes. Judicial activism that relies on "fundamental interest" arguments leaves to the court decisions about its own scope of power in shaping public policy. More specifically, the court's power in the area of protecting "discrete and insular minorities," which emerges from a footnote in *United States v. Carolene Products* (1938), allows the court to recognize minority status in a variety of ways and shape policy to protect the identified minorities (Campbell and Fischel 1996).

Under this interpretation of court activism, the political system is viewed as controlled by special interests which shape policy in a manner that benefits a select group of citizens to the disadvantage of citizens who are either not represented in the decision-making process or whose interests are weakly represented. The aforementioned evidence notwithstanding, this theoretical perspective of local government finance and political processes argues that districts with high property valuations are wealthy districts. Citizens in wealthy districts, in turn, would not see an economic benefit to centralizing the education funding process because it would likely result in increased tax costs and decreased fiscal autonomy. Responding to interest group demands, state legislatures would likely not support funding equalization approaches. Thus, equality of educational opportunity would have to be achieved through court activism.

In their 1996 article, "Preferences for School Finance Systems: Voters versus Judges," Colin Campbell and William Fischel found no evidence to support the justification for judicial activism in their New Hampshire case study. Districts that had a high tax base were not overrepresented in the state legislature. In studying the gubernatorial race in which a Democratic candidate actively supported centralization of school funding, the authors found the exact opposite of what conventional wisdom might dictate. When controlling for party identification and socioeconomic characteristics of voters, school districts with higher property valuations were in fact significantly more likely to vote for the Democratic candidate.

Assuming that funding equalization in public school districts would not have appeared without court-initiated guidelines, let us further assume that state legislative representation is biased in favor of high socioeconomic districts unwilling to tax themselves at a higher rate, so as to adequately support equalization of funding. In other words, let us draw two conclusions for which the evidence in the literature is not present. Independent of the evidence and drawing upon supposition alone, is there any solid foundation to the argument that equalization of school resources has the intended impact on communities subject to redistribution of resources and on educational outcomes?

The central goal of redistribution of resources is to achieve equity in some form. Equity can be viewed in terms of either horizontal equity or vertical equity. Horizontal equity relates to the availability of resources within units of government or perhaps within regions with similar demographic characteristics and/or similar levels of need in terms of public goods and services. Vertical equity relates to the issue of taxation across units of government or region with different levels of socioeconomic status. In terms of school districts, do poorer districts pay a larger percentage of their income to government than do wealthier districts? Certainly, wealthier districts have on average a greater ability to pay for their public services, such as education, than do poorer districts. Additionally, poorer districts frequently require greater resources in order to deal with the impact of various poverty-related contingencies that impact educational achievement than is the case in wealthier districts. The redistribution function in taxation and in resource allocation among and between levels of government is frequently intended to alleviate the inequities in both revenue collection and public policy outcomes; but, is it in fact justifiable in terms of equity, efficiency, or even morality?

William Oakland (1994) concluded that the arguments made in support of redistribution of resources across school districts are weak and limited. Horizontal equity, for instance, would require a great deal more than the simple transfer of funds from one school district to another. Horizontal inequities are often related to a whole host of privately owned goods and services. The achievement of horizontal equity, therefore, would require the redistribution of private sector goods. Private differentiation is unlikely to be successfully equalized through redistribution, and it is unclear that horizontal equity is a justifiable or achievable goal in school district finance.

Additionally, vertical equity often fails to produce real benefits to the poor. The transfer of wealth to poor communities for improved public service provision usually produces a net benefit for the service providers, who are generally not poor. In this instance, the poor gain whatever benefit is likely produced from changes in service provision. In educational research, it is not evident that per pupil expenditures have any lasting impact on educational outcomes, which further confirms Oakland's (1994) thesis.

Vertical equity is usually measured in terms of average socioeconomic status in a particular school district compared with other school districts. The problem with this approach is that it tends to ignore the variation in socioeconomic status that is likely to be present within school districts. The redistribution of resources from a wealthy school district, therefore, might result in limited resources for poor individuals within that district. Alternatively, wealthy individuals within poor school districts will either benefit at the expense of poor individuals from the wealthy school district or opt out of public schools and enroll their children at available private schools. In either case, measuring vertical equity may only partially capture the socioeconomic status of individuals within school districts.

Oakland also points out that educational opportunity is partially a function of the nature of community. In urban school districts, for instance, school violence may serve to constrain school organizations. The result of disruptive student behavior may be lower average student test scores. But is this a function of the relative poverty of the school district or the behavior of students within those schools? In other words, would greater resources result in significant alterations in student behavior? According to Oakland, a more reasonable alternative would be programs designed to target the poor rather than focusing on district level resource redistribution efforts.

Supporters of school finance equalization take a distinctly different view of public services. While the critics of equalization—like Oakland—identify a variety of factors *external* to the operation of school organizations and the promotion of educational policies designed to meet the needs of disadvantaged students, proponents of aid equalization are often narrowly focused in their work. Ladd and Yinger (1994) identify two different forms of equity, absent from Oakland's critique: categorical equity and distributional equity. *Categorical equity* focuses on equalization of public service spending across jurisdictions, while *distributional equity* emphasizes economic outcomes shaped by public policy. In both instances, the aid equalization advocates focus on the quality of public services. It is assumed that quality of public service plays a significant role in shaping the lives of citizens: "the real incomes of all low income households are depressed by the fact that they receive low quality public services, and raising that quality of public services . . . boosts the real incomes of all low income households" (Ladd and Yinger 1994: 219). Furthermore, equalization advocates believe that it is a central goal of government to ensure that a "state's most fundamental responsibility in education is to ensure that every student receives a minimum acceptable level of educational services."

Proponents of equalization do not view resource parity independently of outcomes. In other words, both categorical and distributional equity must be emphasized in order to achieve equitable outcomes. In that sense, there is a pressing need to study the "need-capacity gap" (Ladd and Yinger 1994: 213). Poor inner-city school district's often face a number of educational challenges, ranging from school violence to limited English proficiency to the effects of poverty on student learning. The resource needs of such schools are frequently quite great, but the resource availability—according to the pro-equalization advocates—is limited. Therefore, there is a large need-capacity gap. Conversely, suburban school districts often face fewer obstacles in the educational process. The attractiveness of suburban school districts leads to the recruiting and retention of highly qualified staff. Additionally, resource availability is likely to be much greater in suburban school districts, reducing or possibly eliminating the need-capacity gap. The advocates of equalization, therefore, propose the transfer of wealth from well-to-do districts to poorer—frequently, inner-city school districts—with the primary goal of achieving equalization of education quality and realizing equitable educational outcomes.

The assumption that expenditure per pupil equalization across school districts and even the attempt to close the need-resource gap are the primary factors shaping distributional equity is likely to be inaccurate. A large portion of school district expenditures are not directly related to basic education. There are a variety of environmental factors and school-related factors that are likely to shape per pupil expenditures for basic education. There is an economy of scale that shapes penditures, which may result in a larger portion of dollars per pupil expended for administration and teachers in smaller school districts.

Conversely, large urban school districts may spend a smaller portion of their resources per pupil on limited English proficiency students or teachers' salaries but a greater amount of their overall budget in these areas. School districts face different types of environmental constraints, which will in turn shape budgetary priorities. Student attendance patterns may influence per pupil expenditures for basic education as well as influence performance measures. Such exogenous factors are frequently beyond the grasp of school districts, but nevertheless shape their expenditures and outcomes. Interdistrict comparisons are frequently misleading simply because one is not necessarily comparing two or more similar entities—the 'apples and oranges' problem. In such a case, achieving distributional equity may or may not be directly related to public policy choices.

Categorical equity is difficult to measure, especially when taking the need-resource gap into account. Equity in expenditure may mistakenly assume that resources are prioritized in the same manner. Resources may be directed to a large degree towards reducing environmental pressures on the promotion of school districts' core goals—namely, educational excellence. In extremely distressed school districts, reducing the student dropout rate may supercede the goal of achievement on standardized examinations. If students are not regularly present at school, then it is obviously difficult to educate them. Thus, extremely challenging organizational environments may require adjustment to educational priorities and the adoption of alternative measures of school district success. Despite the introduction of the need-resource gap, the ability to gauge accurately categorical equity will be flawed, particularly when there is no uniform measure of organizational output (Downes and Pogue 1994).

Additionally, there is some evidence that indicates that attempts to equalize school spending may have actually produced a greater crisis in educational finance. When combined with the impact of Proposition 13, state mandated limits on school district expenditures resulted in reduced per pupil expenditures for elementary and secondary education in California. Additionally, enrollment growth was not matched with increased spending. Therefore, per pupil expenditures were nearly $1,000 lower than if equalization efforts had not been introduced. While state characteristics and other public policy may impact school expenditures, it is certainly not clear that centralization of school finance necessary to promote equalization goals has actually led to increased per pupil expenditures. Equalization may or may not result in greater fairness in terms of quality of education opportunity; but, it tends to ignore the need for greater educational spending for basic education in nearly all school districts (Silva and Sonstelie 1995).

While the justification for state court involvement in funding equalization may not stand up to closer scrutiny, the fact remains that the courts have become actively involved in shaping school funding decisions. Between 1972 and 1992, state courts in sixteen states (including the State of Washington) ordered funding reforms for public education, and twenty-one states have initiated legislative reform of school funding—further evidence in support of the Campbell and Fischel (1996) argument. But is there a different outcome in states that have court-initiated reform when compared with states that have legislature-initiated reform?

There is conclusive evidence that court-initiated reforms have produced greater funding equity than have legislature-initiated reforms. Legislative school funding reforms at times begin as a revolt against property taxes. Court-initiated reforms, however, are the function of litigation directly related to equity issues and are therefore more focused. Court activism may not be viewed as an abrogation of legislative authority. The fact that a larger proportion of states have engaged in legislative-initiated reform is an indication that legislatures often consider funding centralization to be appealing and are not averse to court support for this type of reform. Therefore, it is possible that the courts are not engaged in unwanted judicial activism but rather are acting in support of prevailing political sentiments (Evans et al. 1997).

In instituting school funding reforms, state legislatures and courts are focusing primary attention on the issue of equity. In the process, less attention might be focused on the issues of efficiency and the responsiveness of school districts to local citizens and their needs. Contingency theory would predict that organizations will choose a more stable funding source over one that is less stable. Local funding is potentially more unstable than state or federal funding. In the process of pursuing stable funding sources, school organizations will likely adopt the goals and priorities of the state and federal funding agencies and to some degree place less emphasis on local citizen demands.

Several states that have adopted centralized funding reforms have attempted to alleviate the problem of accountability to local citizens through the maintenance of local supplemental levies. The State of Washington still maintains local supplemental levy elections. Additionally, local school districts benefit from timber sales in their districts and bond issues for capital projects. Thus, local control is enhanced through the maintenance of a small but significant proportion of school funds coming from local voters. While there is some concern that even limited local control can have a deleterious impact on equity, a recent study of Michigan reforms demonstrates that the maintenance of a nominal proportion of local funding does not result in unequal educational opportunities (Courant and Loeb 1997).

Strict state formula funding guidelines act as an unintentional limitation on the promotion of equity in education. The goal of social equity is frequently constrained by resource equity and the pursuit of efficiency. Even after efforts to promote funding equity have been firmly established, the evidence would indicate that test score performance in poorer school districts is not improving dramatically. Critics charge that large inner city schools are constrained by their own bloated administrative staffs, which produces economic inefficiency and ineffective outcomes. Duncombe and Yinger (1997) found that large urban school districts in New York are to some degree less efficient than less urbanized and smaller school districts, but that may be the result of factors other than unresponsive rent-seeking administrative staff. Large urban school districts face more problems than do smaller less urban districts and require more resources to solve those problems. The pursuit of outcome equity is inappropriately measured in terms of efficiency because the two measures are not compatible. In order to solve the problems of urban schools, their funding formula should be more generous in light of the multiple contraints which such schools regularly face.

Test score improvement is not the sole measure of school performance and is not the primary reason why the courts and state legislatures have engaged in dramatic education funding reforms. In education finance cases, the courts have focused attention on issues of social justice (i.e., equality of opportunity), while state legislative actions often react to calls for property tax relief. A secondary impact of state usurpation of school financing has been to concentrate control of educational policy in the hands of state-level education bureaucrats, politicians, and teachers' unions. It is more efficient for interest groups such as teachers' unions to shape education policy in a centralized system than in a geographically and politically fragmented system of fairly autonomous school districts. For education bureaucrats and state-level politicians, funding of local schools implies a degree of control over how those monies are spent and the establishment of general and specific goals and outcomes for primary and secondary education.

Student performance is neither directly not consistently linked to school funding or staffing ratios (Simon et al. 1999). The equalization of funding in the State of California does not appear to have produced improved student achievement. In their zeal to equalize educational opportunity, the courts left the impression that monetary resources were a critical explanation for student achievement. In essence, the lessons of history were lost on state legislators, executives, and the courts. The common thread in the education policy histories indicate that centralization does not produce successful schools (Spring 1976). In fact, the movement to centralize funding and educational policy has tended to parallel a growing crisis in public education. Empirically, it would be difficult to demonstrate that centralization has been the root cause of educational decline. Yet, it is hard to imagine that the correlative evidence is entirely coincidental.

Neither human capital nor family social capital is directly related to school funding, staffing, or programming in the short term, but the longer term evidence indicates that funding equity is related to improved human capital in school district environments. Reductions in the local tax burden associated with increased state funding appear to be beneficial to local economies. If the earlier analyses are correct, therefore, elevated human capital in turn leads to greater opportunities for students. Fernandez and Rogerson (1997) predicted a 10 percent rise in aggregate welfare following the adoption of state school funding systems. The impact of state-centered school finance systems does appear to have a long-term significant redistributive impact on local schools and communities.

While dissatisfied citizens have the option of "exiting" underfunded and/or underperforming school systems, the ability of lower income citizens to transfer their children to preferred schools is often not feasible. The evidence presented by Fernandez and Rogerson (1997) acknowledges these limitations and demonstrates that the redistributive function of state-centered school financing is both practical and effective.

Since the commencement of the Cold War, school funding and centralization of educational policy have been critical parts of the student achievement debate. School finance, in particular, became the foundation upon which uniformity in pedagogy (i.e., core technologies) and curriculum (i.e., core mission) was established. Additionally, financial arrangements have led to metamorphoses in the essential nature of school district organizations. Increasingly, school district administration is externally focused, studying practical organizational responses to state and federal resource providers, and the regulations and standards by which those levels of government will ascertain the success or failure at the local level.

The emergence of equitable educational outcomes as the *novus voco* in the educational policy debate introduced school districts to federal and state courts. Educational finance was no longer a tool used to shape pedagogy and curriculum, but a key weapon in the battle against poverty and racial inequality. In other words, educational finance has become more redistributive in its policy intents.

Clinton Administration education initiatives appear to be driven by two primary goals. First, educational equity is a central theme in many of the administration's education initiatives. The 21st Century schools programs that were initiated during the Bush Administration and perpetuated in the Clinton years, focus primarily on the need to link social services with education policy. Many of the Clinton administration's education reform proposals are based on the work of public school advocates attempting to replicate private school success by adopting those elements of private schools which they firmly believe will produce improved student achievement.

Initiatives to reduce class size have become increasingly prevalent as a result of President Clinton's education agenda. Smaller class sizes will allow for greater teacher-student interaction, particularly for students in early grades. Following the same general logic upon which Head Start is based, it is a generally accepted belief in the education policy literature that efforts to shape student learning at a young age will reduce the inequities in student achievement in high school and beyond (Mosteller 1995). In 1998, President Clinton pushed for federal assistance to school districts nationwide—particularly poor school districts—to reduce class size and hire additional teachers. The Clinton proposal would provide nearly $13 billion in matching funds to school districts. It is not clear that reduced classroom sizes would lead to improved student achievement. The National Center for Educational Statistics (1998) indicates that classroom size has been decreasing for several years, while test scores have remained either stagnant or have demonstrated noticeable declines.

In 1995, the student/teacher ratio was approximately 27:1—30:1 in elementary schools and 21:1 in high schools. By 1998, the estimated overall student/teacher ratio in public schools was 17:1—19:1 in elementary schools and 15:1 in high schools. While the current ratio for public schools is higher than those found in private schools (16:1 in elementary schools and 11:1 in high schools), there is little evidence that the decline in student teacher ratios has led to improved student performance in public schools. The Clinton proposal would attempt to achieve classroom size parity between public and private schools, which will reduce the demands placed on teachers; but will structural reforms alleviate the impact of sociocultural influences on student achievement? Additionally, classroom size reforms do not address the stress on administration to mitigate the effects of disorderly behavior or to effectively manage a larger teaching staff.

More teachers means that there will be a need for more classrooms. The physical plant of schools is financed by state and local taxpayers through capital project bonds, which must be approved by state legislatures and local voters. Capital projects are frequently very expensive long-term endeavors with equally long-term goals. Both state legislators and local voters are frequently leery of long-term debt, and often must be convinced that the goals of such projects are worthwhile and the costs are manageable. Additionally, voters in poorer school districts—districts that are frequently with the greatest infrastructure needs—are frequently disgruntled with government and tend to 'vote down' local ballot initiatives to express their angst with government.

In order to reduce the impact of socioeconomic disadvantage on the ability of schools to finance their capital projects, the "Clinton Administration proposed in early 1998 to underwrite approximately $22 billion in zero-interest school construction bonds" (Temple 1998: 522-523). While there is a strong correlation between student achievement and the decay of school buildings, it is unlikely that the relationship is causal. Funding equalization efforts in St. Louis, Missouri, for example, produced a number of new school buildings for inner city neighborhoods. Nevertheless, there was no corresponding improvement in student achievement in these schools. Poor building conditions are more common in urban environments, which tend to enroll a larger proportion of individuals with lower levels of student achievement, and who are more likely to come from families with lower socioeconomic status. Wealthier families are more likely to send their children to private schools when they find the quality of the decaying inner city schools to be undesirable.

The condition of public school buildings may not be entirely a function of neglect on the part of policymakers serving the needs of the affluent. Tax equalization efforts in education financing place limits on the levy amounts raised in wealthy school districts. Additionally, substantial portions of school district revenues come from state and federal sources. Therefore, an alternative explanation for the physical decay of public schools in poorer districts may be related to the prioritization of funds. Teachers' salaries in inner city schools are frequently higher than in suburban and rural school districts, in part due to the need to attract and retain high quality instructors. Schools operating in urban settings are often associated with more heterogeneous student populations suffering from poverty-related disadvantages. Teachers in such environments operate under a great deal of stress due to the fact that their pupils' educational needs are both varied and not easily met through conventional methods of instruction. Money that could be spent on improving the school infrastructure is often directed towards meeting the more pressing issue of fending off environmental threats to organizational core goals. Core technologies (i.e., instructional staff and education-related resources) might take priority over improvements in the condition of school buildings.

Grade retention is another recent proposal that has received attention. So-called 'social promotion' has been particularly prevalent since the education equality movement first began with the passage of the Elementary and Secondary Education Act of 1966. The theory behind social promotion is that the life chances of students—particularly poor and minority students—would be adversely impacted if they were unable to successfully graduate from school with their peers. In reality, social promotion has been devastating because it ineffectively deals with students who are not meeting expected achievement levels. Moving students to the next grade level does little more than pass the 'problem' to the next level of teachers. It likely does not motivate students to excel and does little more than add yet another layer of incomprehensible material on top of the already incomprehensible material which they failed to master in previous school years.

Conversely, grade retention may not be the best method of dealing with students who are unable to meet educational standards. Removed from their peer group and identified as 'failures,' students may withdraw from the educational experience and drop out of school (Temple 1998: 523). The development of 'alternative schools' represent a workable education initiative designed to reduce problems associated with nontraditional students who may require greater time and resources to meet academic requirements necessary for graduation from high school. Nontraditional schools, rather than grade retention, will be particularly important in the coming years as the 'crack baby' and 'fetal alcohol syndrome' student cohorts (to name but two groups of students likely to face serious challenges in the educational process) become a larger proportion of the public school student population.

A variety of issues surrounding school district funding have been discussed here, as well as current proposals for improving student achievement, one measure of school organizational success. Success is defined in this instance as the ability of the organization—namely, a school or school district—to achieve its organizational core mission. How does funding fit into a discussion of organization? According to the 'classical' approach, organization was really a matter of identifying structures, functions, and interplay between the two. An organization was viewed from a mechanistic perspective—if it did not operate effectively, the organization would be altered in some fashion, often along structural or functional lines. Reorganization of this type is often very expensive and time-consuming. If such efforts are to be undertaken at all, they are usually the last resort. In older organizations, a pattern of ossification sets in over time. Personnel become 'conservers,' resistant to changing methods of operation or alternations in the core goals and technologies associated with the organization and its methodology (Downs 1957). Public school districts are old organizations, yet they are being called upon to respond to new pressures and needs. In measuring change, therefore, studying functions and structures is not likely to tell us very much about public schools. Functions and structures rarely change appreciably unless the organization is impacted by some fairly dramatic turns of event. Resources, however, are much more likely to change over time.

While budgeting appears to be incremental, new policies usually mean new sources of revenue. Court decisions that call for funding equity will have an almost immediate impact on school budgets and will alter the sources of revenue. Whereas nearly 70 percent of school district revenues came from local sources thirty years ago, the states currently provide over 60 percent of school district revenues. Local and federal sources account for roughly one-fifth of school district budgets. In short, revenue—where it comes from and what it is intended for—is a convenient method of studying school organization. Organizations run on money, and while structures and functions may nominally remain the same, resources and personnel often reflect organizational adaptation.

Resources and resource providers shape the organizational goals and technologies of school districts.   While the broadly defined goals of the organization likely remain the same, the narrowly defined short term goals of schools are shaped by resources. Resources produce new technologies in some instances. Vice President Al Gore's efforts to wire schools for the Internet will shape pedagogy and curriculum and shape the goal of computer literacy and information management in new ways.

Therefore, a discussion of resources is an integral part of organization. Organizations seek steady resource providers because they are shaped by resource providers. The goal of achieving equity in elementary and secondary education is grounded in the notion that resources are critical to achieving equal opportunities and outcomes. Resource provision in this model is based on need, while revenue collection is based on progressive taxation (i.e., ability to pay).

In order to better understand Washington State schools, therefore, it is necessary to define their structures, functions, and sources of revenue. Additionally, it is important to understand the intended uses of the resources. Through a better understanding of the goals attached to school funds, we will more likely be able to determine the short-term goals of public elementary and secondary education.

FUNDING WASHINGTON'S SCHOOL DISTRICTS: ORGANIZATION AND RESOURCES

The Office of Superintendent of Public Instruction (OSPI) in the State of Washington is perhaps one of the most well-developed state-level education offices nationwide. Over the last ten years, OSPI has completely reorganized its information management systems. Nearly all the school district-level data for Washington's 296 school districts are now available at the OSPI Internet site. In addition to financial and student achievement data, OSPI publishes most of its technical reports and bulletins on the World Wide Web.

The *Organization and Financing of Washington Public Schools* (Billings et al. 1996) is an excellent reference for both current and historical state education policy. The Common School Manual (CSM) is another valuable source of information, which is a compendium of Revised Code of Washington (RCW) and administrative procedures related to the operation of public school districts and the execution of elementary and secondary education policy. The CSM is updated annually and is available through the Office of Superintendent of Public Instruction, State of Washington.

The legal foundation of public school finance in Washington is based in the State Constitution, laws, and administrative code. The state constitution clearly defines the responsibility of the state to provide education to all children who live within the state borders, "without distinction or preference on account of race, color, caste, or sex" (Billings et al. 1996: 5). The power to finance public schools resides in the state legislature (Washington State Constitution, Article IX), while the direct executive power is vested in the Superintendent of Public Instruction.

Title 28A of the RCW deals with the common school system—"public schools operating a program for kindergarten through twelfth grade or any part thereof." (Billings et al. 1996: 5). On the basis of RCW 28A, the OSPI is required to submit a proposed budget to the legislature, which meets biannually. While OSPI develops detailed proposals, the governor has the power to rewrite much of the budget request. OSPI is required by the RCW to submit to the state legislature the governor's proposed education budget.

In addition to defining the process by which financing of public schools will be accomplished, RCW 28A clearly outlines the *core mission* of public school districts through the Basic Education Act:

The goal of the Basic Education Act for schools of the state of Washington…shall be to provide students with the opportunity to become responsible citizens, to contribute to their own economic well-being and to that of their families and communities and to enjoy productive and satisfying lives. To these ends, the goals of each school district, with the involvement of parents and community members, shall be to provide opportunities for all students to develop the knowledge and skills essential to:
1. Know and apply the core concepts and principles of mathematics; social, physical, and life sciences; civics and history; arts; and health and fitness.
2. Think analytically, logically, and creatively, and to integrate experience and knowledge to form reasoned judgments and solve problems.
3. Understand the importance of work and how performance, effort, and decisions affect future career and educational opportunities. (RCW 28A.150.210)

The legislative intent surrounding the general goals is to adopt a pragmatic approach to education. Unlike the relatively uniform curriculum and pedagogy employed by schools for most of the nineteenth and twentieth centuries, the state legislature recognizes the need for considerable flexibility in approaches to learning. School curriculum should reflect the needs of the students. Basic education identifies the need to provide foundational educational tools to students but also recognizes that students must be prepared for their future educational and life goals (RCW 28A.150.210 c336). Educational organizations, therefore, do not operate as closed systems; administrators and teachers must be aware of social and economic trends in the communities in which they operate as well as remain vigilant to the changing goals of their student population.

The state legislature does not entirely place the burden of education on the shoulders of public schools. It codifies important prerequisites to effective education on local communities. Specifically, there is a need for students to exhibit honesty and trustworthiness. Students should be respectful of the law and display respect for others as well as for themselves. Finally, the state legislature explicitly recognizes the "family as the basis of society" (RCW 28A.150.211). Curiously, the state code specifically states that the exemplification of such values and traits "essential to individual liberty, fulfillment, and happiness" (RCW 28A.150.211) are "not intended to be assessed or be standards for graduation."

In essence, the State absolves itself from the role of providing a "moral education." While there are certain individual traits necessary to preserving a strong community and a strong democracy, those traits are instilled through nongovernmental institutions, such as family, community, and possibly religious organizations. The role of the public school, therefore, is primarily directed towards instruction in basic knowledge necessary to live a productive life but not necessarily a "moral" life—an important distinction that will be discussed later in this book.

RCW 28A delineates a required number of credit hours that must be completed prior to the successful completion of high school, the length of the school year (180 days), the FTE-based funding formula for school districts, and the levels of competency that must be met by students at various grade levels. As students progress from elementary school through high school, the percentage of required courses in basic skills (e.g., mathematics, reading, vocabulary) declines from 90 percent to 60 percent. Work and life skills courses become a larger percentage of course offerings in high school and are concentrated in areas such as: "industrial arts, home and family life education, business and office education...agricultural education, health occupations education, vocational education, trade and industrial education, technical education, and career education" (RCW 28A.150.220.1B).

The responsibility for the successful implementation of the Basic Education Act guidelines lies with local school district boards of directors. The boards of directors must adopt educational performance standards and guidelines that are consistent with the State Board of Education. Local school boards establish personnel guidelines related to hiring standards and performance measurement. The school boards also approve curricula that are beneficial to local student needs and evaluate "text books, teaching aids, handouts, or other printed material" when parents or legal guardians object to materials being employed in the learning process (RCW 28A.150.230.2f).

In order to coordinate the efforts of school districts, the state has established Educational Service Districts (ESDs). The boundaries of ESDs essentially follow Congressional boundaries; thus, Washington currently has 9 ESDs. ESDs have either seven or nine member boards, depending on the service district members' preference. ESDs are intended to coordinate the efforts of individual school districts.   Learning materials and equipment are often shared among school districts, which reduces the cost of education and expands opportunity. ESD's are funded by state and federal grants, which can be used to expand curriculum offerings and make available educational tools for school districts within the ESD (RCW 28A.310.010).

While local school boards and ESDs work to create greater educational opportunity at the local level, the goal of the State Board of Education (SBE) is to coordinate the public school mission and operations in the 296 school districts across the state. The board codifies the more specific educational requirements through administrative rules and guidelines related to everything from curriculum to teacher training. Graduation requirements are generally determined by the SBE. Most important, the board is responsible for the allocation of state general and special funds to ESDs and school districts (Billings et al. 1996: 11). The SBE is comprised of one member from each of the nine ESDs, the Superintendent of Public Instruction, and one representative from private schools.

The state Superintendent of Public Instruction (SPI) focuses her efforts on coordinating the technical aspects of the educational process. In accordance with state guidelines, Washington State pupils are tested to determine if they are meeting educational standards set for their grade level. The SPI administers and evaluates student performance on standardized basic education examinations to determine if pupils are meeting grade level competency standards. In terms of finance, the SPI is charged with monitoring school district budgets for reasons of accountability as well as for future budget requests from the state legislature. Policy analysts at OSPI carefully study apportionment of funds to ensure that school districts are obtaining needed local, state, and federal funds and are spending those funds in accordance with educational goals often attached to those funds. OSPI finance analysts also monitor local levies to determine if they are meeting state guidelines in terms of election outcomes and levy rates.

The organization of school district personnel is typically divided between teaching and administrative responsibilities. District organization is highly dependent on the size of the school district, as well as the number and type of ancillary responsibilities school district superintendents, administrative personnel, and teachers must fulfill. Budget size usually reflects the size and scope of school district functional complexity. Functional complexity reflects environmental constraint factors limiting the ability of school district organizations to accomplish educational goals by directing resource expenditure to core operation functions (e.g., teachers operating in traditional classroom settings).

To illustrate better what is meant by functional complexity, let me provide a few examples. While subject to State Board of Education approval, school districts negotiate contracts with nonpublic agencies (NPAs) to provide supplemental education to students. Education centers provide learning opportunities to public school dropouts in a nontraditional learning environment. Homeschooled students must be monitored by school districts to determine if the pupils are meeting educational standards set by state and local agencies. School districts with middle and high schools frequently have athletic programs engaged in inter- and intradistrict competitions, which require resources for equipment and frequently draw on the talents of full-time or part-time athletic directors as well as employing teachers as team coaches. In all three instances, resources and personnel are not used to fund the most direct methods of achieving core educational goals as defined by state and local administrative and elected officials. Local school districts, superintendents, school boards, parents, and concerned citizens must in some way manage to match local and state level demands on public school district organizations in order to arrive at a satisfactory organizational schema.

Frequently, it is at the local level—not the state level—where demands or constraints on school districts determine organizational complexity. State-level demands on schools and school districts are generally uniform across all school districts, thus serving as a constant level and source of environmental complexity to which all school districts must respond. Local level demands or organizational environment constraints are highly variable and have a tremendous impact on school district organization and resource allocation beyond the monies earmarked for basic education. Resource allocation is one method of measuring the functional complexity paralleling school district responses to various—frequently local-level—demands or constraints.

FINANCING SCHOOL DISTRICTS

The budget process for school districts typically begins in July. School districts must prepare their budgets and submit them to ESDs for review. Districts must simultaneously make their preliminary budget available to the public for comment. ESD personnel pre-audit the school district budgets and report back to individual districts in August, noting discrepancies or inaccuracies. The school districts have three work weeks to correct their budgets and return them to the ESDs for final approval. The ESDs file copies of the school district budgets with OSPI in September (Billings et al. 1996: 22-23).

Following approval of the school district budget by OSPI or by local budget review committees (used for small school districts operating without a high school), school district budgets are implemented. School districts must report their financial status on a monthly and annual basis to OSPI. Each school district must report the status of the seven primary fund groups in their budget document: general fund, capital projects fund, debt service fund, special revenue fund, transportation vehicle fund, expendable trust funds, and nonexpendable trust funds (Billings et al. 1996: 25).

Based on monthly school district financial reports, OSPI submits allocation requests to the state treasurer for each school district in the state. Federal and state monies intended for each school district are then transmitted to treasurers in their respective counties. Monthly financial status reports are then submitted by OSPI to the state and county treasurers and the ESD budget office personnel. The reports detail the current operating expenditures within each fund group for each school district. The reports are intended to ensure that resource expenditures match to resource allocations, thus assisting district administrators maintain a high degree of consistency in their district's rate of expenditure. Trust funds may produce a larger than expected cash flow due to fluctuations in financial markets, thus enlarging school district budgets. Local school levy passage (or failure) has a potentially tremendous impact on school budgets and will likely be reflected in monthly financial statements. Most important, increased or decreased enrollment—which alters school districts' state level funding for basic education—and personnel changes may produce significant alterations in funding formulas and lead to the adjustment of budget priorities (Billings et al. 1996: 28-30).

Nearly half of the state budget is allocated to public elementary and secondary education. The state funding is designed to provide school districts with resources necessary to meet the requirements outlined in the Basic Education Act as well as finance school district personnel, taking into account school district size, student-to-teacher ratios, and the education and seniority of staff members. Additionally, the state provides funds for school personnel fringe benefits, employee insurance, substitute teacher pay (calculated using an enrollment-based formula), and nonemployee-related costs (e.g., textbooks, staff travel, instructional supplies, etc.).

The state also makes budget allowances—on a per pupil basis—for students falling under state guidelines for special education. Pupil transportation, arranged by local school district administrators, is financed by the state. The Local Effort Assistance Program (LEA) provides funds to school districts with above average local tax rates "due to low property valuations" (Billings, et al. 1996: 55). LEA funds are calculated on the basis of the property tax rate in a particular school district in relation to the average property tax rate in the state.

Given that the state has established proficiency requirements in its Basic Education Act, funds have been set aside for underperforming school districts so that they may provide remedial education programs for their pupils. The formula is based on the school districts' average test score performance on the statewide standardized examinations. In essence, the learning assistance program (LAP) provides approximately 92 percent of the $378.05 per pupil allocated for remedial education. In addition to test score performance, a poverty factor based on free and reduced lunch program enrollment is used to calculate remedial education funding.

The federal and state governments provide funding for bilingual education. Student eligibility for the program is based on several factors. The student must have a primary language other than English and must be underperforming in English language skills tests. A student performing above the thirty-fifth percentile in English language skills is not eligible for the bilingual education program. Additionally, a student cannot be enrolled in bilingual education for more than three years unless he or she consistently performs below the thirty-fifth percentile on the state grade-level competency examinations. The state rate for bilingual education is approximately $646 per pupil per school year (Billings et al. 1996: 57).

LOCAL FINANCING: MAINTENANCE AND OPERATION SUPPLEMENTAL LEVIES

Prior to 1977, local maintenance and operations (M&O) levies provided a substantial portion of local school district funding. In that year, the Seattle School District failed to pass its M&O levy, leading to a lawsuit against the state filed by the school district in the state courts. The Seattle School District contended that the state did not provide sufficient revenues to school districts to guarantee equality in education opportunity in terms of basic education offerings. The court decided in favor of the school district in the 1977 case. In subsequent decisions written in 1983 and 1988, the state courts ordered the legislature to expand its definition of basic education. The new definition must include bilingual, remedial, and special education programs, but the courts also clearly delineated programs that were not to be considered to fall under the definition of basic education, such as extracurricular activities, and food service. The state courts have also forced the state to create a 'safety net' for schools which are underfunded (Billings et al. 1996: 7-9).

State funding of local school districts for basic education went from approximately 50 percent of the M&O budget to nearly 80 percent in the mid-1990's. While local M&O levies fell precipitously by the early 1980's following the *Doran* decision, but in the 1990's local school supplementary levy rates steadily increased. In 1975, school district levy rates were as high as $1,100 per pupil. Increased state funding following *Doran* led to a dramatic reduction in local levy rates, falling to approximately $340 per pupil in 1980.[1]

Despite the fact that the state and federal government provide substantial funding for programs that were specifically excluded from the court definition of basic education, the local levy rates have increased dramatically since 1980. The state legislature had placed a levy lid—a limitation on local levy rates—when it assumed the dominant role in funding basic education in 1977. Nevertheless, the legislature has amended the levy rate limitation ten times in the last twenty years, which has led to marked increases in local school district levies. There was a dramatic decline in local school district property tax value assessment from 1977 to 1980; but despite the fact that the state funds basic education and other ancillary school functions, the assessed valuation in 1996 is virtually the same as it was in 1975.

The tax rate per $1,000 assessed value also fell following the *Doran* decision. In 1981, the tax rate bottomed out at $1.39. By 1996, however, the tax rate had increased by nearly 90 percent to $2.62 per thousand dollars assessed value—and this despite the fact that assessed values had increased by an astounding 152 percent in real dollars. The increased school district assessed property values appear to have permitted school districts to enlarge their budget constraints. School districts have taken advantage of the budgetary expansion,

---

1. Dollar figures are in 1996 dollars.

despite the fact that the state pays for a growing portion of their core technologies (i.e., teachers' salaries) and core mission (i.e., basic education).

An initial reaction to these relatively dramatic increases might be: "What are *they* doing with the money?"—a question which when posed to discontented voters, particularly to those individuals who most directly pay these increased tax bills, often produces talk of a tax revolt.   In the State of Washington, however, tax revolt initiatives have been relatively unsuccessful, the most recent property tax initiatives appearing on the state ballot in 1996. Voters do not appear to be overwhelmingly upset with the costs of government, although there was overwhelming support for a recent ballot measure designed to reduce auto-licensing fees. School levies require voter approval, which means that despite the dramatic increases in local costs for the maintenance of school districts, the amount of money involved does not seem to be of overwhelming concern to voters. Apparently, a majority of voters approve of the increased costs and are satisfied with organizational outcomes.

Economies of scale do not seem to play a role in the increased levies. In other words, the amount per pupil does not seem to respond to the fact that the number of public school pupils has increased by nearly 17 percent since 1975 and by 26 percent since 1986—the year in which state public school enrollment began its tremendous ascent. Controlling for inflation, the dollar amount levied per pupil still increases. The model is fairly simple—a lagged dependent variable, inflation index, and enrollment log transformed—but it explains 87 percent of the variance in the dependent variable, dollars per pupil levied.

An alternative explanation for levy increases is that public school budgets are incrementally increasing, perhaps due to administrative assertiveness.   In the private sector, executives pursue profit-maximization strategies, while in the public sector organizational entrepreneurs seek to maximize their budgets, producing organizational slack that can be used for a variety of new and existing purposes. Public choice theorists frequently test the latter theory with the expectation that they will find support for the budget-maximization theory. The evidence does not offer consistent support to the theory, but organizational slack—if that is a plausible explanation for the levy increases in Washington—does not necessarily mean that public schools are budget maximizing for the personal gain of administrators and teachers. Salaries have been fixed by state law. Thus, the monies raised from local levies are likely being used for purposes other than personnel.

Herbert Simon and James March hypothesized that organizational slack serves to protect an organization and its central mission from unexpected changes or from environmental complexity. As discussed in the previous chapter, organizational complexity and environmental constraints facing public schools have increased and have made it difficult for public schools to meet their core mission. Increased complexity produces a greater need for resources, a need that appears to nullify any economy of scale that might exist for public schools. Growth in school enrollments is one form of constraint that might exist for public schools. In many cases, schools are literally outgrowing their physical buildings; but this form of complexity is not likely to be reflected in M&O levies. Rather, an analysis of bond levies might produce evidence of enrollment growth as a form of constraint. Poverty and limited English proficiency are two other sources of constraint on public schools; yet the impact of these social and educational dilemmas are supported by state and federal monies. Decreased support from the state is a third possible constraint, but one that by law cannot occur for basic education programming.

A final source of constraint on public schools to be addressed here is what I refer to as the *relative social environmental order* present in the school district environment. Social environmental order refers to the community social capital, family social capital, and human capital, all of which I have discussed to a large degree in the previous chapter. Disorder has a deleterious impact on the learning process, distracting students from the core goals of formal education. The education process disintegrates into education-by-contingency, where teachers and administrators are responding to an ever-changing and often unpredictable learning environment.   Schools lose their ability to produce a tangible output and can no longer causally link core technologies with outcomes.

As student populations grow, the variety and intensity of contingencies facing school administrators and teachers is likely to increase. Therefore, in my simple model of levy amount per pupil, student enrollment represents increasing probability of complexity.   The inflation factor in the model represents a constraint of quite a different type—namely, a decline in resource capacity. Under the norms of rationality, school districts would pursue larger levies as inflation increased and as organizational complexity increased with the goal of reducing the impact of *social environmental disorder* on the formal educational process and student achievement.

Of course, the ability to obtain the local resources necessary to pursue organizational buffering and create order in an environment that tends increasingly towards entropy is highly dependent on the ability of school districts to convince voters that the requested levy amount is reasonable. What one finds, however, is that voting behavior in local school district levy elections is explained by economic and sociological schools of thought. The former theoretical approach is based in rate bargaining, while the latter explanation is rooted in theories of voter discontent. Previous research offers some support to both explanatory methods, but neither approach offers much hope to school administrators pursuing organizational slack.

VOTING BEHAVIOR IN LOCAL FINANCIAL ELECTIONS

In *An Economic Theory of Democracy* (1957), Anthony Downs argues that citizens tend to pursue their economic self-interest in public programs and policies through the voting mechanism. The Downsian model posits that voters are able to affect the price of government quite effectively through vote choice. Voters will tend to reject measures that the majority consider to be too costly, and will support measures that are perceived to provide a benefit greater than the costs of providing the particular good or service. Proponents and opponents of particular ballot measures seek to garner the support of the theoretical 'median voter'—in essence, the individual vote that will result in either the victory or the defeat of the ballot issue in question (Holcombe 1980: 261).

Charles Tiebout (1956) delineated an early application of the median voter model in his theoretical analysis of local government expenditures. Tiebout argued that voting behavior could be equated directly to consumer behavior in the marketplace. Under ideal conditions, aggregate voter preference sets would approximate a normal curve. As with marketplace consumers, voters will seek to maximize their benefit and minimize their cost, at times understating preferences so as to "enjoy the goods while avoiding the tax" (Tiebout 1956: 417).

Those voters who are not satisfied with existing levels of service either must seek to remedy this through the election process or, failing to do that, move to a community with service and tax levels determined to be satisfactory vis-à-vis their own preference sets. It must be noted here, however, that the cost associated with local school levies is likely to be insignificant when compared to the cost of relocation.

Prospective voters employ information to determine: a) the cost of voting in a particular election (Frey and Pommerehne 1982); b) the benefits that would emerge from a particular vote choice (Rubinfeld and Thomas 1980); and, c) the likelihood that the election outcomes would be favorable to the individual voter in question (Filer and Kenny 1980). As information costs decline, the costs of decision making and participation are reduced and voter turnout is likely to increase (Matsusaka 1995). While perhaps not absolutely complete, information held by voters is assumed to be accurate (an assumption countered by Niskanen 1971). Furthermore, voters may not actively pursue existing reputable information sources (Dalton 1977).

Despite generally acknowledged information constraints, the existing literature suggests rather strongly that voters tend to approach school district levies in a rational manner in most instances. As Downs (1967) postulated, voter turnout for elections is related to the perceived benefit associated with election participation in relation to the perceived costs associated with gathering information and the effort necessary to participate in the election itself. Despite the general applicability of rational actor reasoning to voter behavior in school levy elections, the process of establishing a tax rate through local school finance elections is somewhat different from that of most other tax measures.

If a school finance levy fails, district administrators may resubmit the measure; in the State of Washington, for example, school finance measures may be re-submitted three times (i.e., there may be up to four attempts per year). Romer and Rosenthal (1979) argue that this process often leads to rate-bargaining between school administrators and local voters. Downsian theory would indicate that if voters reject a levy because costs are judged to be too high, then subsequent levies should witness a decline in the proposed tax rate, a central hypothesis that is partially supported by Romer and Rosenthal (1979). Eventually, voters will accept a proposed tax rate that is considered to be a fair cost given the perceived benefit.

Despite the central focus on tax-cost considerations, Downsian approaches to school levy voting include social and economic factors used as control variables to account for interdistrict differences. Social and political characteristics have been shown to be related to local government expenditure levels (Megdal 1983). The general affluence of communities appeared to have a positive impact on spending levels in the majority of the states analyzed (Bergstrom and Goodman 1973).

Tax share elasticity was negatively related to local public policy spending levels in nearly all cases (Bergstrom and Goodman 1973), an observation which is supported in some more recent studies (Denzau and Grier 1984). The relative stability of residency, the age of community residents, and the proportion of minorities in the population were all factors which were significantly related to expenditure levels. Individual choices play a role in shaping tax levels and bureaucratic expenditures, but only within the broader context and constraints of the community in which the individual dwells.

It has been demonstrated that as the number of levy attempts increases, the probability of passage increases, apparently independent of tax rate adjustments (Romer and Rosenthal 1979). Voters may begin to lose interest in repeated elections, and turnout among negative voters tends to decline. Additionally, repeated elections afford school administrators the time necessary to disseminate information to voters, which would outline the benefits associated with levy passage. Finally, due to either information deficiencies or ignorance (Dalton 1977), voters generally may not be capable of drawing cognitive connections between total tax cost and proposed supplementary levy rates (Lankford 1986).

Testing the Downsian model, Rubinfeld and Thomas (1980) indicate that neither tax cost nor community-mindedness offered particularly strong explanations for school finance election outcomes. Voting in local school finance elections may not be consistently related to the direct benefits resulting from a particular election outcome. Nevertheless, controlling for social and economic conditions, self interest—associated with the direct impact of tax-costs—appears to play a minor role in the decisions to participate and to vote in levy elections (Bergstrom et al. 1982; Rubinfeld, 1977; Peterson 1973).

Sociology-based analyses of school district elections in particular and voting behavior in general, do not focus primarily on tax cost. Rather, their concern is associated with voter differences when explaining participation and election outcomes. The nature of the community in which the voter resides is also of cardinal importance in the sociologically oriented analyses.

Participation in a school district levy election can be used by voters to reflect their preferences in at least two general ways. Voters can demonstrate support for a proposed level of funding and perhaps for the goals and outputs of the organizations seeking public support. Conversely, the levy may be viewed as a forum to express frustration (with funding levels and/or organization goals and performance)—a form of protest vote.

Socioeconomic variations that exist across school districts offer some explanation for protest votes. Dissent of this nature is less prevalent in school districts with higher socioeconomic status (SES). In the latter case, protest votes in school levy elections tend to reflect a limited sense of political efficacy on the part of citizens and/or a sense of disenfranchisement on the part of community denizens (Lutz and Iannaccone 1978; Minar 1966; Horton and Thompson 1962).

In terms of substantive democracy, disaffection is likely to be indicative of public institutions operating at odds with their organizational environment. Chronic dissonance could reflect a systematically unresponsive policymaking process, likely contributing to suboptimal organizational outcomes over a given period of time. For such reasons, Lutz and Iannaccone (1978) place significant emphasis on the nature of the organizational environment; in their view organizational performance may be largely a function of environmental conditions and associated inputs into the system (Easton 1965).

Studying referenda voting patterns at the state and local level, Hahn and Kamieniecki (1987) found that social and economic political correlates are significantly related to local school levy election outcomes. Properly designated indicators reflecting variations in SES characteristics across school districts might represent the potential for political disenchantment and conflict for reasons previously stated.

In addition to negative voting, socioeconomic indicators offer some explanation for the decline in voter turnout (Chen 1992; Hill and Luttbeg 1983; Langton 1980). Sidney Verba and others have concluded that socioeconomic status to a substantial extent explain variations in voter turnout, levels of perceived political efficacy, and support for and/or confidence in existing governmental institutions (Verba and Nie 1972; Verba et al. 1993). The relationship between SES and voter turnout may vary depending on when the election occurs and the issue being decided (Filer and Kenny 1980).

Income level and occupational type offer less powerful explanations for voter turnout than does education level. Wolfinger and Rosenstone (1980) conclude that the relationship between income and educational attainment is highly variable. Additionally, the public choice literature generally concludes that economic indifference—particularly in the case of supplementary public school district levies—may actually result in lower levels of turnout among high income individuals, unless the cost of the proposed levy is sufficiently high to warrant participation.

The level of education of the individual voter, however, "increases one's capacity for understanding and working with complex, abstract, and intangible subjects such as politics. This heightens one's ability to pay attention to politics, to understand politics, and to gather the information necessary for making political choices" (Wolfinger and Rosenstone 1980: 35). Teixeira (1987) found that socioeconomic status and voter age played a statistically significant but fairly minor role vis-à-vis other SES factors, in explaining the decline in voter turnout in presidential elections. The decline in voters' perceived political efficacy, however, remained a salient explanatory factor.

Given the high percentage of school district levies that eventually succeed—either after one election or as many as four attempts in a given year— 'voting a levy down' may serve primarily as a form of protest vote that is largely unrelated to tax cost. School district supplementary levy support has declined significantly in Washington school districts. Levy support was fairly steady from 1991 to 1994—averaging roughly 71 percent support—but the level of support declined to approximately 66 percent in 1996. As mentioned earlier, levy rates steadily increased during the 1990's. In 1991, the mean first attempt levy rate was $2.65 per thousand dollars assessed value. By 1995, the average first attempt levy rate was $3.10 per thousand dollars assessed value. As noted in the preceding review of the school finance literature, tax cost influences voter support for school levies. The economic theories of voting behavior hypothesize that voters tend to reject increased costs of government. Demographic data indicate that the population of Washington is becoming older. The proportion of residents over the age of 55 increased during the 1990's. As noted earlier, older voters tend to reject school levies because they do not see a direct benefit from increased expenditures for schools; with a few exceptions, these voters do not have school-aged children at home. The charts presented here would offer support to the economic perspective—voters are beginning to indicate that local education costs are too high.

The sociological models of voting behavior are offered some support as well. The proportion of students living in poverty has steadily increased over the last ten years. The proportion of students eligible for the Federal Free and Reduced Lunch Program—a very solid poverty indicator—increased from 32 percent in 1990 to over 38 percent in 1995. Children living in poverty usually come from low income homes and neighborhoods. The increase in the poverty figures is inversely related to voter support for school levies. It would appear, therefore, that the voter disaffection argument is offered some support.

The poverty indicator parallels almost exactly the rise in school district levy rates. The rate increase for school supplementary levies is likely to be related to the increased environmental constraints facing public school districts in Washington. School administrators are not likely to be building organizational 'slack' or 'rent-seeking'; rather, they are simply trying to obtain the resources necessary to combat a real threat to the core mission and technologies of their organizations.

CONCLUSION

Paradoxically, the voting literature and the evidence presented demonstrate that as the environmental constraints—particularly constraints related to socioeconomic disparity—increase, the legitimacy of the goals and costs of public schools decline in the minds of local voters. Without the steady supply of needed fiscal resources, public schools populated with a high percentage of at-risk students are likely to become even more severely constrained. The local finance argument tends to collapse in light of this evidence. A state-centered model of public school finance would more likely offer public schools a steady and sufficient resource base, but the legitimacy of the education enterprise is a function of the local citizenry.

Resources should not serve as a constraint on public school organizations. The tremendous efforts to equalize funding for basic education have been largely successful, which is good news for public school organizations and their student populations. Nevertheless, the local levy vote patterns offer further insight into the problems facing school districts—namely, the issue of legitimacy. Even if resource provision is removed as a credible constraint on public school organizations, there are a whole host of other constraints that remain. A school district may be well-funded but not strongly supported by local citizens. While the evidence indicates that local funding may not be the answer—due in large part to the serious funding disparities that would potentially emerge—that should not be a signal to education policymakers that the local level should be entirely by-passed. Local citizens and voters will offer legitimacy to school district organizations if performance is of high quality. While funding dictates organization goals, funding bodies (i.e., state level bureaucracy) should not exclude the local voice through the funding process. Resources should be provided in a manner that allows for local variations in educational goals. Local citizen-stakeholders must retain an active role in the education goal-setting process if the legitimacy of the local school is to be preserved.

Appendix 4.1
Median Levy Rate in Washington School Districts, 1990-1996

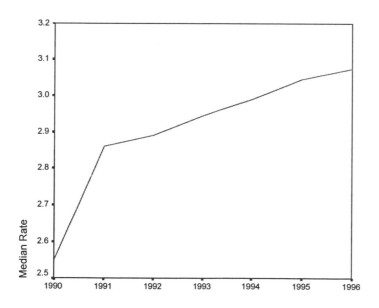

Appendix 4.2
Median Percentage of Voters in Favor of First Attempt Levy in Washington State School Districts, 1990-1996

Appendix 4.3
Time Series Model of Levy Amounts in Washington State, 1975-1996

	B	t
Consumer Price Index	0.481	4.63***
Levy Amount (Differenced)	0.232	2.76*
Enrollment (Logged)	0.513	5.10***

R^2=0.89
Adjusted R^2=0.87
N=20

***p<0.001, *p<0.05

WORKS CITED

Bergstrom, T. and Goodman, R. 1973. "Private Demand for Public Goods," *American Economic Review*. 63: 280-296.

Bergstrom, T., Rubinfeld, D. and Shapiro, P. 1982. "Micro-Based Estimates of Demand Functions for Local School Expenditures," *Econometrica*. 50: 1183-1205.

Billings, J., Roberts, M., Schley, R., Case, T., Shish, S., Molohon, J., and Hauntz, D. 1996. *Organization and Financing of Washington Public Schools*. Olympia, WA: Office of the Superintendent of Public Instruction.

Campbell, C. and Fishel, W. 1996. "Preferences for School Finance Systems: Voters versus Judges," *National Tax Journal*. 49(1): 1-15.

Chen, K. 1992. *Political Alienation and Voting Turnout in the United States: 1960-1988*. San Francisco, CA: Mellen Research University Press.

Courant, P. and Loeb, S. 1997. "Centralization of School Finance in Michigan," *Journal of Policy Analysis and Management*. 16(1): 114-136.

Dalton, T. 1977. "Citizen Ignorance and Political Activity," *Public Choice*. 15: 85-99.

Denzau, A. and Grier, K. 1984. "Determinants of Local School Spending: Some Consistent Estimates," *Public Choice*. 44: 375-383.

Downes, T. and Pogue, T. 1994. "Adjusting School Aid Formulas for the Higher Cost of Educating Disadvantaged Students," *National Tax Journal*. 47(1): 89-110.

Downs, A. 1957. *An Economic Theory of Democracy*. New York: HarperCollins.

_____. 1967. *Inside Bureaucracy*. New York: Little, Brown.

Duncombe, W. and Yinger, J. 1997. "Why Is It so Hard to Help Central City Schools?" *Journal of Policy Analysis and Management*. 16(1): 85-113.

Easton, D. 1965. *A Framework for Political Analysis*. Englewood Cliffs, NJ: Prentice-Hall.

Evans, W., Murray, S., and Schwab, R. 1997. "Schoolhouses, Courthouses, and Statehouses After *Serrano*," *Journal of Policy Analysis and Management* 16(1): 10-31.

Filer, J. and Kenny, L. 1980. "Voter Turnout and the Benefits of Voting," *Public Choice*. 35: 575-585.

Frey, B. and Pommerehne, W. 1982. "How Powerful Are Public Bureaucrats as Voters?" *Public Choice*. 38: 253-262.

Hahn, H. and Kamieniecki, S. 1987. *Referendum Voting: Social Status and Policy Preferences*. New York: Greenwood Press.

Hill, D. and Luttbeg, N. 1983. *Trends in American Electoral Behavior*, Second Edition. New York: Peacock Publishers.

Holcombe, R. 1980. "An Empirical Test of the Median Voter Model," *Economic Inquiry*. 18: 260-274.

Horton, J. and Thompson, W. 1962. "Powerlessness and Political Negativism: A Study of Defeated Local Referendums," *American Journal of Sociology.* 67: 485-493.

Ladd, H. and Yinger, J. 1994. "The Case for Equalizing Aid," *National Tax Journal.* 47(1): 211-224.

Langton, K. 1980. *Political Participation and Learning.* North Quincy, MA: The Christopher Publishing House.

Lankford, R. 1986. "Property Taxes Tax-Cost Illusion and Desired Education Expenditures," *Public Choice.* 49: 79-97.

Lutz, F. and Iannaccone, L. 1978. *Public Participation in Local School Districts: The Dissatisfaction Theory of Democracy.* Lexington, MA: Lexington Books.

Matsusaka, J. 1995. "Explaining Voter Turnout Patterns: An Information Theory," *Public Choice.* 84: 91-117.

Megdal, S. 1983. "The Determination of Local Public Expenditures and the Principal Agent Relation: A Case Study," *Public Choice.* 40: 71-87.

Minar, D. 1966. "The Community Basis of Conflict in School System Politics," *American Sociological Review.* 31: 822-835.

Mosteller, R. 1995. "The Tennessee Study of Class Size in Early School Grades." In *The Future of Children: Critical Issues for Children and Youths,* 5. Los Angeles, CA: Center for the Future of Children, Packard Foundation, 113-127.

National Center for Educational Statistics. 1998. *Digest of Educational Statistics.* Washington, DC: U.S. Department of Education.

Niskanen, W. 1971. *Bureaucracy and Representative Government.* Chicago, IL: Aldine and Atherton.

Oakland, W. 1994. "Fiscal Equalization: An Empty Box?" *National Tax Journal.* 57(1): 199-210.

Peterson, G. 1973. "Voter Demand for Public School Expenditures," in J. Jackson (ed.), *Public Needs and Private Behavior in Metropolitan Areas.* Cambridge, MA: Ballinger, 99-119.

Piele, P. and Hall, J. 1973. *Budgets, Bonds, and Ballots: Voting Behavior in School Financial Elections.* Toronto: Lexington Books.

Romer, T. and Rosenthal, H. 1979. "Bureaucrats versus Voters: On the Political Economy of Resource Allocation by Direct Democracy," *Quarterly Journal of Economics.* 93: 563-587.

Rubinfeld, D. 1977. "Voting in a Local School Election: A Micro Analysis," *Review of Economics and Statistics.* 59: 30-42.

Rubinfeld, D. and Thomas, J. 1980. "On the Economics of Voter Turnout in Local School Elections," *Public Choice.* 35: 315-331.

Silva, F. and Sonstelie, J. 1995. "Did *Serrano* Cause a Decline in School Spending?" *National Tax Journal.* 48(2): 199-215.

Simon, C., Lovrich, N., and Yap, E. 1999. "Public School Organizational Performance and Social Capital: A Comparative Outlier Analysis of Washington State School Districts." Paper presented at the Annual Meeting of the Western Political Science Association.

Spring, J. 1976. *The Sorting Machine: National Education Policy Since 1945.* New York: David McKay Co.

Teixeira, R. 1987. *Why Americans Don't Vote: Turnout Decline in the United States, 1960-1984.* New York: Greenwood Press.

Temple, J. 1998. "Recent Clinton Urban Education Initiatives and the Role of School Quality in Metropolitan Finance," *The National Tax Journal.* 51(3): 517-529.

Tiebout, C. 1956. "A Pure Theory of Local Expenditures," *Journal of Political Economy.* 64: 416-424.

Verba, S. and Nie, N. 1972. *Participation in America: Political Democracy and Social Equality.* New York: Harper & Row.

Verba, S., Scholzman, K., Brady, H. and Nie, N. 1993. "Citizen Activity: Who Participates?   What Do They Say?" *American Political Science Review.* 87(2): 303-318.

Wolfinger, R. and Rosenstone, S. 1980. *Who Votes?* New Haven, CT: Yale University Press.

COURT CASES

San Antonio Independent School District v. Rodriguez (1973) [411 U.S. 1]

Seattle School District No. 1 et al., Respondents v. The State of Washington et al., Appellants (1978) [90 Wn P.2d 476; 585 P.2d 71]

Serrano v. Priest (1976) [18 Cal.3d 728; 135 Cal.Rptr. 345; 557 P.2d 929]

U.S. v. Carolene Products (1938) [304 U.S. 144]

Chapter 5

Findings

Chubb and Moe (1990) and Smith and Meier (1994, 1995) look at public school administration *in toto*.   In the first instance, administration is viewed as the nefarious bureaucracy, primarily designed to maintain the organizational status quo and respond to the needs of powerful interest groups (e.g., teachers' unions). In the latter case, administration is viewed from a contingency theory perspective.   Smith and Meier (1994) argue that public school administration serves to maintain the organizational core mission, and actively responds to the needs of their clientele (e.g., students).

Each of the regression models of central administration reported here explains a sizeable portion of the variance in central administrative expenditures. Regression models of public school district central administration for school districts in the State of Washington explain approximately 71 percent of the variance in central administration expenditures per pupil (see Appendix).   The variables employed represent four critical dimensions outlined by contingency theorists: core technology, administrative unit capacity, resource providers, and environmental constraint.   Teachers are the primary core technology in elementary and secondary education. First, expenditures for classroom technologies and special programs are closely related to resource provision. Resource allocations reflect an organizational commitment to particular goals and more importantly a commitment to human resources—school administrators, teachers, and school-aged children and their parents.   Programmatic expenditures for particular educational purposes and classroom technologies are only truly effective if a school organization has made a commitment to those individuals who will use those educational tools in classroom instruction— namely, teachers.

Resources have increased, but on average the general proportion of the resource pie changed very little between 1991 and 1995.   Nevertheless, resources are a critical element in understanding administration.   If the contingency theory model is accurate, then there should not be any significant change in the relationship between central administrative expenditures and resource providers. In fact, no significant change was observed. Stable resource providers at the federal and state level were negatively related to the size of central administrative expenditures.   In other words, fewer resources were committed to central school district administration as the proportion of school resources from federal and state sources rose. Consistency in resource provision means that schools need to spend less time and energy searching for resources.

While efforts to equalize resources for basic education has had a hand in reducing the search process for school districts operating in economically disadvantaged communities, basic education is not the only function of public schools.   There are a number of ancillary activities requiring additional resources that are obtained from the local level via supplemental school district levies.   If the norms of rationality hold, then central administrative expenditures should be lower in school districts in which voters are supportive of school district supplemental levies.   In all but one instance—the 1992-1993 central administration model—levy support was negatively related to central administration.

School districts operating in supportive environments do not require larger central administrative expenditures in order to engage in resource-seeking activities.   It costs less to run a school if the community being served by the school is supportive of the organization, its goals, and methods of achieving those goals.   As we have entered into an era of skepticism about public schools and their ability to produce high quality education, how will this impact the school organization?   The models reported here indicate that a less supportive school environment results in greater administrative expenditures—resources needed to educate students are diverted to administrative departments within the school district.

In the 1991 central administration model, I was able to use a poverty indicator generated by the U.S. Census Special Tabulation for Washington School Districts 1990.   Unfortunately, the Census does not produce poverty estimates for school districts in Washington on a yearly basis.   Therefore, I substituted the free and reduced lunch data in the 1992-1995 models of central administration.   The proportion of students enrolled in the free and reduced lunch program is considered to be an acceptable measure of the proportion of students living in poverty. The relationship between free and reduced lunch enrollments and per pupil expenditures for central administration was not significant in the 1991-1995 models.

The findings are consistent with the general expectations of contingency theory. Public schools are open systems organizations that respond to the constraints related to core organizational goals and tasks and environmental constraints that limit the ability to achieve educational purposes. Nevertheless, does effective administrative capacity and responsiveness necessarily produce improved organizational outputs?   The goals of administration are quite a bit different than the goals and tasks of classroom teachers.   Administrators deal with resources and environmental constraints—critical functions of school district administrators. Additionally, administrators must be good leaders, identifying the goals of the organization and ensuring that those goals are accomplished.

Conversely, teaching staff are often more concerned with the day-to-day education process. It could be stated with a high degree of confidence that teachers would prefer orderly to disorderly classrooms. Ideally, students would come to school physically and mentally prepared for the education process and eager to learn, and schools would provide teachers with consistently high quality educational resources (e.g., good textbooks, computers, paper, writing instruments, multi-media tools, etc.).   Teachers would prefer to be less concerned about classroom order and the acquisition of basic learning materials. Finally, teachers would prefer to spend less time having to generate student enthusiasm about the learning process, and less time having to justify the learning process and curriculum to students and their parents.

Effective administration would have a positive impact on student achievement because it would reduce the constraints placed upon the classroom teacher. Resources would be consistent, classrooms orderly, and students quite possibly enthused due to a highly effective school administrator promoting organizational goals within the school as well as convincing parents and interested citizens of the legitimacy and importance of the public school in the local community. Highly effective administration, however, is not a constant or 'given' element in school organizations—or any organization, for that matter.

In an open systems organization, functions of school administrators must be adapted so as to effectively respond to ever-changing environment constraints. Certainly, federal and state resources are stable; local resource provision is largely a function of how voters view the school district. If voters feel that the school is not functioning in an effective and efficient manner, the ability of administrators to successfully pass local levies will be hampered. What appears to be more frequently the case in Washington, however, relates to levy rates. Despite the fact that basic education is paid for largely through state funds, local schools are asking for ever-larger supplement levies, as seen in the charts reported in the Chapter 4 Appendix.   Conversely, levy support has dropped considerably. In times of relative stability, staff functions should be along the same dimension, reflecting consistency in function within the organization. Administrative function should be fairly benign during times of stability, allowing teachers to accomplish the core organizational tasks. In times of instability, administrative capacity is directed towards the various constraints imposed on the organization by the environment.

UNDERSTANDING ORGANIZATIONAL OUTCOMES

In order to determine the dimensions of organizational influence on student achievement, fifteen explanatory variables were identified in the OSPI school district personnel and general demographic data reports. District staffing reports provide a detailed record of personnel in terms of their function, average salary, contract days, and Legislative Evaluation and Accountability Program (LEAP) factor.[1] The number of full time equivalent (FTE) for each job category was required to determine the per pupil presence of various types of personnel in a school district. Nearly all school districts had a superintendent, which was duty code 101. Other district personnel working in the superintendents' offices fell under duty code 102 (e.g., assistant superintendents).   Building administrators (i.e., principals) fell under duty code 201, and other building administrators fell under duty code 202 (e.g., vice principals and deans of students).

Administrative personnel fulfill the executive and managerial functions within school districts. Central and building administrators are primarily tasked to limiting environmental constraints on teachers as they go about achieving the core missions of the school organization. Central administration in particular is the primary organizational-environmental interface for the school organization. Central administrators must seek to maintain resource stability and promote the legitimacy of school district goals and functions to local citizens. Additionally, central administrators must promote school levies and actively seek their passage. Building administrators alternatively must maintain order within their schools and promote the core mission of the education process.

Teaching staff fell under personnel duty code 301. Teaching personnel represent the most critical core technology and human resource in the education process. Absent a well-trained, committed, and experienced teaching staff, the education process would fail to accomplish its central goals. There are limits to how successfully teachers can adapt the learning process—due to constraints associated with time, resources, and organizational rules. For instance, a teacher working within the traditional classroom frequently cannot single-handedly help a student overcome the effects of poverty and limited English proficiency. Policy analysts frequently laud the extraordinary teacher and his or her students for overcoming seemingly insurmountable obstacles through the employment of extraordinary talents and personal drive.   As much as the praise is often deserved, such circumstances and the outcomes produced should be interpreted in the manner in which they are related: truly extraordinary events that cannot be duplicated easily on a daily basis in classrooms across America. Consistently high quality outcomes are a function of consistent and high quality human and monetary resources.

Given the limitations under which teachers commonly operate, there is a need for experienced administrative staff to support the educational process. Elementary and secondary education organizations have been termed "loosely coupled" (Harmon 1981). In other words, teachers operate in a manner that is largely independent of administrative oversight.   Nevertheless, an effective

---

[1] Established in 1977, the Legislative Evaluation and Accountability Program is a research arm attached to the Washington State legislature. In this case, the LEAP factor is a measure of the staff education and experience mix for classified and certificated staff in school districts.

administrator is one who knows when to step in to aid teachers in their efforts to provide quality education in an orderly environment.

As illustrated in previous chapters, the school environment is dynamic. In my analysis of Washington State, I found that students have become increasingly concerned about drug use, absenteeism, and cutting class. While weapons violations went down over the course of the 1990's, the deadly gun violence captured in media reports clearly had an impact on students—they are increasingly concerned about the potential for disorderly behavior in schools. Under these conditions, an experienced administrative staff would likely attempt to limit the impact of school violence on the learning process with the help of counselors, student psychologists, and community disorder officers.

An organization operating in a relatively stable environment with consistent resource provision would likely experience fairly stable internal processes. Staff experience, core technologies, environment constraints, and staff size per pupil would be easily identified as unified concepts or factors. An experienced staff would contribute to better educational outcomes. Ideally, schools would not have to develop supplemental education programs and would not have to contract out to private learning services to help students overcome learning disabilities frequently associated with poverty. The student/teacher ratio would be relatively small, providing students with greater opportunity for individual one-on-one learning with instructors.

The experience level of teachers and administrators is captured in this analysis through the LEAP factor, which relates to the average pay grade of personnel within that job category. Pay grade is a function of education level and tenure. For this analysis, LEAP does a wonderful job of capturing the multi-dimensionality of 'experience.' Formal classroom experience for teachers and administrators is a critical element in effectively operating in the ever-changing learning process. New classroom technologies must be understandable to the teacher if the technology is going to have the intended impact on students. Teachers, therefore, must be well-educated and life-long learners. Formal education, however, cannot replace practical experience in the classroom.

Teachers must be able to determine "what works and what does not work," a task that can only be achieved through the trial and error of the educational process conducted under typical classroom conditions common for each teacher. Despite our best efforts to discover it, there is no 'one best way' to educate—circumstances vary and practices must respond to unique and changing conditions. The LEAP factor is an effective method of capturing the two dimensions of teacher and administrator experience: formal training and practical experience in school settings.

Resource distribution is an important part of organizational core functions and boundary spanning activities. Resources can be expressed in at least two different ways: human resources and technological resources. In both instances, resources cost money and the distribution of financial resources is therefore one of the best uniform measures of organizational priorities. An organization with a well-paid staff is an organization that values human resources. Conversely, an organization with state-of-the-art technology is an organization that values technological resources.   Human and technological resources are not mutually exclusive. It is possible to value both resource types and to finance core technologies that demonstrate equitable valuation.   It is equally possible that neither technology is highly valued and is not well-financed, which may be a function of organizational priorities, resources, or environmental constraints.   Studying the distribution of resources for schools that operate under resource or other forms of environmental constraints is not an exercise in assigning blame to administrators, teachers, public sector unions, voters, or elected officials.   It is an attempt to understand what happens to organizational priorities under conditions of economic deprivation. I do not plan to spend significant time on the issue of resource-starved school districts. In this particular instance, I am primarily interested in studying resource provision for core technologies that attempt to remedy the environmental constraints which limit the ability of public schools to produce a quality output: namely, academic excellence.

To this end, three categories of resource expenditure are identified—contractual services, supplies, and instructional materials. All three variables are measured in terms of dollars per pupil expended. *Contractual services* relates to expenditures for privately operated learning programs which are designed to assist students with basic skills proficiency in areas such as language arts (i.e., reading and verbal ability) and mathematics. *Supplies* designates expenditures for educational tools needed to instruct students.   In schools with greater constraints on the learning process, a larger proportion of the budget is frequently dedicated to educational supplies and instructional materials. Educational technologies as a proportion of the school budget, however, are generally negatively related to per pupil expenditures for teachers. Budgeting is frequently a zero-sum game: one program area loses resources while other areas may gain resources—or some program areas gain resources at a rate greater than other program areas. In theory, public budgeting should involve the pursuit of Pareto-optimal outcomes in which some areas gain resources, but none generally loses resources. In practice, however, budgeting is about making tough choices. In this instance, teachers appear to lose out to other instructional technologies. They may not be actually losing resources, but teachers may not be gaining resources, which could be interpreted as a form of loss in terms of prioritization in the organizational budgeting processes and outcomes. That is not to say that teachers should be the top priority in terms of core technology in all instances. It simply means that some technologies are advanced as a priority while other technologies—in this case, teachers—are not. There is no clear and consistent evidence that smaller student/teacher ratios are *the* answer when it comes to improved student performance. Therefore, it is not particularly surprising that under different circumstances, different core technologies are given greater weight.   What remains unclear is the issue of the relationship between core technologies and outcomes.

When I refer to 'circumstances,' I am generally referring to environmental constraints under which school districts must operate. Environmental constraints relate to factors which are both closely connected to student outcomes as well as more general measures of community support for the school district as an organization. Parental education is one of the most important factors in predicting student achievment. Students whose parents have attended college and attained college degrees usually have a higher level of human capital or socioeconomic status. Higher socioeconomic status translates into greater educational opportunities and life experiences for children. Additionally, parents who have attended college frequently see the value in educational achievement beyond high school graduation. Parents often serve as role models for their children, which would lead the children of college-educated parents to be more likely to seek post-secondary educational opportunities.

If the value of education is reinforced by parents and/or legal guardians and education opportunities are made available to children beyond the opportunities provided at their school, then the constraints on the educational process within schools will be significantly reduced. Teachers and administrators will spend less time having to maintain order within their school environments. Less time will have to be spent legitimizing the educational process, while more time could be dedicated to learning. The circumstances under which a school operates are significant contributing factors to outcomes.

Four measures of environmental circumstances have been chosen for this study. The percentage of *mothers with some college experience or a college degree* is a measure of family human capital and general socioeconomic status. The percentage of *school children in the district who are enrolled in the free and reduced lunch program* is another measure of socioeconomic status in the school district. Districts with a higher percentage of students enrolled in this program are generally districts with severe socioeconomic deprivation. The *dropout* rate is included as a third measure of socioeconomic status within school districts. Finally, *voter support for school district levies* is included as a measure of general community support. As discussed previously, school districts with serious economic disparity are generally less supportive of school district supplemental levies than school districts with higher levels of socioeconomic status. Additionally, rate bargaining theory indicates that voters may vote down levies for cost-related factors, which is in some ways a measure of worth. A well-supported institution is an institution that citizens feel is worth financing. Additionally, an organization that is trusted and that requests a particular level of resources will gain citizen support because citizens believe that the request is made in good faith.

During the 1990's budgeting in Washington's public schools appears to have involved some trade-offs in terms of resource allocation. On average (note: median value employed), school budgets grew by approximately 1.6 percent in constant 1996 dollars between 1991 and 1994, while school enrollment rose by over 15 percent during the same time period. In other words, the situation appears to have been more than a simple zero sum game in which some parties won while others lost. In fact, public school students in 1994 were probably not receiving the same educational opportunities as their 1991 counterparts.

When budget constraints tighten, organizations are frequently forced to reconsider their priorities, subsequently reflected in organizational financial arrangements.   Suborganizations within schools that are not performing what are considered to be core tasks often lose their budget priority within the organization.   Central administration expenditures were severely curtailed between 1992 and 1994, falling more than 25 percent in that two-year period. Building administration fell approximately 8 percent between 1991 and 1993, but rose slightly by 1994. Boundary spanning organizations lost roughly 12 percent of their real dollar per pupil expenditure between 1991 and 1994. Teaching expenditures, however, rose by about 5 percent—public schools in Washington directed their resources to core technologies when resources become scarce. The increase in teaching expenditures is also a function of state mandates regarding student-to-teacher ratios as discussed earlier in the book. Student/teacher ratios fell from 18.8 pupils per teacher in 1991 to 18.2 pupils per teacher in 1994—a 3.2 percent decline in the student/teacher ratio.

When resources become tight, organizations are more likely to lose experienced personnel. Administrators become frustrated with the limitations on their ability to accomplish their goals.   In shifting priorities away from administrative functions towards core technologies, the public school system has hired new teaching staff.   Typically, the new teachers are young individuals, often with limited full-time instructional experience.   Reduced administrative capacity may prove to be problematic when the composition of teaching staff changes fairly rapidly. Working in loosely coupled organizations, public school administrative staff have limited control over teachers—with constraints on administrative budgets and less experienced administrators, public schools are likely to drift away from administrative order, limiting their ability to effectively influence organizational outputs.

As hypothesized, the budget constraints of the early 1990's paralleled the loss of experienced administrative personnel as measured by average LEAP factors for school districts.   The median LEAP factor for school district superintendents fell from roughly 2.22 in 1991 to just under 2.10 in 1994. The LEAP factor for school principals fell from 2.07 to 1.98 in 1994. For reasons largely related to the increased hiring of teachers to reduce the student/teacher ratios in Washington schools, the LEAP factor for teachers fell approximately 5 percent between 1991 and 1994. Personnel and budgetary changes are likely to have a tremendous impact on the ability of schools to consistently produce academic excellence, largely due to the inability of the organization to operate under stable internal organizational conditions, let alone the changing nature of the school organizational environment.

Resource expenditures for supplies rose very modestly between 1991 and 1994, while resource expenditures for instructional materials and contractual services declined substantially.   Schools were hiring more teachers—many of them with limited experience—but not offering a larger pool of resources to accomplish educational goals.   With contractual service budgets declining, teachers were increasingly required to accomplish educational challenges—such as teaching students with learning disabilities—that until only quite recently were deemed beyond the abilities of the average teacher operating in a conventional classroom with limited time and resources.

        In the State of Washington, environmental constraints on public schools
did not become more severe during the early 1990's, possibly due to the efforts
of school counselors and other boundary spanners whose goal is to retain at-risk
students.   Public school boundary spanners accomplish their mission by
directing students towards alternative public schools with nontraditional
classrooms or simply helping students cope with personal or family problems
that affect their desire to remain in school. For the most part, boundary spanners
attempt to limit the impact of environmental constraints using nonpunitive
techniques. Conversely, school principals and deans of students primarily wield
negative reinforcement tools to shape student behavior.

        The percentage of mothers with some college education increased from
approximately 28 percent to over 30 percent between 1991 and 1994.   With an
increasing percentage of school-aged children's parents having obtained a
college degree, the importance of education is more likely to be reinforced
within the home environment. Additionally, college-educated parents generally
have higher incomes and professional employment.   Higher socioeconomic
status is associated with greater extracurricular educational opportunities for
children, which reinforces and illuminates further concepts and information
learned in the formal educational environment of the school.

        Improved parental education levels, however, did not appear to
diminish the impact of poverty within Washington school districts. Employing
data from the free and reduced lunch program, the proportion of school children
participating in the nutrition program noticeably increased from a median school
district enrollment of 31.5 percent of pupils in 1991 to 35 percent in 1994. The
11 percent increase in nutrition program eligibility, however, increased between
1991 and 1993, with no substantial change from 1994 to 1995. Nevertheless,
the figures would tend to indicate that Washington schools, as with other schools
across the nation, continue to face the challenges that often accompany
socioeconomic disparity. The increase in poverty and the increased proportion
of students' mothers who have attended or graduated from college would tend to
support the contention that there is a growing socioeconomic gap that will likely
impact educational outcomes.

        In a more general sense, school district communities are increasingly
supportive of local public schools. One method of measuring the level of
community support involves a simple analysis of school district supplemental
levy election results. As mentioned in the previous chapter, Washington allows
school districts up to four elections per year to gain support for successful levy
passage. Levy requests generally pass by the fourth attempt; thus, studying levy
support in the *initial* attempt would provide some clues regarding community
support for local school district finance measures.

        The median level of support for school district supplemental levies
increased between 1991 and 1994 from 72 percent to over 74 percent (Note: The
1995-1996 school year witnessed a tremendous decline in first attempt levy
support).   At first glance, this increased level of voter support offers some
encouraging evidence that public schools are actively supported by their
communities. Perhaps less encouraging, however, is evidence that voter turnout

in supplemental levy elections fell precipitously over the four-year period, from a 63 percent first attempt levy turnout rate in 1991 to a fairly low 52 percent turnout rate in 1994. Over that same period of time, levy rates and levy amounts requested rose substantially. Voters are not voting levies down per se; they are simply choosing not to vote. Those individuals who are voting, however, are very supportive of public school funding. Nevertheless, the fairly strict Washington State levy passage rules that were still in place during the period made it difficult for levies to succeed in their first attempt.

Contingency theory indicates that under these conditions of uncertainty, organizational administrators must devote greater resources to boundary-spanning activities directed at voters. Voters may or may not be parents, and the evidence would indicate that parents—individuals who have a vested interest in the success or failure of the education enterprise—are more likely to vote for levies. Beyond the resource-related factor, low voter turnout might be indicative of communities that increasingly lack a sense of loyalty to the public school enterprise. Public organizations that lack public support are less likely to produce desirable outcomes.

By way of conclusion, the organizational constraints on public schools are dynamic. Internally, public schools in Washington witnessed a decline in staff experience and education levels as indicated by the LEAP factor data. Central administration expenditures per pupil declined, while per pupil expenditures for school administrators (e.g., principals) declined marginally. While expenditures for teachers increased, the LEAP data indicate that the level of teacher experience declined. Hence a small administrative staff was charged with coordinating the activities of less experienced teachers. External environmental constraints did not improve a great deal. While a growing proportion of public school children's parents have attended college, the effects of poverty remained. Finally, the more general school district community was less supportive for public school levies. Contingency theory would indicate that over the four-year period under study, public schools in the State of Washington faced growing internal and external dilemmas in 1994 compared to 1991.

How do school districts react to such changing conditions? Given that this study is almost exclusively guided by financial data, the answer to the question will not be found in interview responses or other forms of qualitative data. It is likely that qualitative data would effectively describe the dynamic nature of public school organizations, because administrators and teachers may not be entirely aware of how their roles change on a year-to-year basis. Budget data, however, offer a very clear understanding of where resources are directed. A statistical approach known as factor analysis will indicate how certain general categories of expenditure are related to other general categories of expenditure. Expenditure patterns provide some understanding of how organizational expenditures reflect environmental constraints. Stable organizations should reflect a fairly constant relationship between expenditure categories.

In the rotated factor matrix tables listed in the Appendix, the organizational and environmental variables appear to represent four concepts: organizational core technologies, administrative expenditures, staff experience, and environmental constraints. The organizational core technology factor indicates that strong core technologies relate to higher per pupil expenditures for supplies, instructional materials, and contractual services. Teachers must be amply supplied with the tools needed to complete their core tasks. Private contractors offer services that are designed to offer remedial and special education programs to students who cannot be educated under normal classroom conditions. The factor indicates that *smaller* classroom size is indicative of a stronger organizational commitment to the core technology of public schools.

Per pupil expenditures for central administrative, building, and boundary spanning staff are identified as a second factor in the rotated factor matrix. Central and building administrative staff included in the analysis are superintendents, principals, and the supporting administrative personnel (excluding secretarial staff) in the respective offices. Administrative 'boundary spanners' represented dollars per pupil expenditures for four different staff duty codes: community disorder specialists, (such as building security personnel), psychiatrists, counselors, and library/media specialists. In boundary spanning roles, the four personnel categories represent organizational efforts to limit the impact of environmental constraints on the educational process. Psychiatrists offer support to emotionally troubled students, helping them to cope with problems that occur in their everyday lives. Counselors frequently help students pursue post-secondary educational options, directing students to a variety of opportunities that are compatible with students' stated career aspirations. Library staff frequently help students access information sources beyond those materials supplied in daily classroom activities. Developing research skills is critical when introducing students to more proactive educational experiences that are likely to be highly beneficial to them in their careers. Finally, the community disorder specialist expenditures represent an organizational effort to maintain order within schools. The factor loadings are all in the positive direction, which would indicate that in 1991-1992, there were no significant resource trade-offs in terms of financing personnel in these three categories.

The third factor relates to administrative staff experience level, specifically the experience of staff executives (i.e., superintendents and principals). Staff experience is positively related to school levy support. In other words, experienced organizational leaders play a large role in gaining needed resources for public schools. Organizational leaders attempt to legitimize the core mission and processes of schools to concerned parents and other attentive community members.

The environmental constraint factor was composed of three variables. School district dropout rates exhibited a positive factor loading, while the parental educational variable produced a negative factor loading. In other words, larger positive factor scores produced by this factor would indicate a greater environmental constraint on public school districts' core missions and technologies. The poverty measure (i.e., proportion of students eligible for the free and reduced lunch program) produced a positive loading, consistent with the dropout rate loading. This factor represents the environmental constraints primarily associated with the impact of socioeconomic disparity.

The 1991-1992 factor analysis exhibits a fairly stable organizational pattern. Core technologies, administrative staff, and environmental constraints are fairly easily identified. By 1992-1993, this model begins to change slightly. Core technology is still an easily identifiable factor in the analysis, but administrative capacity becomes inconsistent. Dollars per pupil commitments to administration change, perhaps due to the changing nature of environmental constraints. Dropout rates are fairly stable across the time period under study, but parental education goes up significantly, as does the poverty rate in student populations. As noted earlier, the gap between affluent and poor students appears to grow, which would set up a new set of crises for administrative staff. The 1992-1993 and 1994-1995 factor analyses tend to support the contention that public school districts are becoming divided by socioeconomic class. There does not appear to be a unifying principle regarding administrative capacity because schools are in all likelihood seeking unique remedies to highly divergent constraints. The negative factor loading for central administrative expenditures per pupil in the core technology factor would indicate that administratively derived solutions are receiving lower priority—resource expenditures for core technologies are increasingly viewed as the solution to limiting the impact of environmental constraints such as poverty. This finding is supported by the central administrative expenditure line chart discussed previously—school resources are being concentrated in one of the most critical points of school-student contact: the classroom.

ORGANIZATIONAL OUTPUTS

Student performance on standardized examinations is a rather poor measure of student achievement (Orlich and Carroll 1991). Nevertheless, the authors concede that to date, performance on standardized examinations is one of the few generally accepted measurements available to education policy researchers. This study will employ aggregate district level measures of fourth and eighth grade student achievement on the Comprehensive Test of Basic Skills (CTBS) as a primary measure of school district organizational output.

For the purposes of this study, I employed aggregate school district percentile rankings on the CTBS at the fourth and eighth grade levels. The aggregate measure is not part of an attempt to explain the performance of individual pupils in these school districts, as that would violate accepted methodology, resulting in an ecological fallacy. The CTBS results will, however, serve as a measure of general school district performance. Specifically, the aggregate measure reflects on the *quality* of organizational output.

The education policy literature could fill volumes when it comes to predicting individual student achievement, but it generally falls short of explaining even half of the variation in individual success. In part, this is due to the weakness in measurement, producing statistical models that lack the power and completeness to offer a strong and consistent explanation. Recognizing these dilemmas, this study does not attempt to solve the riddle of individual performance, and thus focuses attention on organizational performance. Through the use of statistical models and structural contingency theory—a variant of open systems organizational theory—is it feasible to arrive at a better understanding of why schools produce particular outputs?

The factor analysis of the explanatory or 'independent' variables, as discussed previously in this chapter, produced varying results. A next step in analysis is to link the changing organizational and environmental dimensions (i.e., 'circumstances') with organizational output. As discussed in the theoretical chapter, organizations tend to avoid uncertainty, fearing the unknown and possibly deleterious impact of rapid change on a structure that is not designed for such circumstances. Public organizations are bound by constitutional, statutory, and administrative law, and are financed to a significant degree in a fairly formulaic manner—as if schools operated in a stable environment and enjoyed fairly uniform operational conditions—due in large part to concerns about educational equity in the provision of basic education. In fact, the organizational and environmental dimensions discussed have a tremendous impact on school organizational performance.

The results of the statistical regression analysis support the contention that public school organizations respond to and are shaped by core technologies and environmental circumstances in several ways. The maintenance of high quality core technologies is critical to the performance of nearly all organizations. In the case of production lines, the core technologies most critical to the organization are mechanical devices, but schools are not production lines. The core technology in public schools is a high-quality teaching staff. As noted previously, good teachers are experienced and well-educated, which is reflected in the LEAP factor statistic, but there is more to the core technology of public schools than just high-quality and experienced teachers. The entire organizational staff—administrators and teachers—operates most effectively as a unit if all the key personnel are highly experienced and well-educated.

In the statistical models of aggregate district level student performance on the three testing areas (verbal, mathematics, and reading) at both the fourth and eighth grade levels, the staff experience indicator—related to average LEAP factors for administrative and teaching personnel at the district level—had a positive and significant impact on performance. School districts that retain experienced administrative and teaching staff produced higher student performance, when controlling for environmental constraints. The finding has important implications for proponents of plans to reduce class size. Simply hiring additional teaching staff may not provide the 'quick fix' to perceived underperformance. Rather, teachers and staff must be committed to a long career in education—preferably a career in a single school. The relationships that develop among staff members are a critical part of maintaining organizational stability and high performance.

The core technologies factor is negatively related to aggregate student performance in the 1991-1992 models. The positive factor loadings in this instance were related to expenditures for instructional materials, contractual learning-related services, classroom supplies, and the overall dollars per pupil expended. Student teacher ratio had a negative factor loading, which means that higher student teacher ratios were negatively related to student performance. The expenditure loadings indicate that the core technology factor is a measure of resource expenditure priorities made under conditions of environment-related constraints. Classrooms populated by challenged learners would likely require greater resources for instruction-related materials and supplies. If the educational goals of teachers are not being met within the traditional classroom, it is necessary to contract out for additional teaching support staff and related services. The trade-off, however, is that resources diverted for instructional materials, supplies, and contractual services appear to reduce resources expended for full-time teaching staff. The model demonstrates that experienced and well-educated human resources are of greater importance as core technologies than supplies and instructional materials. Expenditures for supplies and instructional materials may represent a quick-fix mentality in public schools, in a political atmosphere that rewards the quick fix and punishes long-term planning which may or may not produce short-term gains.

Administrative size is generally not a significant contributor in the models of student performance. In other words, the per pupil administrative capacity may be less important than the relative *experience* and *knowledge* of the administrators. The administrative capacity factor includes staffing for the central office, principals' offices, and ancillary staff in counseling, psychology, library services, and school community protection. This findings is clearly consistent with findings in the organizational theory literature, which regularly emphasize a need for quality personnel rather than focusing on the size of administration. Administrative capacity relates to the ability of administrative staff to meet organizational goals. At a certain point, size of administration is important when studying workload, but perhaps a more experienced administrative staff can reduce workload through proactive efforts to eliminate problems before they fully develop.

The environmental constraint factor has a negative impact on district level student achievement in all testing areas reported. Environmental constraints are typically outside of the direct control of school districts; yet the impact of environmental constraints is greater than school-related factors. Schools are often criticized for their policy or staffing choices, which are often mistakenly believed to lead to specific student performance outcomes; but such criticisms ignore the true complexities surrounding the education process. Students are not 'equal' in their capacity to learn when they matriculate. Education is not a uniform process with predictable outcomes. The findings reported here would indicate that *ceteris paribus*; school-related factors accounted for a relatively small proportion of the variance in aggregate district level student performance in 1993. Two school-related factors that exhibited the greatest influence were core technologies (i.e., student-teacher ratio and instructional materials and supplies) and staff experience.

Total district enrollment generally did not play a significant role in explaining performance on standardized examinations, with the exceptions being eighth grade reading and verbal. Controlling for the effects of core technologies, staff experience, and environmental constraints on performance, enrollment was negatively related to student achievement on the aggregate district level 1993 eighth grade reading and verbal portions of the examination. Large school settings do not appear to be beneficial in this testing area. The finding may be statistically significant but irrelevant in theoretical or practical terms. Given that enrollment is significant in only one case out of six performance measures explored, the finding would need to be replicated in another testing year to be considered worthy of further discussion.

It is not possible to make a direct comparison of the 1993 models of aggregate district level student performance on standardized examinations with the 1994 results because the scaled explanatory variables are different. As noted in the factor analysis discussion, school districts and the conditions under which they operate change. Dynamic organizations adapt to their environments, which would necessitate changing roles and responsibilities for school personnel. James Q. Wilson (1989) argued that public schools are 'coping organizations,' responding to the environmental circumstances with which they are faced, which is demonstrated in the factor analyses of the explanatory variables. "Coping organizations" are shaped by their environments, rather than shaping their environments to suit their organizational needs.   To some degree, these expectations would indicate that schools are governed to a larger degree by chaos and complexity than by stable and predictable conditions and operational systems.

In the 1994 model of fourth grade student performance on the standardized reading examination, the three scaled explanatory variables were statistically significant in two of the three testing areas. Core technology had a negative factor loading for much the same reasons as discussed in relation to the 1992 models—monies spent for instructional materials and supplies were related to higher student-teacher ratios. The organizational environment had a strong positive relationship to performance. Finally, school staff experience and education levels displayed a strong positive relationship with aggregate student performance. The models of 1994 fourth grade performance on the verbal and mathematics portions of the standardized examination were slightly different from the reading score model. In both verbal and mathematics, enrollment size did not appear to make a significant difference in explaining outcomes. The eighth grade models were not dissimilar from the fourth grade analysis.

The 1992-1993 factor analysis confirms that central and building administrators have become part of school districts' core technology. Larger student-to-teacher ratios are associated with larger administrative capacity. Administration may grow in order to limit environmental constraints that classroom teachers are unable to manage. Environmental constraints had a consistently negative and statistically significant impact on district-level student performance in all testing areas at the fourth and eighth grade levels. The environmental constraint factor remained fairly stable in the three factor analyses conducted, which would indicate that the factor rotations are producing theoretically valid and reliable scaled indicators. The findings indicate, however, that efforts of education policymakers and practitioners have not been entirely successful in their efforts to reduce the impact of socioeconomic status on student learning.

The relationship between the experience of administrative personnel and teaching staff and student performance would indicate that staff experience plays a significant role in explaining aggregate fourth grade student performance, but is not statistically related to the performance of eighth graders. The findings also indicate that teaching staff are on average highly committed to their mission; experienced and well-educated teachers are being retained in lower performing middle schools, which—based on evidence presented earlier—tend to witness serious problems with disorderly student behavior. It is encouraging to find that experienced teaching staff are being retained in poorer performing middle schools, limiting the impact of aberrant student behavior.

CONCLUSION

Three central factors in explaining macro-organizational structure and performance are personnel, resources, and circumstances. Organizations tend to operate more effectively when high quality personnel are retained at all levels. The development and effectiveness of informal communication patterns are partially governed by the stability of staffing. Teaching and administrative staffs that have shared a career together in the same school district may be better able to coordinate their efforts to promote the core mission of elementary and secondary education.

Resources are also a critical factor in explaining outcomes. Critics and proponents of public schools generally hold highly divergent views regarding the effective use of tax dollars in various education programs.   While this book does not pursue the extant policy debates, the prioritization of resource expenditures clearly leads to important trade-offs in public education.   The findings reported here would indicate that the single most important core technology in public schools is the teaching staff. Other core-technology related expenditures—instructional materials and supplies—reflect a weakened commitment to teaching and an increased reliance on alternative pedagogical and curricular strategies, often producing less significant impacts on organizational performance.

The nature of the task environment is the most important contributing factor in explaining school district performance. The task environment of public schools cannot be controlled by school organizations. Despite nearly forty years of public policies designed to reduce inequality in educational opportunity, socioeconomic status will likely continue to have a strong impact on our educational process and outcomes.

The evidence reported here also demonstrates the very fragile nature of public schools. Efforts to reduce classroom size are noble and highly valuable efforts to improve student performance; but we cannot expect a short-term fix as a result.   If the evidence reported here is an accurate reflection of school organizational behavior, new teaching and administrative staff are probably not the 'magic bullet.' High quality faculty and administrators must be retained, so as to build organizational stability. Additionally, the task environment— particularly, local voters—must be made aware of the long-term dimension to educational reform. Instability in the task environment and massive reform of the core technologies will have a negative impact on schools and student performance.

Appendix 5.1
Organizational and Environmental Dimensions, 1991-1992

Variable	Technical Core	Administrative Capacity	Organizational Environment	Staff Exp.
Central Administration		0.973		
Building Administration		0.880		
Org. Buffer Units		0.948		
Dollars Per Pupil	0.833			
Classroom Supplies	0.874			
Instructional Materials	0.843			
Contractual Services	0.890			
Student/Teacher Ratio	-0.838			
Dropout Rate			-0.578	
Free & Reduced Meals			-0.558	
Levy Support			0.577	
Mother's Education			0.695	
Superintendents' LEAP				0.644
Principals' LEAP				0.600
Teachers' LEAP				0.730

Variance Explained=64.72%; Rotation: Varimax; Converged in 5 iterations; N=296.

Appendix 5.2
Organizational and Environmental Dimensions, 1992-1993

Variable	Core Tech.	Environmental Conditions	Staff Experience
Central Administration	-0.645		
Building Administration			
Org. Buffer Units			
Dollars Per Pupil	0.915		
Classroom Supplies	0.851		
Instructional Materials	0.660		
Contractual Services	0.771		
Student/Teacher Ratio	-0.844		
Dropout Rate		-0.571	
Free & Reduced Meals	0.435	-0.628	
Levy Support		0.607	
Mother's Education		0.650	
Superintendents' LEAP			0.499
Principals' LEAP			0.594
Teachers' LEAP			0.800

Variance Explained=48.67%; Rotation: Varimax; Converged in 5 iterations; N=296.

Appendix 5.3
Organizational and Environmental Dimensions, 1994-1995

Variable	Core Tech.	Protecting Core Tech.	Environ. Constraint	Org/Environ. Interface	Staff Exp.
Central Administration		0.619			
Building Administration		0.657			
Org. Buffer Units				0.850	
Dollars Per Pupil	0.889				
Classroom Supplies		-0.630			
Instructional Materials	0.730				
Contractual Services	0.921				
Student/Teacher Ratio	-0.627	0.335		0.530	
Dropout Rate			0.610		
Free & Reduced Meals		-0.524	0.523		
Levy Support			-0.644		
Mother's Education		0.361	-0.518		
Superintendents' LEAP				0.349	0.270
Principals' LEAP					0.784
Teachers' LEAP					0.524

Variance Explained=56.25%; Rotation: Varimax; Converged in 8 iterations; N=296.

Appendix 5.4
Central Administration, 1991-1992

	B	t
Building Administration	-0.443	-4.50***
Building Administration (squared)	0.361	3.90***
Teaching Expenditure	0.763	16.75***
Teaching Support Expenditure	0.055	1.43
State General Purpose Revenue	-0.205	-4.42***
State Special Purpose Revenue	-0.165	-3.58***
Poverty	0.030	-0.08
Levy Support	-0.063	-1.75@
Enrollment (Logged)	-0.131	-2.81**

R^2=0.77
Adj. R^2=0.76
N=246 (Districts with enrollment greater than 50 students)

Appendix 5.5
Central Administration, 1992-1993

	B	t
Building Administration	-0.493	-4.20***
Building Administration (squared)	0.336	2.79**
Teaching Expenditure	0.785	15.11***
Teaching Support Expenditure	0.082	1.88@
State General Purpose Revenue	-0.120	-2.42*
State Special Purpose Revenue	-0.166	-3.35***
Poverty	0.007	0.16
Levy Support	-0.051	-1.41
Enrollment (Logged)	-0.142	-2.52**

R^2=0.75
Adj. R^2=0.74
N=235 (Districts with Enrollment Greater than 50 students)

Appendix 5.6
Central Administration, 1994-1995

	B	t
Building Administration	-0.405	-3.06**
Building Administration (squared)	0.303	2.19*
Teaching Expenditure	0.671	11.65***
Teaching Support Expenditure	0.101	2.11*
State General Purpose Revenue	-0.132	-2.37*
State Special Purpose Revenue	-0.155	-2.96**
Poverty	-0.005	-0.10
Levy Support	-0.090	-2.22*
Enrollment (Logged)	-0.192	-3.19**

R^2=0.68
Adj. R^2=0.66
N=257 (Districts with Enrollment Greater than 50 students)

Appendix 5.7

Model of Aggregate District Level Student Performance, 1993: Fourth Grade Reading

Organizational Dimension	B	SE B	BETA	t
Core Technologies[2]	-3.97	1.28	-0.210	-3.11**
Administrative Capacity	0.45	0.51	0.043	0.89
Staff Experience	2.05	0.63	0.173	3.23***
Environmental Constraint	-6.40	0.54	-0.579	-11.94***
Enrollment (Logged)	-0.29	0.58	-0.036	-0.50

Constant= 48.22 (p<0.001)
F= 36.22 (p<0.001)
R^2 = 0.42
Adj. R^2 = 0.41
N= 257

Appendix 5.8

Model of Aggregate District Level Student Performance, 1993: Fourth Grade Verbal

Organizational Dimension	B	SE B	BETA	t
Core Technologies	-3.91	1.44	-0.189	-2.71**
Administrative Capacity	0.88	0.57	0.076	1.54
Staff Experience	2.26	0.72	0.174	3.16**
Environmental Constraint	-6.46	0.61	-0.535	-10.69***
Enrollment (Logged)	0.05	0.65	0.005	0.07

Constant=44.64 (p<0.001)
F= 31.23 (p<0.001)
R^2 = 0.38
Adj. R^2 = 0.37
N= 257

---

[2] Core Technologies: A negative coefficient means that school districts with higher student/teacher ratios and greater resource expenditures for supplies, contractual services, and instructional materials are performing at a lower level on standardized examinations.

Appendix 5.9
Model of Aggregate District Level Student Performance, 1993: Fourth Grade Math

Organizational Dimension	B	SE B	BETA	t
Core Technologies	-2.21	1.61	-0.103	-1.38
Administrative Capacity	0.71	0.64	0.059	1.12
Staff Experience	2.60	0.80	0.192	3.25***
Environmental Constraint	-5.65	0.67	-0.451	-8.38***
Enrollment (Logged)	0.39	0.73	0.04	0.54

Constant= 39.06 (p<0.001)
F= 20.15 (p<0.001)
$R^2 = 0.29$
Adj. $R^2 = 0.27$
N= 257

Appendix 5.10
Model of Aggregate District Level Student Performance, 1993: Eighth Grade Reading

Organizational Dimension	B	SE B	BETA	t
Core Technologies	-7.50	1.22	-0.384	-6.13***
Administrative Capacity	-0.27	0.44	-0.028	-0.61
Staff Experience	2.58	0.60	0.222	4.30***
Environmental Constraint	-6.42	0.47	-0.626	-13.70***
Enrollment (Logged)	-1.63	0.53	-0.210	-3.05**

Constant= 63.71 (p<0.001)
F= 49.26 (p<0.001)
$R^2 = 0.51$
Adj. $R^2 = 0.50$
N= 243

Appendix 5.11
Model of Aggregate District Level Student Performance, 1993: Eighth Grade Verbal

Organizational Dimension	B	SE B	BETA	t
Core Technologies	-6.98	1.28	-0.370	-5.46***
Administrative Capacity	0.05	0.46	0.005	0.11
Staff Experience	2.67	0.63	0.239	4.28***
Environmental Constraint	-5.35	0.49	-0.541	-10.93***
Enrollment (Logged)	-1.34	0.56	-0.180	-2.41*

Constant= 57.18 (p<0.001)
F= 34.76 (p<0.001)
$R^2 = 0.42$
Adj. $R^2 = 0.41$
N= 244

Appendix 5.12
Model of Aggregate District Level Student Performance, 1993: Eighth Grade Math

Organizational Dimension	B	SE B	BETA	t
Core Technologies	-3.60	1.58	-0.173	-2.29*
Administrative Capacity	-0.06	0.57	-0.006	-0.11
Staff Experience	1.48	0.77	0.119	1.91@
Environmental Constraint	-5.35	0.60	-0.489	-8.86***
Enrollment (Logged)	-0.40	0.69	-0.049	-0.59

Constant= 51.15 (p<0.001)
F= 18.59 (p<0.001)
$R^2 = 0.28$
Adj. $R^2 = 0.27$
N= 244

Appendix 5.13
Model of Aggregate District Level Student Performance, 1994: Fourth Grade Reading

Organizational Dimension	B	SE B	BETA	t
Core Technologies	-3.55	0.89	-0.302	-4.00***
Environmental Constraint	-6.26	0.62	-0.532	-10.14***
Staff Experience	2.44	0.65	0.208	3.76
Enrollment (Logged)	-3.21	1.54	-0.165	-2.09*

Constant= 56.47 (p<0.001)
F= 31.58 (p<0.001)
$R^2 = 0.34$
Adj. $R^2 = 0.33$
N= 254

Appendix 5.14
Model of Aggregate District Level Student Performance, 1994: Fourth Grade Verbal

Organizational Dimension	B	SE B	BETA	t
Core Technologies	-4.19	0.93	-0.337	-4.50***
Environmental Constraint	-6.11	0.65	-0.492	-9.46***
Staff Experience	2.62	0.68	0.211	3.86***
Enrollment (Logged)	-1.73	1.61	-0.084	0.28

Constant= 50.76 (p<0.001)
F= 33.34 (p<0.001)
$R^2 = 0.35$
Adj. $R^2 = 0.34$
N=254

Appendix 5.15
Model of Aggregate District Level Student Performance, 1994: Fourth Grade Math

Organizational Dimension	B	SE B	BETA	t
Core Technologies	-2.40	1.07	-0.179	-2.24*
Environmental Constraint	-5.75	0.74	-0.430	-7.74***
Staff Experience	3.07	0.78	0.229	3.93***
Enrollment (Logged)	-0.60	1.85	-0.027	-0.33

Constant= 44.52 (p<0.001)
F= 21.62 (p<0.001)
$R^2 = 0.26$
Adj. $R^2 = 0.25$
N=254

Appendix 5.16
Model of Aggregate District Level Student Performance, 1994: Eighth Grade Reading

Organizational Dimension	B	SE B	BETA	t
Core Technologies	-4.54	0.80	-0.397	-5.07***
Environmental Constraint	-6.38	0.53	-0.607	-12.13***
Staff Experience	2.96	0.58	0.274	5.13***
Enrollment (Logged)	-6.13	1.35	-0.334	-4.54***

Constant= 75.54 (p<0.001)
F= 44.76 (p<0.001)
$R^2 = 0.43$
Adj. $R^2 = 0.42$
N=242

Appendix 5. 17
Model of Aggregate District Level Student Performance, 1994: Eighth Grade Verbal

Organizational Dimension	B	SE B	BETA	t
Core Technologies	-3.78	0.83	-0.328	-4.55***
Environmental Constraint	-6.20	0.55	-0.585	-11.30***
Staff Experience	2.09	0.60	0.192	3.48***
Enrollment (Logged)	-3.69	1.41	-0.200	-2.62**

Constant= 61.80 (p<0.001)
F= 37.81 (p<0.001)
$R^2 = 0.39$
Adj. $R^2 = 0.38$
N=242

Appendix 5.18
Model of Aggregate District Level Student Performance, 1994: Eighth Grade Math

Organizational Dimension	B	SE B	BETA	t
Core Technologies	-3.10	0.50	-0.250	-3.27***
Environmental Constraint	-6.03	0.63	-0.528	-9.61***
Staff Experience	2.76	0.69	0.236	4.02***
Enrollment (Logged)	-4.22	1.61	-0.212	-2.63**

Constant= 63.81 (p<0.001)
F= 27.05 (p<0.001)
$R^2 = 0.31$
Adj. $R^2 = 0.30$
N=242

Appendix 5.19
Model of Aggregate District Level Student Performance, 1995: Fourth Grade Reading

Organizational Dimension	B	SE B	BETA	t
Core Technologies	1.27	1.85	0.050	0.69
Protecting Tech. Core	3.02	0.89	0.256	3.41***
Environmental Constraint	-5.03	0.59	-0.444	-8.81***
Org./Environmental Interface	1.17	0.61	0.100	1.93@
Staff Experience	1.76	0.59	0.151	2.96**
Enrollment (Logged)	1.06	0.79	0.130	1.35

Constant= 38.63 (p<0.001)
F= 23.83 (p<0.001)
$R^2 = 0.36$
Adj. $R^2 = 0.34$
N= 264

Appendix 5.20
Model of Aggregate District Level Student Performance, 1995: Fourth Grade Verbal

Organizational Dimension	B	SE B	BETA	t
Core Technologies	3.86	2.07	0.138	1.86@
Protecting Tech. Core	1.97	0.99	0.151	1.98*
Environmental Constraint	-5.66	0.66	-0.436	-8.54***
Org./Environmental Interface	1.80	0.68	0.139	2.64**
Staff Experience	1.62	0.67	0.126	2.43*
Enrollment (Logged)	2.22	0.88	0.246	2.51*

Constant= 30.65 (p<0.001)
F= 22.04 (p<0.001)
$R^2 = 0.34$
Adj. $R^2 = 0.32$
N= 264

Appendix 5.21
Model of Aggregate District Level Student Performance, 1995: Fourth Grade Math

Organizational Dimension	B	SE B	BETA	t
Core Technologies	5.25	2.28	0.173	2.30*
Protecting Tech. Core	1.94	1.09	0.138	1.77@
Environmental Constraint	-5.60	0.73	-0.401	-7.70***
Org./Environmental Interface	1.08	0.75	0.077	1.44
Staff Experience	1.33	0.74	0.096	1.81@
Enrollment (Logged)	2.90	0.97	0.299	2.98**

Constant= 23.69 (p<0.001)
F= 19.52 (p<0.001)
$R^2 = 0.31$
Adj. $R^2 = 0.30$
N= 263

Appendix 5.22
Model of Aggregate District Level Student Performance, 1995: Eighth Grade Reading

Organizational Dimension	B	SE B	BETA	t
Core Technologies	-1.88	1.82	-0.075	-1.03
Protecting Tech. Core	5.99	0.91	0.529	6.48***
Environmental Constraint	-5.50	0.56	-0.500	-9.86***
Org./Environmental Interface	0.86	0.56	0.080	1.54
Staff Experience	1.23	0.62	0.102	1.99*
Enrollment (Logged)	-2.31	0.83	-0.290	-2.79**

Constant= 69.11 (p<0.001)
F= 26.15 (p<0.001)
$R^2 = 0.39$
Adj. $R^2 = 0.38$
N= 251

Appendix 5.23
Model of Aggregate District Level Student Performance, 1995: Eighth Grade Verbal

Organizational Dimension	B	SE B	BETA	t
Core Technologies	-1.30	1.79	-0.054	-0.72
Protecting Tech. Core	5.82	0.90	0.541	6.51***
Environmental Constraint	-4.67	0.55	-0.439	-8.52***
Org./Environmental Interface	0.80	0.55	0.077	1.46
Staff Experience	1.72	0.60	0.149	2.85**
Enrollment (Logged)	-1.98	0.82	-0.257	-2.43*

Constant= 63.75 (p<0.001)
F= 23.73 (p<0.001)
$R^2 = 0.37$
Adj. $R^2 = 0.35$
N= 251

Appendix 5.24
Model of Aggregate District Level Student Performance, 1995: Eighth Grade Math

Organizational Dimension	B	SE B	BETA	t
Core Technologies	-1.90	2.14	-0.068	-0.89
Protecting Tech. Core	5.75	1.03	0.481	5.56***
Environmental Constraint	-5.23	0.64	-0.441	-8.19***
Org./Environmental Interface	0.75	0.64	0.065	1.18
Staff Experience	1.96	0.70	0.152	2.80**
Enrollment (Logged)	-2.35	0.94	-0.273	-2.50*

Constant= 66.51 (p<0.001)
F= 19.05 (p<0.001)
R^2 = 0.32
Adj. R^2 = 0.30
N=250

WORKS CITED

Chubb, J. and Moe, T. 1990. *Politics, Markets, and America's Schools.* Washington, DC: The Brookings Institution.

Downs, A. 1967. *Inside Bureaucracy.* New York: Little, Brown.

Harmon, E. 1981. "Organizational Control in Educational Systems: A Case Study of Governance in Schools," in S. Bacharach (ed.), *Organizational Behavior in Schools and School Districts.* New York: Praeger, 245-276.

Orlich, D. and Carroll, J. 1991. *Report to the State Board of Education on the Schools for the 21st Century Program: Supplement: Defining School Productivity: Alternative Indicators for Policy-Makers.* Olympia: Washington State Board of Education.

Pennings, J. 1992. "Structural Contingency Theory: A Reappraisal," *Research in Organizational Behavior.* 14: 267-309.

Simon, H. 1976. *Administrative Behavior: A Study of Decision-Making Processes in Administrative Organizations.* New York: Free Press.

Smith, K. and Meier, K. 1994. "Politics, Bureaucrats, and Schools," *Public Administration Review.* 54(6): 551-558.

_____. 1995. *The Case Against School Choice: Politics, Markets, and Fools.* Armonk, NY: M.E. Sharpe.

Thompson, J. 1967. *Organizations in Action: Social Science Bases of Administrative Theory.* New York: McGraw-Hill.

Wilson, J. 1989. *Bureaucracy: What Government Agencies Do and How They Do It.* New York: Basic Books.

Chapter 6

Privatization: The 'Virtue of Competition' Hypothesis

INTRODUCTION

Over the last twenty years the privatization of public services has become an important new element in public policymaking; this is particularly the case in education. In the field of public policy, privatization has assumed many different forms. Free market approaches often advocate the elimination of traditional public school hegemony in favor of an openly competitive approach to education featuring vouchers and the easy formation of schooling alternatives. Public school advocates of greater choice for parents propose 'privatization' schemes such as partnerships between schools and businesses and easy contracting out for particular educational services. Both approaches to pedagogical and administrative reform claim similar outcomes for their proposals—namely, greater equity, cost-effectiveness, and improved academic performance.

The focus of this chapter relates to the effect of private school competition on public school performance. School choice advocates claim that the presence of viable private school alternatives within public school districts will lead to improved student performance in public schools as well as private schools. Conversely, public school advocates find that private school competition leads to 'creaming' and greater inequality of educational opportunity. This chapter will focus on the issue of improved public school student performance in relation to private school enrollment in school districts in the State of Washington.

The education policy literature indicates that the result of the various free market approaches to privatization in education might be a worsening of public school performance via the loss of fiscal resources and as a consequence of the phenomenon of 'creaming.' Critics of free market approaches to privatization argue that Milton Friedman's (1955) notion of increased freedom with increased 'choice' would likely have the opposite effect, either by enlarging the resources gap between public and private schools or through a new form of socioeconomic (and oftentimes racial) segregation.

As with most other states, the State of Washington has not adopted a full free market approach to educational choice. There has been some movement towards intradistrict choice, which allows students—particularly those students in county school districts—the opportunity to transfer from one school to another. Many of the students who exercise their choice of schools feel empowered by the opportunity presented. Students actively consider their career and life goals, scrutinize their options, and make a fairly educated choice of schools. Under this limited system of choice, it is evident that students actively consider their individual good rather than collective good, which may or may not be consistent with the goals of some policymakers and public school advocates.

One of the goals of public education policy in Washington and in other states has been to serve as a 'melting pot.' Students from different racial, cultural, and socioeconomic backgrounds attend public school. Through school-related interaction, it is hoped that greater political and social tolerance will develop among student populations. Public school students tend to hold significantly more tolerant attitudes towards historically excluded minority populations. Intra-district choice, however, has a tendency to produce a creaming effect, as students begin to segregate themselves on the basis of their career goals and academic abilities. The effect becomes even more significant when a large portion of the student population from a given district competes for a limited number of openings in highly desirable schools.

Additionally, the added costs of intradistrict choice provide policy analysts with greater insight into the resource needs associated with implementing a full-scale choice system. On average, intradistrict choice presents an added cost of nearly $500 per pupil in the State of Washington. Based on the average cost per pupil in terms of basic education (approximately $6000 per pupil per school year), intradistrict choice represents about an 8 percent increase in educational costs. The benefits—in terms of student performance—related to the policy of intradistrict choice cannot be determined due to data limitations.

Intradistrict choice is the only form of state financed school choice in the State of Washington. It is a geographically limited choice mechanism, which means that the policy is not available to all students. As an experimental policy, however, it does offer some hope for greater responsiveness on the part of public schools to their clientele. Responsiveness, however, means that schools must allow themselves to be constrained by environmental demands. The environmental constraints on public school districts may be limited if intradistrict choice adopts a magnet school approach and narrowly focuses schools' core missions and technologies. Narrowly defined goals, however, may be at odds with the historic goals of public schools.

While intradistrict choice is the sole choice mechanism available to Washington students, there are a number of alternative approaches available. Private schooling and homeschooling—the latter was discussed earlier—are options available to parents who can afford to pay private school tuition or who are willing to make the economic sacrifice of relying on a single wage-earner for their household.   In the former case, there is generally an economic bias. Wealthier parents or legal guardians are more likely to be able to afford the option of private school.   In the latter case, there is a clear social and economic bias present.   Single parent households are unlikely to be able to pursue homeschooling as an option.   Generally, single parents do not have the time to stay at home with their children during the day because of work commitments. Due to economic constraints, single parents are more likely to have two or more jobs, which means that simply rearranging work schedules would have a limited impact on their ability to exercise the homeschooling option.

Particularly since the desegregation of public schools, equality of educational opportunity has been a critical priority in elementary and secondary education policy in the United States.   For more than fifty years, the progress towards real equality of opportunity has been faced with numerous obstacles. Parents, students, and concerned citizens recognize that desegregation does not in and of itself produce equal outcomes.   Equal financing for basic education has been unable to effectively overcome the environmentally related obstacles to academic success.

Additionally, the equality issue has become less focused on group-based issues and is increasingly associated with individual-based priorities. Group-based emphasis has some role in shaping the educational choice debate, primarily in the form of the deep-seated concern of racial and ethnic minorities that educational outcomes tend to fall out along racial and economic lines. Public schools—particularly in the inner city and in rural areas—lack the additional resources necessary for well-developed science and technology programs providing requisite skills for so-called New Economy jobs. Racial and ethnic minority groups concentrated in 'low tech' schools recognize the gravity of the situation they face—namely, the growing potential for technology-based ghettoization in the rapidly changing Information Age.   In his book *Future Shock*, Alvin Toffler (1971) discusses the very high potential for individuals to fall behind in technological skills and knowledge, resulting in social and economic isolation—a concern that is becoming increasingly evident to racial and ethnic minorities, who for centuries have experienced the horrors of political, economic, and social exclusion.

Equality has taken on a new meaning in our new world.   Education is frequently viewed as a commodity that will ensure individual success.   In the past, education was viewed as a tool for the cultural assimilation of recent immigrants who had left traditionalistic cultures and who now found themselves dwelling in a free society with new social and political norms.   Today, however, education is viewed as a requisite tool in achieving economic success—at the very least it is the "key" to a middle class existence and the economic and social opportunities that frequently parallel it.   In a product-oriented world, education has come to be viewed as something that can be readily purchased, a product with a guaranteed impact if one only pays the amount on the price tag.   Under these conditions, the free market paradigm would lead one to view equality in terms of opportunity to *purchase* the commodity 'education.' For free market economists, their education policy acolytes in public policy and political science, and supporters among elected officials and the general populace, the direct provision of education has been delegitimized as a method of achieving social and economic equal opportunity. For these individuals, parity is best achieved through lifting budget constraints via vouchers or tax credits.

Current choice mechanisms in Washington school districts are not equally available to all students. Therefore, the education marketplace is not equally open to all individuals. Parents or legal guardians with higher socioeconomic status have greater flexibility in terms of educational choices than do parents or legal guardians with lower socioeconomic status. How has the education marketplace changed to deal with these new pressures and concerns emanating from the environment? As discussed, public schools have responded with limited educational choice and have attempted to focus greater attention on outcomes, particularly since the 1993 legislative effort to reform elementary and secondary education in the state. School district budgets increasingly emphasize classroom technology and high tech training for students and teachers.

It is unclear as to whether citizens feel that this has been a sufficient effort to reestablish the legitimacy and relevance of public schools in the eyes of the parents of school-aged children and other concerned citizens. There has been an increasing number of private primary and secondary schools in the state and an increase in private school enrollment over the past two decades. Privatization advocates see the rise of private school options as an opportunity to pursue a full-scale reframing of publicly provided elementary and secondary education. As Tiebout (1956) theorized, citizens or consumers will 'vote with their feet.' If they find a better or less expensive service provider (preferably, both cheaper and better), they will relocate in a manner which will allow them to enjoy the increased benefits and/or lower costs. While Tiebout was primarily discussing intergovernmental competition at the state and local level, the privatization advocates arguably see the movement towards private school options as evidence that the benefits of a private school education outweigh the added cost of pursuing the market-based option.

For private school advocates, the exodus from public schools to private schools is indicative of public concerns regarding the legitimacy and functionality of public schools. The largest problem facing privatization scholars, however, is the continued existence of public schools as near monopoly providers of elementary and secondary education. The resources currently directed to public schools are predominantly the result of taxation, which tends to draw down the budget constraints of potential private school customers, thus limiting their ability to choose between private and public school providers. From the privatization advocates' view, the movement towards private school options is an underrepresentation of the crisis of legitimacy facing public schools—in other words, more parents would choose private schools if they could afford to send their children to these alternative institutions. As mentioned previously, vouchers have become a preferred method among private school advocates of introducing increased choice into the elementary and secondary education marketplace, while simultaneously weakening the public school monopoly.   In essence, the whole approach is designed to pursue private methods of achieving what has historically been considered a 'public good.'

Throughout the course of the 1990's, private school advocates and public school apologists in the State of Washington have debated their respective policy proposals.   The early 1990's found many public school apologists on the defensive.   The Coleman Report of nearly a decade earlier and the recommendations of the President's Commission on Privatization (Linowes 1988) left public school advocates with only one feasible option—namely, to address the concerns of elected officials, policy analysts, attentive citizens, and parents of school-aged children through public education reform.   In Washington, then-Governor Booth Gardner advocated the reduction, but not the elimination, of state-level regulation of local schools and school districts.   In Gardner's view, the introduction of greater autonomy for public schools must be accompanied by an increased emphasis on accountability, which could be achieved through the increased emphasis on state-level monitoring and evaluation of student achievement as measured by standardized examinations (Gardner 1991: A15).

The election of Bill Clinton in 1992 led to Goals 2000, an effort to encourage greater flexibility and the pursuit of innovative approaches to service delivery in public schools.   Goals 2000 (Educate America Act) identified other factors besides standardized examination performance as a measure of school success.   Dropout and graduation rates were considered to be significant measures of programmatic success.   The program was voluntary and did not impose new education standards for participating schools.   Additionally, the program focused on vocational training, through job training programs designed to retain and graduate vocational education students with the basic skills needed to pursue a career in a trade (*Seattle Times* 1994: B8).

In Washington, the Schools for the 21st Century Program was funded largely through federal and state grants designed to encourage schools and districts involved in the experimental pilot program to pursue innovative methods of educating their students, while enlarging the scope and time commitment to local level policymaking.   State-level regulations were relaxed for these pilot program participants.   Among other things, Schools for the 21st Century attempted to link social service organizations with public schools.   In essence, social services would coordinate its efforts with public schools and provide an effective organizational buffer for public schools' core organizational mission.   Beyond the anecdotal evidence, however, it is unclear as to how effective was the effort at coordination.   As evidenced in the previous chapter, socioeconomic conditions in public school districts' organizational environments seriously impede the ability of schools to achieve their core goals.

In terms of test score performance, there was no significant increase in aggregate student performance on standardized examinations in the participating schools and school districts, when compared with nonparticipating schools and districts (Simon and May 1996).   The school districts participating in the pilot program were among the most severely constrained school districts in the State of Washington, characterized by large percentages of students living in poverty and sizeable limited English proficiency (LEP) student populations. It appears that the policymakers involved in the pilot program participant selection process chose the most severely constrained school districts, with the idea that if the program could work in those districts, it could work elsewhere in the public education system. The strategy may have doomed the program in its effort to produce a measurable gain in student performance as a result of a major public education policy reform. In turn, the limited success of the program is likely to have encouraged private school advocates in their efforts to pursue market-based approaches to reform.

Privatization alternatives were a central issue in the 1996 general election, demonstrated best by two state-level political races and two prominent ballot initiatives. The governor's race was between a very socially conservative Republican candidate, Ellen Craswell—who supported private school vouchers—and a moderate New Democrat, Gary Locke. Craswell's candidacy was marked by significant religious rhetoric, calling for a renewal of Judeo-Christian moral education. Public school secularism was less attractive than private—frequently, religious-school options. The Republican candidate couched most of her reasons for supporting school choice in economic equity—namely, individuals who chose to homeschool or send their children to private schools should not have to "pay twice" (Paulson 1995: B2). Craswell was also opposed to innovative public school policies and stated that she would repeal outcome-based education plans if elected governor.

Conversely, Democratic candidate for governor and eventual election winner Gary Locke was and remains an ardent supporter of public schools. He supports the use of innovative education policies designed to build 21st-century schools. A New Democrat, Locke is cautious about education policy and tempers his support for education with a strong appeal for student achievement testing to best measure the degree to which education innovations either must be fine-tuned, reinforced, or abandoned. During both his 1996 candidacy and his subsequent term as governor, Locke remained supportive of a public solution to education reform, rather than adopting the free market solutions proffered by privatization advocates.

In terms of education policy, the Superintendent of Public Instruction election paralleled the issue debates occurring in the gubernatorial race. Ron Taber's candidacy was an attempt to introduce widespread private school competition into the state's 296 school districts. Taber advocated the use of private school vouchers as a means to make private school options more accessible to school children from middle and low income families. He claimed to be a supporter of good schools, either public or private. From his perspective, there were and are many good public schools in the State of Washington. However, the poor quality schools generally serve a clientele which cannot afford to choose private school alternatives better-suited to the particular needs of their school-aged children. The use of public education monies for private school vouchers would introduce competition for both resources and students, and encourage underperforming public schools to improve their performance. Based on the evidence presented in the previous chapter, it is apparent that Taber's argument omitted one important detail—namely, public school performance tends to be a function of environmental constraints, such as relative socioeconomic disparities. Low income families can neither afford private school alternatives, nor is it likely that competition for resources between public and private schools would result in improved student performance in public schools. Rather, positive changes in environmental conditions (i.e., family human and social capital) would likely reduce the constraints placed on the core technologies of school organizations, resulting in improved student performance.

Taber was the author of Initiative 173, which, had it passed, would have resulted in a ten-year phase-in of a statewide voucher program. Initially, the privatization plan was to be introduced at the elementary school level. Eventually, middle and high school students would have been given the opportunity to participate in school choice. At the elementary school level, the voucher would cover 100 percent of the costs of education. Middle school student vouchers would cover 90 percent of student costs, while high school vouchers would cover 80 percent. "If a parent can't pay the tuition gap, the public school is always ready to carry out its mandate to provide tuition-free education" (Taber 1996: G1).

The voucher program proposed by Taber in Initiative 173 claimed a $1 billion savings to the state if roughly 40 percent of elementary and secondary school students used the voucher option. Tuition vouchers would cost approximately $3,400 per student per school year compared to the nearly $6,000 per pupil per school year spent in the public schools. In Taber's view, the public school monopoly must be broken in order to promote the interests of a free society. He pointed to the large proportion of Seattle public school teachers—approximately 40 percent of those teachers and administrators making greater than $70,000 per year—who sent their children to private schools as evidence that the public school system was failing to achieve its core mission (Taber 1996: G1).

A charter school proposal—Initiative 177—was also on the 1996 general election ballot, which represented a third option in the education policy debate. Charter schools are one method of equalizing the choice options for students in districts without intradistrict choice. Despite a campaign costing ballot measure supporters $2.5 million, Initiatives 173 and 177 failed to gain the necessary support from voters, paralleling Taber's election loss in the Superintendent of Public Instruction race (Holt 1996: A15).

Taber's opponent in the 1996 Superintendent of Public Instruction race was Terry Bergeson, the former president of the Washington Education Association and an ardent supporter of public schools (Holt 1996: A15). Bergeson was adamantly opposed to the introduction of voucher or charter school options. She felt that competition for limited resources would cause more harm than good to public school organizations and their students.

Bergeson's approach recognized the open systems characteristics of public schools and a system which was best characterized at the building and classroom level by the intensive technology organizational model and the mediating technology organizational model at the district and state level. Despite the failure of the privatization initiatives, it would appear that Bergeson was aware of the serious crisis of legitimacy facing public schools—her opponent had succeeded in establishing a well-organized and well-funded campaign, and the public was made aware of a viable alternative to the public school system.   Consistent with principles of rationality, Bergeson sought to coopt or at the very least collaborate with powerful interests operating in the organizational environment.   "As the state's schools chief, Bergeson said citizens can expect her to be an outspoken leader who rallies the education establishment, business, and the media into a powerful coalition that focuses on a few high-priority issues, goes to the Legislature and gets them accomplished" (Iwasaki 1996: A15).

In addition to building strong support in the public school organizational environment, Bergeson sought to rebuild the core technologies of public education. She supported the use of innovative methods of improving public schools in the state and increasing resources for technology in the classroom. Student dropout rates must be reduced through retention programs and the development of more alternative schools for at-risk students. Finally, public schools must be monitored to determine the programmatic success or failure. As Superintendent of Public Instruction, Terry Bergeson has pursued the implementation of more stringent student testing methods. Under her leadership, Washington public schools have pursued the implementation of outcome based education and the development of the Washington Student Learning examination (WASL) to determine if students are meeting grade level competency.

Bergeson's election victory, however, does not signal the legitimization of the public school system in the minds of Washington voters. As with other states, Washington's public schools continue to face serious challenges to the learning process, and the ability of public schools to effectively deal with these challenges remains unclear. Voters in the state rejected a change in the school finance formula relating to the passage of local school levies, which may signal growing voter skepticism about local public school finance. While not in favor of abandoning public schools, voters may not understand why schools need greater resources.

Cultural and economic changes in the last five years appear to have had a tremendous impact on the public's attitude towards public schools. Economic expansion and the meteoric growth of service-related industries have created a society increasingly fickle in their loyalty to public or private organizations. Support for outcome-based education reflects this cultural change—consumers want to know what they will receive in return for their money. Focusing on tangible output, however, is a double-edged sword—poor performance is almost immediately followed by declining support for the institution in question.   A 1997 Gallup Poll found that for the first time, a majority of parents of school-aged children support the use of tax money for private school vouchers. The support was greatest among women, blacks, and the poor—groups that have traditionally been ardent supporters of public schools (Ross 1997: 4). The support was lowest among suburbanites, persons over 50 years old, and individuals that did not have children (Greene 1997: 2).

Parents, concerned citizens, and elected officials are becoming more aware of the role that family social capital plays in academic achievement. Since the 1950's, the parent-adolescent relationship has changed dramatically. The 'working mother' and the 'single mother'/'single parent' phenomena have placed serious constraints on the ability to nurture and maintain stable family relationships, which are so critical to student success. It is very possible that the growing awareness among voters and policymakers regarding the link between family social and economic conditions and student achievement is related to increased support for private school vouchers and other privatization alternatives. There is a growing public interest in the education process and outcomes, but it does not appear to have led to a greater understanding of why public schools are linked to particular levels of student achievement—levels which are alternately reported as either disappointingly stagnant or alarming low.

Albert Hirschman (1970) once argued that customers or clients have two general options when dissatisfied with the level of service they receive or the quality or cost of the products obtained through interactions with an organization. If they have a high level of loyalty to an organization, they exercise 'voice'—in essence, expressing their dissatisfaction with the quality of the goods or services. Conversely, they can 'exit,' terminating their relationship with the organization so as to pursue alternate providers. The exit option is most commonly exercised by individuals who either lack loyalty to a given organization or who fail to achieve their goals through voice (i.e., through feedback to the organization).

Based on Hirschman's theoretical explanation, one could argue that the growing popularity of privatization alternatives may be related to both the growing awareness of the importance of active involvement of family in shaping children's educational achievement and future success. Additionally, there is a sense that public schools are not responsive to the concerns of their clientele. Many of the privatization advocates employ this observation in their arguments. Whether this observation is accurate or not, public school organizations need to be aware of the environmental constraints that they face in this regard. One method of dealing with such constraints has been discussed earlier—the reinvention of public education through innovative programming. A second method—one that has become more visible as support for school vouchers and charter schools has become more evident—would be the use of legal challenges to the privatization plans.

It is not especially surprising that this alternative has been employed. The "scope of conflict" (Schattschneider, 1960) tends to enlarge in both range and size when an individual or group engaged in a heated policy battle finds themselves at a disadvantage. There have been a series of legal challenges to vouchers and charter schools. The locus of legal challenge relates to the use of vouchers in religious schools. Both opponents and supporters of privatization plans have employed the separation of church and state as a wedge issue in the debate over vouchers and charter schools.

In Washington, religion and education policy were more than casually related in the 1996 gubernatorial race. The GOP gubernatorial candidate Ellen Craswell argued that moral education should be a central part of elementary and secondary education; hence her support of the use of publicly financed vouchers for private school—frequently operated by religious organizations—and reduced support for secular public schools. Having failed to pass the privatization initiatives in 1996, Washington's privatization lobby has been unsuccessful in achieving significant legislative action that would lead to the statewide implementation of a voucher or charter school program. Therefore, the state has not experienced First Amendment litigation regarding the constitutionality of publicly supported vouchers used in private religious-based schools or the creation of charter schools operated by religious organizations.

The judicial reaction to privatization has been mixed. A cursory analysis of recent court decisions nationwide leads one to conclude that privatization plans are being significantly weakened by decisions in state and federal courts, but the opposite might in fact be the case. In the past decade, the Supreme Court has passed a number of rulings indicating that constitutional legal theory is moving towards state-centered federalism. In the case of privatization, therefore, it is likely that the majority of Court members would prefer to avoid making a final ruling on either the constitutionality or unconstitutionality of voucher or charter school programs, preferring to leave the decision to state-level policy makers and courts.

In 1998, the Wisconsin Supreme Court decided that the use of voucher aid for religious schools in Milwaukee was not in violation of the state constitution. The U.S. Supreme Court has not heard this case on appeal and it is not likely that it will grant a writ of certiorari. In essence, the Wisconsin decision stands. For the opponents of privatization, the court's silence in this case has been interpreted as tacit approval of state aid to private religious schools and would allow for the further development of voucher programs and charter schools nationwide.

However, the Court appeared to clarify its position in 1999, finding that Maine and Vermont statutes restricting the use of voucher monies in religious schools not to be in violation of the First Amendment's Free Exercise Clause. The Court did not use the opportunity presented to it to establish a precedent regarding the constitutionality of voucher systems, but chose instead to offer implied support for a state-level policy decision. In essence, the Court is offering support for a more state-centered approach to federalism, giving the states a wide berth in establishing their own priorities regarding elementary and secondary education policy.

The manner in which the Florida case regarding vouchers is handled should provide critical evidence for the aforementioned supposition. A Florida state court judge found that the state voucher plan was unconstitutional because it violated the "mandate that the state provide a free education through a system of 'public schools.' Under the state constitution, he wrote, "Tax dollars may not be used to send the children of this state to private schools" (Halifax 2000: A7). The decision was appealed to Florida's First District Court of Appeal, which essentially ruled that the voucher law was constitutional, and referred the case back to the lower court system for further adjudication (Hegarty 2000). Based on previously related evidence and expectations, should the Florida case proceed to the Federal court system, the courts are likely to take a 'hands-off' approach—particularly if the Republican candidate wins the presidential elections and makes conservative appointments to the Federal bench.

A 1999 Ohio case, however, does offer some evidence of the manner in which the federal courts might get involved in the implementation of privatization plans. In the Ohio case, Federal District Court judge Solomon Oliver, Jr. found that the state's publicly funded voucher program was unconstitutional because the program offered no true private secular choice. In other words, the preponderance of the fifty-eight private schools involved in the choice program were religious schools, thus limiting the alternatives available to children and parents preferring secular private school options. In this case, however, the courts are defining what 'choice' means by identifying what it does not mean—namely, choice is a wide diversity in educational options—but the courts are not saying *carte blanche* "privatization is unconstitutional." For the moment, it would appear that voucher and charter school options have lost the battle. The decision on who won the privatization war, however, remains to be seen and may be decided largely by the judicial appointments of the next president.

PRIVATIZATION ALTERNATIVES: THE ACADEMIC DEBATE

The debate over privatization is perhaps not as bifurcated as it initially appears. The education literature provides some evidence that privatization means different things to different scholars (Lieberman 1989). On the more progressive end of the spectrum, privatization can entail partnerships with business leaders and local industries with the goal of making primary and secondary education more supportive of workplace needs. Public school contracts with private industry for grounds maintenance and cafeteria concession, the creation of magnet and alternative schools, the liberalization of homeschool options, and other regular and temporary services are examples of a more restricted conceptualization of privatization in public education.

At issue for those who wish to restrict privatization is the continued cultivation of the basic values associated with the maintenance of social equity and a sense of community through public education. The education literature in this area often promotes parent-school collaboration and encourages the development of community empowerment in the education arena. Unlike the top-down reforms of the 1950's and the somewhat insulated goal of national defense through education, which spawned a distinctly bureaucratic approach to education, theorists in this arena find evidence of a clear relationship between students' living environment (i.e., socioeconomic condition as well as a sense of community) with student performance in the classroom. This is consistent with findings reported in the Comprehensive School Improvement Program, which was sponsored by the Ford Foundation in the 1960's and early 1970's (Meade 1972). Advocates of this viewpoint deem privatization of the public schools harmful when it further exacerbates socioeconomic inequality and leads to a decline in community spirit.

Contemporary conservative advocates for education reform often call for a high degree of privatization of primary and secondary education. They ground their approach to education reform in economics and libertarian philosophy (Smith 1982: 126), appealing to the promotion of equality and diversity through private means. In terms of economics, market-based reformers tend to equate "free markets" with economic efficiency and individual liberty, concluding that the freedom to choose schools is part of a democratic education.

Advocates of market-based reform often employ the work of Milton Friedman (1955), who argued that the virtual monopoly held by public schools unwisely and unnecessarily limits individual freedom. Instead of promoting equality, the system encourages inequality inasmuch as only wealthier individuals can freely exercise their freedom to exit the public school system by attending private schools. While Friedman recognized that government should require a minimum level of education for the purpose of preserving an understanding of regime norms and values, he argued that educational requirements beyond that goal hamper individual spirit and initiative. Friedman insisted that a free market approach would enlarge the scope of individual choice and promote freedom, equity, and efficient service delivery in virtually every area of economic life, particularly education.

A Nation at Risk (National Committee on Excellence in Education 1983) provided the basis for a renewed emphasis on alternative methods of dealing with the perception of declining educational achievement in America. While the report concluded that there was a need for more stringent educational requirements and a return to some of the top-down themes of an earlier time period, a great deal of reflection and criticism of education reforms during the previous twenty years was evidenced in the study. While the report did not emphasize the privatization movement cultivated by Friedman (1955), it is quite possible that *A Nation at Risk* generated a genuine sense of urgency within the education policy arena, thereby rekindling privatization as a legitimate and acceptable policy innovation.

The Reagan administration, generally supportive of a devolution of power to the states and local governments, went a step further with education policy by recommending a school voucher method of finance (Linowes 1988). President Reagan believed that by leaving educational choice up to parents, local efforts to address poor school performance would lead to the proliferation of educational options for parents to consider. The Report of the President's Commission on Privatization, entitled *Privatization: Toward More Effective Government* (1988), emphasized the need to form contracts with private sector industries for the provision of particular government services (e.g., prison construction and management) while still retaining a large degree of power over the contractees. In the case of education, however, this oversight function was not discussed, nor was the notion of the semi-privatization of ancillary services.

The privatization of education efforts witnessed during the 1980's and 1990's has attracted support from a wide variety of groups (Cookson 1994: 20-35). Economic conservatives and middle class white suburbanites in some cases were joined by disaffected blacks—such as Annette 'Polly' Williams in the State of Wisconsin—who saw school choice as an effective method of exiting an unresponsive public school system (Matland 1995). State governors such as Tommy Thompson in Wisconsin and Pete Wilson in California have also advocated choice-based reforms in their state's public education systems. Public school educators in New York City (a distinctly 'liberal' group) saw school choice—in the form of alternative and charter schools of diverse character—as an effective method of revitalizing public support for public schools. The different motivations for advocating school choice tend to reflect different expected outcomes resulting from choice. Some observers have argued that these reforms might lead to confusion and disappointment for those individuals viewing choice as a panacea for the perceived ills of the public school system (Honig 1994; Dougherty and Sostre 1992).

Without entering into a full discussion of the various manifestations of privatization in education, it is important to mention a few of the most prominent alternatives proffered. The voucher system is possibly the most revolutionary approach. In its ideal form, parents would be able to use a state-provided education voucher to send their children to any public or private school of their choice. Theoretically, the government would provide transportation to and from these schools in order to increase accessibility and scope of choice (Chubb and Moe 1990; Lieberman 1989). Charter schools operate under more restricted conditions, with stipulations in their state charter regarding expected educational outcomes. Finally, magnet schools are public schools that operate on a semi-private basis with other public schools; they are given greater flexibility in their curricula, operations, and teaching methods than conventional schools, and are designed to attract cross-district enrollments of students when parents wish to exit the public school jurisdiction to which their children are assigned to gain access to the educational offerings and facilities of the magnet school.

The criticisms of education privatization proposals range from the strictly empirical to the broadly philosophical. Analyzing one the strongest empirical arguments favoring school choice, Kevin Smith and Kenneth Meier (1995, 1994) offer strong evidence indicating that few if any of the findings reported in John Chubb and Terry Moe (1990) are replicable. Smith and Meier (1995) take serious issue with the individual level of analysis employed by the market-favoring proponents of school choice, concluding that educational policy outcomes are properly studied at the aggregate level of analysis.

Other critics charge that the privatization of elementary and secondary education does not appear to lead to greater equality of educational opportunity. The effective use of choice by citizens requires that information on schooling options is clearly available and understandable to parents and students of all socioeconomic backgrounds. The operative assumption is that parents and students will be motivated primarily by a desire to maximize favorable educational outcomes for their children and will choose schools that have the highest probability of achieving this individual-level goal. The evidence in the literature indicates that these assumptions are not often met in practice. Parents' socioeconomic status and their expectations of schools and of their children are often reflected in their decision to exit from a particular school and to matriculate elsewhere (Martinez et al. 1995). If choice decisions are not uniformly rational, the outcomes of permitting greater school choice would lead to greater educational inequality (Bierlien 1993: 120).

Critics of school choice proposals often note that the market-based approaches to school reform assume that parents and students are economic maximizers who base their choices solely on their individual desires. If emotive considerations are factored into the choice equation, a whole variety of motivations can be attributed to choice. A sense of community and the loyalty attributed to interpersonal relationships may provide a clearer explanation for a particular choice than simply concern for long-term individual economic gain (Lee 1995; Matland 1995; Wells and Crain 1992).

If educational choices are not made in a manner consistent with individual economic rationality, and if the cognitive abilities of parents and guardians who are making these choices is not roughly uniform, the long-term consequences of educational choice could lead to a less equitable and less democratic society (Honig 1994; Kane 1992; Levin 1983). Less popular schools with limited resources could become the only option for students who, for a whole host of reasons beyond their control, could not compete effectively for admission to the more resource-rich schools. The "creaming" of the most talented students from disadvantaged area schools might lead to increased racial and economic segregation and a loss of positive role models in settings where they could potentially make the most difference (Lee 1995; Smith and Meier 1995).

FOCUS OF CHAPTER

One of the fundamental complaints leveled by advocates of education privatization is that the public schools have a virtual monopoly on available education resources. In this environment, public schools have little motivation to pursue higher performance standards or become more efficient. In addition to providing greater consumer freedom, school choice advocates argue that the privatization of education will introduce competition into the education marketplace. Forced to compete with emerging private schools, public schools will become less bureaucratic and more competitive (Chubb and Moe 1990).

Chubb and Moe (1990) found that school bureaucracy size is inversely related to student performance. They concluded that more efficient private schools with smaller bureaucracies would generate higher levels of student achievement. While similar results have been reported by Gary Anderson and associates (1991), Smith and Meier (1994) found evidence of the opposite pattern—namely, a positive relationship between student performance and the size of school administrative staff. It is quite likely, given these contradictory findings, that the relationship between student performance and size of school bureaucracy is moderated by other variables that were not considered by Chubb and Moe (1990).

Critics of school choice argue that the privatization of education will lead to creaming reflected in lower average standardized test scores in public schools (Couch et al. 1993). Controlling for parental education, dollars expended per pupil, poverty rate, and population density, Jim Couch and his colleagues found that there was a weak but statistically significant relationship between student test score performance in public schools and the percentage of students enrolled in private schools in 100 counties in North Carolina (Newmark 1995: 365). This evidence supports the notion that public school student performance will improve if there is a competitive environment.

Employing the same North Carolina data, however, Craig Newmark (1995) concluded that the relationship between public school student performance and the presence of private school competition was not consistent across testing areas. Newmark found that aggregate mean levels of parental education and poverty rates were two of the strongest predictors of student achievement, and his findings are consistent with the critics of school choice and other forms of privatization. They tend to argue that public education is not an isolated activity, but rather must be assessed in the context of the broader social environment in which it occurs (Meade 1972).

The effect of the presence of private school competition within a public school district on public school student achievement is directly relevant to the education privatization debate because it centers squarely on the fundamental question of inequality in educational outcomes that many fear might emerge from a market-based approach to education. In many respects, the "virtue of competition" argument is theoretically much stronger than the "bureaucracy stifles success" critique offered by Chubb and Moe (1990). The latter argument has been effectively criticized by Smith and Meier (1994, 1995), but the former argument should be analyzed further. While Craig Newmark (1995) seemed to indicate that the "virtue of competition" argument was specious on the basis of his North Carolina findings, further analysis is necessary in other state settings.

FINDINGS

In their analyses, Couch and colleagues (1993) and Craig Newmark (1995) employed a cross-sectional design in their work, focusing on a single year's test scores in North Carolina school districts. As demonstrated in the previous chapter, school districts change over time. Personnel changes, resources, and student population characteristics have a substantial impact on organizational performance. The impact of private school competition on public school performance is best discussed in terms of multi-year analyses.

Newmark (1995) and Christopher Simon and Nicholas Lovrich (1996) demonstrate that private school competition does not have a consistent impact on student performance.   In some testing areas, private school competition appears to be negatively related to student performance in public schools, while in other instances there is virtually no relationship present.   In regression analysis, the statistical relationship between a dependent variable (the variable one wishes to explain) and an independent variable (a variable one uses to explain changes in dependent variables, controlling for the impact of other variables) is *only* a statistical relationship and is assigned *causality* through theoretical explanations.   In other words, if the relationship between private school enrollment and public school student performance were positive, the advocates for private schools would likely claim this finding as evidence that the free market competition is good.   The public school apologists would have little to say in this regard, largely because the evidence would simply lead to the acceptance of their null hypothesis.   Conversely, if the relationship between private school enrollment and public school student performance were negative, the apologists for public schools would claim that there is a creaming effect present, and that private schools lead to social and economic inequality.   The private school advocates would view the finding as a statistical aberration, simply fail to accept their preferred hypothesis, and move on to further analysis.

As Newmark (1995) pointed out, the regression models in this instance are extremely fragile and can witness significantly different outcomes when certain assumptions are altered or variables are dropped or added.   In other words, with enough effort, advocates for public schools and free-marketeers can produce a finding acceptable to their individual theoretical positions.   The work in this area appears to be less an issue of scientific inquiry and more an issue of advocacy supported by numbers generated through sophisticated statistical analysis.

The replicative analysis reported here (see Appendix) further emphasizes the concerns addressed above.   In most cases, private school competition has neither a positive nor a negative impact on aggregate district level student performance in the three standardized testing areas in the fourth and eighth grades in 1991, 1993, and 1995.   In less than half of the models reported, dollars per pupil expended in public schools was a significant positive indicator, which would support the arguments made by public school apologists who support increased funding for public schools.   When it was a significant variable, the statistical weight of the dollars per pupil indicator was very apparent—in one instance, it had greater weight than did the parental education indicator.   There was no clear relationship between dollars per pupil expended and test score performance.   It was a significant indicator in models at both grade levels studied and in all three testing areas at various times in the three school years analyzed.

Private school enrollment was frequently not a significant contributor to the models.   In the 1995 fourth grade verbal and mathematics models, private school enrollment was *positively* related to aggregate student performance. Private school enrollment was *negatively* related to performance measures at the eighth grade level in the 1991 reading and verbal examinations—in all other instances, it had no significant impact in the statistical analysis.   The urban variable was significant in only one testing area in one year—the 1993 eighth grade reading examination.

There were only two variables in the models that were consistently significant and had the strongest relationship to student performance—the parental education indicator and the poverty indicator. As expected, parental education was positively related to aggregate student performance, while poverty was negatively related. As the Ford Foundation concluded some thirty years ago, education goes beyond the formal processes occurring within schools. School children spend a substantial portion of their time with adult members of their families, who reinforce the value of education through encouragement, tutoring, and serving as role models. The sociology literature has demonstrated repeatedly the clear and consistent connection between family social and human capital and the aspirations of school-aged children and their long-term success.

In short, the evidence presented here would indicate that neither private nor public school approaches serve as *the* solution to our perceived educational woes. The formal instruments and methods by which we educate our children perhaps have less to do with their success than the private and public social and economic conditions surrounding the formal and informal learning process. Socialization experiences appear to have a greater lasting impact on school-aged children than do inchoate and ephemeral administratively derived top-down education policies.

CONCLUSION

The findings reported in this chapter offer credence to the scholarship developed by Newmark (1995). There is no clear evidence that the competition for enrollments generated from the presence of private schools within a public school district results in higher test scores in the public schools. At this point, however, there is no strong evidence of creaming either, which would be indicated by a negative association between private enrollment and public school test scores. The model of fourth grade verbal ability did appear to offer some evidence of a benefit from the presence of competition. The models do support the argument that socioeconomic conditions are better indicators of student performance than the district resources expended per pupil. This latter point is especially true at the eighth grade level. In addition, resources available do seem to be significant contributors to at least one of the three models at the fourth grade level.

This partial confirmation of Newmark's (1995) findings in North Carolina is important for at least two reasons. First, it is further evidence that the advocates of school choice and other privatization plans of this nature may not be justified in claiming "the benefits of competition" (Couch and Shughart 1995; Friedman 1955). Second, it provides some evidence that creaming is not occurring at an appreciable level at this point in Washington school districts that have private school alternatives. The latter finding might reflect the generally low percentage of students currently enrolled in private schools in the State of Washington.

Appendix 6.1
Model of Aggregate District Level Student Performance, 1991: Fourth Grade Math

Variable Name	B	SE B	BETA	T
Dollars Per Pupil Expended	<0.001	0.001	0.004	0.95
% of Mothers w/ Some College +	0.391	0.069	0.430	5.67***
Percent of Children Living In Poverty	-0.532	0.083	-0.457	-6.42***
Percent Living in Urban Area	0.003	0.020	0.001	0.99
Percent in Private School	0.023	0.102	0.014	0.82

Constant= 41.90 (p<0.001)
F= 30.20 (p<0.001)
R^2 = 0.59
Adj. R^2 = 0.57
N= 112

Appendix 6.2
Model of Aggregate District Level Student Performance, 1991: Fourth Grade Reading

Variable Name	B	SE B	BETA	T
Dollars Per Pupil Expended	0.002	0.001	0.100	1.64
% of Mother w/ Some College +	0.352	0.055	0.445	6.42***
Percent of Children Living In Poverty	-0.495	0.066	-0.489	-7.51***
Percent Living in Urban Area	-0.004	0.016	-0.015	-0.25
Percent in Private School	-0.151	0.081	-0.109	-1.87@

Constant= 43.97 (p<0.001)
F= 40.35 (P<0.001)
R^2 = 0.65
Adj. R^2 = 0.64
N= 112

Appendix 6.3
Model of Aggregate District Level Student Performance, 1991: Fourth Grade Verbal

Variable Name	B	SE B	BETA	T
Dollars Per Pupil Expended	<0.001	0.001	0.021	0.31
% of Mothers w/ Some College +	0.385	0.068	0.437	5.65***
Percent of Children Living In Poverty	-0.522	0.081	-0.464	-6.41***
Percent Living in Urban Area	-0.017	0.020	-0.058	-0.87
Percent in Private School	-0.109	0.101	-0.071	-1.08

Constant= 47.31 (p<0.001)
F= 29.10 (p<0.001)
R^2 = 0.58
Adj. R^2 =0.56
N= 110

Appendix 6.4
Model of Aggregate District Level Student Performance, 1993: Fourth Grade Math

Variable Name	B	SE B	BETA	T
Dollars Per Pupil Expended	0.004	0.001	0.255	3.48***
% of Mothers w/ Some College +	2.210	0.810	0.233	2.73**
Percent of Children Living In Poverty	-3.470	0.570	-0.494	-6.10***
Percent Living in Urban Area	-0.006	0.024	-0.019	-0.26
Percent in Private School	0.125	0.126	0.072	1.00

Constant= 30.21 (p<0.001)
F= 21.23 (p<0.001)
R^2 = 0.50
Adj. R^2 = 0.48
N= 110

Appendix 6.5
Model of Aggregate District Level Student Performance, 1993: Fourth Grade Reading

Variable Name	B	SE B	BETA	T
Dollars Per Pupil Expended	0.003	0.001	0.205	3.47***
% of Mothers w/ Some College +	2.87	0.540	0.366	5.32***
Percent of Children Living In Poverty	-3.13	0.381	-0.537	-8.22***
Percent Living in Urban Area	-0.019	0.016	-0.073	-1.22
Percent in Private School	0.028	0.084	0.020	0.34

Constant= 38.46 (p<0.001)
F= 43.76 (p<0.001)
R^2 = 0.68
Adj. R^2 = 0.66
N= 110

Appendix 6.6
Model of Aggregate District Level Student Performance, 1993: Fourth Grade Verbal

Variable Name	B	SE B	BETA	T
Dollars Per Pupil Expended	0.003	0.001	0.205	3.00**
% of Mothers w/ Some College +	2.45	0.690	0.282	3.54***
Percent of Children Living In Poverty	-3.40	0.488	-0.528	-6.97***
Percent Living in Urban Area	-0.017	0.020	-0.058	-0.83
Percent in Private School	0.084	0.107	0.053	0.78

Constant= 38.08 (p<0.001)
F= 27.30 (p<0.001)
R^2 = 0.57
Adj. R^2 = 0.54
N= 110

Appendix 6.7
Model of Aggregate District Level Student Performance, 1995: Fourth Grade Math

Variable Name	B	SE B	BETA	T
Dollars Per Pupil Expended	0.001	0.001	0.062	0.89
% of Mothers w/ Some College +	2.516	0.856	0.233	2.94**
Percent of Children Living In Poverty	-4.400	0.608	-0.545	-7.23***
Percent Living in Urban Area	0.039	0.024	0.106	1.60
Percent in Private School	0.244	0.133	0.124	1.85@

Constant= 42.47 (p<0.001)
F= 26.84 (p<0.001)
$R^2 = 0.55$
Adj. $R^2 = 0.53$
N= 117

Appendix 6.8
Model of Aggregate District Level Student Performance, 1995: Fourth Grade Reading

Variable Name	B	SE B	BETA	T
Dollars Per Pupil Expended	<0.001	<0.001	0.037	0.59
% of Mothers w/ Some College +	2.198	0.649	0.242	3.39***
Percent of Children Living In Poverty	-4.164	0.461	-0.616	-9.03***
Percent Living in Urban Area	0.003	<0.001	0.087	1.45
Percent in Private School	0.131	0.101	0.079	1.30

Constant= 48.96 (p<0.001)
F= 37.90 (p<0.001)
$R^2 = 0.63$
Adj. $R^2 = 0.61$
N= 117

Appendix 6.9
Model of Aggregate District Level Student Performance, 1995: Fourth Grade Verbal

Variable Name	B	SE B	BETA	T
Dollars Per Pupil Expended	0.002	<0.001	0.129	1.99*
% of Mothers w/ Some College +	2.060	0.706	0.215	2.92**
Percent of Children Living In Poverty	-4.193	0.502	-0.588	-8.36***
Percent Living in Urban Area	0.002	<0.001	0.063	1.01
Percent in Private School	0.237	0.110	0.136	2.17*

Constant= 42.00 (p<0.001)
F= 34.10 (p<0.001)
R^2 = 0.60
Adj. R^2 = 0.59
N= 117

Appendix 6.10
Model of Aggregate District Level Student Performance, 1991: Eighth Grade Math

Variable Name	B	SE B	BETA	T
Dollars Per Pupil Expended	<0.001	<0.001	0.061	0.87
% of Mothers w/ Some College +	0.358	0.060	0.450	5.95***
Percent of Children Living In Poverty	-0.445	0.076	-0.424	-5.86***
Percent Living in Urban Area	0.008	0.019	0.031	0.45
Percent in Private School	-0.071	0.009	-0.051	-0.77

Constant= 43.83 (p<0.001)
F= 28.52 (p<0.001)
R^2 = 0.57
Adj. R^2 = 0.55
N= 112

Appendix 6.11
Model of Aggregate District Level Student Performance, 1991: Eighth Grade Reading

Variable Name	B	SE B	BETA	T
Dollars Per Pupil Expended	0.002	0.001	0.177	2.92**
% of Mothers w/ Some College +	0.365	0.048	0.501	7.64***
Percent of Children Living In Poverty	-0.420	0.060	-0.438	-6.97***
Percent Living in Urban Area	-0.002	<0.001	-0.009	-0.16
Percent in Private School	-0.197	0.073	-0.156	-2.69**

Constant= 45.33 (p<0.001)
F= 44.47 (p<0.001)
R^2 = 0.67
Adj. R^2 = 0.66
N=114

Appendix 6.12
Model of Aggregate District Level Student Performance, 1991: Eighth Grade Verbal

Variable Name	B	SE B	BETA	T
Dollars Per Pupil Expended	<0.001	0.001	0.083	1.16
% of Mothers w/ Some College +	0.302	0.056	0.420	5.41***
Percent of Children Living In Poverty	-0.411	0.070	-0.436	-5.83***
Percent Living in Urban Area	0.008	0.001	0.031	0.45
Percent in Private School	-0.143	0.086	-0.114	-1.65@

Constant= 45.04 (p<0.001)
F= 25.63 (p<0.001)
R^2 = 0.55
Adj. R^2 = 0.52
N= 112

Appendix 6.13
Model of Aggregate District Level Student Performance, 1993: Eighth Grade Math

Variable Name	B	SE B	BETA	T
Dollars Per Pupil Expended	-0.001	0.001	-0.089	-1.33
% of Mothers w/ Some College +	0.34	0.07	0.351	4.81***
Percent of Children Living In Poverty	-0.375	0.05	-0.537	-7.30***
Percent Living in Urban Area	0.01	0.02	0.050	0.77
Percent in Private School	0.04	0.10	0.027	0.42

Constant= 58.82 (p<0.001)
F= 33.80 (p<0.001)
R^2 = 0.63
Adj. R^2 = 0.61
N=109

Appendix 6.14
Model of Aggregate District Level Student Performance, 1993: Eighth Grade Reading

Variable Name	B	SE B	BETA	T
Dollars Per Pupil Expended	0.0016	0.001	0.108	1.75@
% of Mothers w/ Some College +	0.320	0.055	0.404	5.89***
Percent of Children Living In Poverty	-0.311	0.039	-0.523	-7.95***
Percent Living in Urban Area	-0.003	0.016	-0.120	-1.97*
Percent in Private School	-0.0079	0.085	-0.006	-0.09

Constant= 50.32 (p<0.001)
F= 41.93 (p<0.001)
R^2 = 0.67
Adj. R^2 = 0.65
N= 109

Appendix 6.15
Model of Aggregate District Level Student Performance, 1993: Eighth Grade Verbal

Variable Name	B	SE B	BETA	T
Dollars Per Pupil Expended	<0.001	0.001	0.027	0.37
% of Mothers w/ Some College +	0.303	0.061	0.405	4.99***
Percent of Children Living In Poverty	-0.251	0.043	-0.448	-5.86***
Percent Living in Urban Area	-0.002	0.018	-0.089	-1.25
Percent in Private School	0.108	0.093	0.082	1.16

Constant= 48.10 (p<0.001)
F= 25.66 (p<0.001)
R^2 = 0.55
Adj. R^2 = 0.53
N=109

Appendix 6.16
Model of Aggregate District Level Student Performance, 1995: Eighth Grade Math

Variable Name	B	SE B	BETA	T
Dollars Per Pupil Expended	0.0013	0.001	0.062	0.89
% of Mothers w/ Some College +	0.252	0.009	0.233	2.94**
Percent of Children Living In Poverty	-0.440	0.061	-0.545	-7.23***
Percent Living in Urban Area	0.039	0.024	0.106	1.60
Percent in Private School	0.244	0.133	0.124	1.84@

Constant= 42.47 (p<0.001)
F= 26.84 (p<0.001)
R^2 = 0.55
Adj. R^2 = 0.53
N=117

Appendix 6.17
Model of Aggregate District Level Student Performance, 1995: Eighth Grade Reading

Variable Name	B	SE B	BETA	T
Dollars Per Pupil Expended	0.0012	0.001	0.076	1.36
% of Mothers w/ Some College +	0.228	0.051	0.287	4.51***
Percent of Children Living In Poverty	-0.381	0.036	-0.644	-10.62***
Percent Living in Urban Area	-0.016	0.014	-0.061	-1.14
Percent in Private School	-0.111	0.078	-0.076	-1.41

Constant= 56.16 (p<0.001)
F= 53.63 (p<0.001)
R^2 = 0.71
Adj. R^2 = 0.69
N= 117

Appendix 6.18
Model of Aggregate District Level Student Performance, 1995: Eighth Grade Verbal

Variable Name	B	SE B	BETA	T
Dollars Per Pupil Expended	-0.002	0.001	-0.145	-2.09*
% of Mothers w/ Some College +	0.370	0.055	0.489	6.77***
Percent of Children Living In Poverty	-0.509	0.103	-0.368	-4.95***
Percent Living in Urban Area	-0.002	0.015	0.008	0.11
Percent in Private School	-0.072	0.095	-0.052	-0.75

Constant= 55.14 (p<001)
F= 25.46 (p<0.001)
R^2 = 0.53
Adj. R^2 = 0.51
N= 117

WORKS CITED

Anderson, G., Shughart III, W., and Tollison, R. 1991.   "Educational Achievement and the Cost of Bureaucracy," *The Journal of Economic Behavior and Organization*. 15: 29-45.

Bierlien, L. 1993. *Controversial Issues in Educational Policy*. Newbury Park, CA: Sage Publications.

Chubb, J. & Moe, T. 1990.   *Politics, Markets, and America's Schools*. Washington, DC: The Brookings Institution.

Cookson, P. 1994.   *School Choice: The Struggle for the Soul of American Education*. New Haven, CT: Yale University.

Couch, J. and Shughart III, W. 1995. "Private School Enrollment and Public School Performance: Reply," *Public Choice*. 82: 375-379.

Couch, J., Shughart III, W., and Williams, A. 1993. "Private School Enrollment and Public School Performance," *Public Choice.* 76: 301-312.

Dougherty, K. and Sostre, L. 1992. "Minerva and the Market: The Sources of the Movement for School Choice," in P. Cookson (ed.), *The Choice Controversy.* Newbury Park, CA: Corwin Press, 24-45.

Friedman, M. 1955. *Capitalism and Freedom.* Chicago, IL: University of Chicago Press.

Gardner, B. 1991. "Gardner's Plan—Monopolistic Nature of Public Schools Must Be Changed." February 7. *The Seattle Times,* A15.

Greene, R. 1997. "Survey: Opposition to Education Vouchers Diminishes." August 26. *The Columbian* (Vancouver, WA), 2.

Halifax, J. 2000. "Florida's Voucher Law Thrown Out." March 14. *The Columbian* (Vancouver, WA), A7.

Hirschman, A. 1970. *Exit, Voice, and Loyalty: Responses to Decline in Firms, Organizations, and States.* Cambridge, MA: Harvard University Press.

Holt, G. 1996. "State Voters Reject Both Charter School and Voucher Initiatives." November 6. *Seattle Post-Intelligencer,* A15.

Honig, J. 1994. *Rethinking School Choice: Limits of the Market Metaphor.* Princeton, NJ: Princeton University Press.

Iwasaki, J. 1996. "Bergeson Maps Out Agenda after Outdistancing Taber." November 6. *Seattle Post-Intelligencer,* A15.

Kane, J. 1992. "Choice: The Fundamentals Revisited," in P. Cookson (ed.), *The Choice Controversy.* Newbury Park, CA: Corwin Press, 46-64.

Lee, V. 1995. "San Antonio School Choice Plans: Rewarding or Creaming?" *Social Science Quarterly.* 76(3): 513-521.

Levin, H. 1983. "Educational Choice and the Pains of Democracy," in T. James and H. Levin (eds.), *Public Dollars for Private Schools: The Case of Tuition Tax Credits.* Philadelphia, PA: Temple University Press, 17-38.

Lieberman, M. 1989. *Privatization and Educational Choice.* New York: St. Martin's Press.

Linowes, D. 1988. *Privatization: Toward More Effective Government.* Washington, DC: President's Commission on Privatization.

Martinez, V., Godwin, R., Kemerer, F., and Perna, L. 1995. "The Consequences of School Choice: Who Leaves and Who Stays in the Inner City," *Social Science Quarterly.* 76(3): 485-501.

Matland, R. 1995. "Exit, Voice, Loyalty, and Neglect in an Urban School System," *Social Science Quarterly.* 76(3): 506-512.

Meade, E. 1972. *A Foundation Goes to School: The Ford Foundation Comprehensive School Improvement Program, 1960-1970.* New York: Ford Foundation.

National Committee on Excellence in Education. 1983. *A Nation at Risk.* Washington, DC: U.S. Government Printing Office.

Newmark, C. 1995. "Another Look at Whether Private Schools Influence Public School Quality: Comment," *Public Choice.* 82: 365-373.

Paulson, M. 1995. "Private Schools, Craswell Says." June 30. *Seattle Post-Intelligencer*, C1.

Ross, S. 1997. "Clinton Wants More Flexibility for Local Schools." October 28. *The Columbian* (Vancouver, WA), 4.

Schattschneider, E. 1960. *The Semi-sovereign People: A Realist's View of Democracy in America*. New York, Holt, Rinehart and Winston.

Seattle Times. 1994. "A New Federal Role in Education Reform." February 27. *The Seattle Times*, B8.

Simon, C. and Lovrich, N. 1996. "Private School Enrollment and Public School Performance: Assessing the Effects of Competition Upon Public School Student Achievement in Washington State," *Policy Studies Journal*. 24(4): 666-678.

Simon, C. and May, D. 1996. "Can Schools Solve Problems They Did Not Create?: Washington State's 'Schools for the 21st Century' Program," *Inroads*. 5: 46-52.

Smith, G. 1982. "Nineteenth Century Opponents of State Education: Prophets of Modern Revisionism," in R. Everhart (ed.), *The Public School Monopoly: A Critical Analysis of Education in American Society*. San Francisco, CA: Institute for Public Policy Research, 109-144.

Smith, K. and Meier, K. 1994. "Politics, Bureaucrats, and Schools," *Public Administration Review*. 54(6): 551-558.

_____. 1995. *The Case Against School Choice: Politics, Markets, and America's Fools*. Armonk, NY: M.E. Sharpe.

Taber, R. 1996. "Election 1996: Initiative 173—School Vouchers Pro and Con: Competition Will Force Public Schools to Improve." October 20. *The News Tribune* (Tacoma, WA), G1.

Tiebout, C. 1956. "A Pure Theory of Local Expenditures," *Journal of Political Economy*. 64: 416-424.

Toffler, A. 1971. *Future Schock*. New York: Bantam Books.

Wells, A. and Crain, R. 1992. "Do Parents Choose School Quality or School Status?" in P. Cookson (ed.), *The Choice Controversy*. Newbury Park, CA: Corwin Press, 65-82.

Chapter 7

Conclusion

This book has analyzed 296 school districts in the State of Washington—just one of fifty states, fairly average in terms of its resources, structure and outcomes. The primary purpose of the study was to test extant theories of organizational behavior as they relate to public school districts. Are public school districts open systems organizations? The statistical evidence presented demonstrates that public schools are open systems organizations, reacting to the demands of their environments. The analysis of public school district administration produced fairly strong statistical models, explaining a sizeable portion of the variance in administrative capacity.

In particular, the evidence tends to come down on the side of public school advocates in this particular case. Public school administration does not appear to be composed of rent seeking bureaucrats. Administrative capacity is a function of environmental conditions. Certainly, if rent seeking were to occur, one would expect to witness the phenomenon most visibly in school districts with higher socioeconomic status—in essence, school districts where voters and parents would have a higher level of economic indifference and would not miss extra tax dollars. In fact, public school district administrative capacity was *greater* in school districts with greater environmental constraints—that is, poorer school districts. Public school districts react to environmental pressures, rather than simply focusing attention on organizational needs and the private goals of school personnel.

The administrative capacity analysis offers a reasonably clear picture of public school districts in action, engaging their environments with the intent of anticipating potentially negative impacts on the core mission and technologies. In our own individual (and, to some degree, collective) minds we have a fairly good idea of what it takes to run a school: good administrators and teachers. Is there any truth to this common wisdom? The answer is clearly "yes," with noteworthy caveats.

Public schools are open systems organizations, and they behave in a manner very similar to 'living' creatures. They have a will to survive; they have purpose; and they seek stability. In fact, the formalization of social, political, and economic endeavors through adaptable or living organizations is one of the greatest accomplishments of humankind. As beings, it appears that most organizations have a life-cycle.

In many respects, age has a lot to do with the apparently ineffective nature of public schools. Despite the fact that some school districts are older than others, our public school paradigm is arguably built on a late eighteenth or early nineteenth century foundation, and the model has not changed significantly. True, we do not line the school desks up, bolt them to the floor, and expect students to simply recite aloud their lessons. We rely to a lesser degree on rote memorization. Progressivism—best exemplified by John Dewey's (1944) work—has led to enormous changes in pedagogy. In the modern era, computers are clearly a new and important technology that are shaping the learning process. Moving beyond the philosophical and technological revolution in education, the basic skeletal structure of a school district has not changed to any significant degree, and neither have the central goals and missions of schools.

Organizational age is an important factor to consider when ascertaining a more cogent understanding of administrative capacity and the ability to produce desired outcomes. Just as with human beings, we have extended (at times, through artificial methods) the life span of both public and private institutions. Certainly, history records the behavior of very old and venerable institutions, some of which are still in our midst, having survived tremendous change. These organizations have survived due to their ability to reinvent themselves or successfully resist any significant forces of change. How an organization deals with the aging process is central to the maintenance of organizational vitality and continued significance.

Change can be a good thing. Growth may be a good thing, too. Nevertheless, one finds that rapid change—specifically, in older organizations— may not always prove to be beneficial, especially in the short term. Should rapid change prove to be beneficial, it may have to be measured over time. One is not going to see an immediate and positive outcome. At times, the organization may appear to be worse off because of the change. Operating in a rapidly changing political and social environment, public schools are having some trouble reacting to change. True, resources are being redirected in a responsive manner, but change often affects public schools' ability to have a strong impact on their young clientele.

There are a number of political forces shaping public schools. At the federal and state levels, there is increased executive pressure to produce positive outcomes. Innovative policy plans such as reduced classroom size may on the surface appear to be fairly innocuous but can change the very nature of the public schools as organizations. The addition of more teachers results in the addition of classrooms. New classrooms may mean new schools and new principals. In essence, the very structure of school districts is becoming larger and more difficult to manage.

Additionally, *informal* organization, which Herbert Simon (1976) indicated is possibly more important than the formal structures and relationships, may be adversely impacted by structural change—at least, in the short run. The organizational culture of a school district will change when the organizational geography is substantially altered. Organizational culture is maintained through structural continuity. Organizational actors understand their role; employees understand the informal operating procedures that make the organization run most effectively. Change the structure of an organization, however, and informal organization and culture are often changed, too. If a school builds a new science wing, teachers may be relocated to new parts of the building. Add another teachers' lounge and informal staff relationships change because patterns of interaction will likely change. Additions to the staff and staff turnover in either the administrative offices or among the teaching staff will likely result in the organizational culture being significantly altered.

The models of public school district organizational performance in Washington effectively measured this phenomenon from the macro-organizational level. In the three years modeled, public school districts in Washington changed. In 1991, organizations were fairly stable. Teaching and administrative staff had their separate functions. The macro-level analysis indicates that neither teaching staff—as part of organizational core technologies—nor administrative capacity had consistent statistically significant relationship with aggregate district level student achievement. Public schools react to their environments, but the reaction in and of itself is less important than the *quality* of the reaction.

Quality is best measured by studying the informal organization that exists within school districts. While this study does not portend to be a micro-level analysis of school districts, it is possible to understand the nature of informal organization through an analysis of the theoretical prerequisites for strong organizational culture. The LEAP factor measures at least two central characteristics pertaining to organizational staff: (1) level of experience, and (2) knowledge. Experience translates into time on the job—time spent within the public school system as an administrator, teacher, or staff member employed in an ancillary organizational unit. Average staff experience plays a tremendously important role in determining the relative strength of organizational culture—informal organizational norms and patterns of staff interaction. In the case of administrative staff, longevity means that administrators have successfully met environmental demands. School district superintendents incapable of effectively dealing with environmental demands—albeit while protecting the organizational core mission—are subject to termination by local school boards or are at the very least pressured into resigning. Assuming the existence of a stable organization (in terms of staff retention and relative size), the longevity of central and building administrators is a reflection of the leadership qualities of the individuals who hold these positions.

School districts with highly educated teaching staff successfully retained by the school district play a substantial role in shaping organizational output. Teachers learn a great deal about their organizational environment and how to educate students through years of practical experience in a particular organizational setting. Additionally, parents and school children become more familiar with teachers over time. Students may find that siblings or even their parents have had the same teacher, which may lead to greater respect for the teaching staff and lead to the conscious or subconscious organizational legitimization by parents, students, community leaders, and other concerned community members.

In the models of student achievement—particularly the 1993 models presented earlier—staff and teacher experience levels played a significant role in outcomes prior to the period of time characterized by growing interest and implementation of macro-structural reforms. To run a school effectively does not necessarily require having a particular administrative or teaching capacity. It does not necessarily mean that a school district must have particular levels of technology in the classroom. The most important factors relate to organizational stability in terms of organizational leaders and teaching staff—the core organizational technology in a school.

To run a school takes good people, people who are—of their own initiative or due to organizational culture and resources—willing to remain loyal to a particular school. Perhaps this finding is not a new revelation in the extant organizational theory literature, but it is something which we seemingly forget from time to time. Certainly Robert Denhardt's book *Pursuit of Significance* (1993) serves as an important reminder that organizational patriotism is related to organizational performance. Additionally, James Q. Wilson—author of *Bureaucracy: What Government Agencies Do and Why They Do It* (1989)— emphasizes the importance of leadership as a critical force in ensuring that organization goals remain vital, that these goals are viewed as legitimate by staff members, and, most important, that organizational missions are met.

The responsibility of meeting organizational commitments does not rest entirely in the hands of school personnel. Environmental actors must be committed to the core mission of public schools. Commitment was measured indirectly in this study, by measuring community support for school district supplemental levies. Levy support offers a partial explanation of the role of community in shaping organizational performance. Without strong public support, administrative capacity necessarily views district voters as a source of environmental constraint. Additionally, community support is also related to organizational output. School districts that are less supportive appear to have lower levels of organizational performance. Effective school districts possess *loyalty* from both internal sources (i.e., staff retention and limited change) and external sources (i.e., parents and community members).

Loyalty and stability cannot always be counted on by school districts. Support for school district levies declined somewhat over the 1990's and school district administrative and teaching staffs became less stable, due to either retirement, resignations, or the influx of additional teachers and administrators. The result has been that school performance is increasingly a function of environmental constraints—that is, schools have become "coping organizations" (Wilson 1989).

If organizational environment plays a larger role in shaping outcomes, then public schools may have become increasingly ineffective mechanisms for accomplishing the goals of *redistributive* public policy. In the past, public elementary and secondary education was viewed as one of the great social, political, and economic equalizers. Many of the greatest American scholars of the twentieth century were educated in public schools. Public schools provided students from various walks of life the opportunity to depart from undesirable social and economic conditions. In essence, public schools were viewed as a critical element in breaking down or at least limiting the possibility of class-based society.

As coping organizations, public schools have become unwitting accomplices in the creation of class-based society. If socioeconomic status plays an increasingly important role in explaining student achievement, then schools become nothing more than reinforcers of the social and economic status quo. If the redistributive function of public elementary and secondary education is to remain viable, stable school organizations must be either maintained or developed. Staff retention and education are critical in maintaining the requisite organizational culture. To the greatest extent possible, policymakers should resist the temptation to pile educational reform on top of education reform. If they cannot fight this temptation, they should at the very least provide an appropriate interval between reforms to permit thorough policy evaluation—policy successes generally do not occur overnight.

The central question for those individuals seeking to maintain public school organizations is, "How do we simultaneously legitimatize school organizations in the eyes of political leaders and community members, and retain critical organizational elements that make public schools successful?" It is a difficult question to answer in theoretical terms, and an equally difficult task to accomplish in practice. To propose a uniform solution would be unreasonable. Top-down one-size-fits-all reforms have generally failed, so why contribute unnecessarily to the proposal graveyard? Solutions, if they exist at all, lie within the grasp of the thousands of school district organizational leaders and staff members across the nation, particularly those individuals committed to the goals of providing a democratic education to their students and helping them to achieve outstanding levels of performance.

Unfortunately, time is not on the side of many public schools in their efforts to reestablish legitimacy. Scoiety is becoming increasingly commodified. The Internet, globalization of commerce, and the growth of materialism have produced the 'point and click' generation. As addressed earlier, the post-Second World War generation was the first generation to become highly mobile and to possess the resources necessary to fulfill their materialistic pleasures. We have, however, moved far beyond buying ice cream at the local soda fountain and watching movies at the local drive-in theater. Youth materialism and youth culture seem to have achieved a new level of demand, and these demands are frequently met with personally earned cash. Youth independence is much greater now than was the case for Generation X (my generation, incidentally). E-commerce has made it possible for companies to rapidly meet customer demand.

At the moment, market-based solutions to demand are rapidly expanding, crossing international borders with increasing ease. Consumer loyalty to a single provider is eroding, making monolithic public schools the hapless victims of a consumer-driven society concerned primarily with high quality products available at reasonable costs. What explains the decline in consumer loyalty when it comes to government organizations such as public schools? At the center of the loyalty issue lies the matter of social values.

Previous generations of parents and school children saw schools as centers for social value, civic, and basic skills education. All three of these areas of education remained at the center of public education curriculum in the nineteenth century public schools and well into the twentieth century. Education, therefore, was tied into the political and social value socialization process, and its importance and legitimacy were an integral part of local community existence. In the process of eliminating social value and civic education from the curriculum—with the intent of making the education process more accessible to *all* students—public schools have become more vulnerable to environmental constraint—the schools are more narrowly focused and subject to even more intense scrutiny.

As it stands now, public school curricula have been wiped clean when it comes to social value and civic education, and there appears to be a declining interest among citizens to pursue non-school-related organizations that would likely provide guidance in these two critical areas. Basic skills education remains the primary focus of public school instruction, and even that area has been the focus of criticism—ranging from disappointment over standardized test score performance to the teaching of sex education. It is unlikely that public schools will regain their role in social value and civic education without a reconfiguration of legal constaints and a restructuring of school organizational goals—perhaps it is no longer desirable to pursue their readmittance into curriculum due to overpoliticization. Nevertheless, the loss of these two elements of the education process will prove to be problematic for public schools, in terms of their ability to meet performance demands and compete with a growing private school presence.

The issue of 'values' has two unique focal points. First, the dearth of social value and civic education in public schools has partially contributed to the decline in organizational legitimacy and has played a role in the erosion of public-oriented values among denizens. Second, the continued battle over anything that remotely relates to social value or civic education increasingly stands as a line of demarcation between those individuals who support public schools and those individuals who advocate privatization. Third, the narrowly focused emphasis on basic skills education has contributed to the commodity image of elementary and secondary education. If the value of the educational process is determined primarily by standardized examinations measuring the ability of students to recall basic facts using fairly mechanical operations, then public schools are no longer unique systems of learning. Under these circumstances, a system is deemed effective if it can produce high quality products at low costs—a quick glance at financial reports and test scores would indicate that public schools are fairly expensive when compared to many private school options.

The increased mobility of society has made the latter option all the more feasible. In the 1950's, economist Charles Tiebout (1956) argued that local government expenditures were subject to intergovernmental competition—in essence, citizens not willing to pay a high price for government services could move to another local government jurisdiction with a lower cost level. One of the most serious critiques facing public choice economists over the years, however, has been the issue of transportation or relocation costs. With improved technology and an increasingly affluent society, the relative costs of transportation or relocation have declined substantially. School choice is now a more viable and possibly desirable option for a larger proportion of school-aged children and their parents.

Increasingly affordable private school alternatives have contributed to the growing pressures on the public school system to adapt if they wish to survive under these circumstances. The ability of public school administration to protect the organizational core technologies and core mission of public schools is limited. The statistical models indicate that public school administrators act to control environmental constraints and establish organizational legitimacy. Despite these apparent efforts, public school legitimacy is not to be found in boundary-spanning activities per se, but rather it is the function of personnel stability. A top priority of public schools, therefore, would be to redevelop their sense of legitimacy through the acquisition and retention of highly qualified staff. To a lesser extent, organizational legitimacy will be found in the expansion of curriculum and to a greater extent in the individuals who operationalize the curriculum.

Beyond the issue of organization legitimacy, however, is the maintenance of consistent resource providers. If private school vouchers and charter schools emerge as publicly financed competitive forces, the resource base of public schools will likely be jeopardized. Limited resources will impact the ability of public schools to compete effectively and to produce high quality student performance. It will also make it difficult to reward and retain outstanding staff members. Administrative boundary-spanning activities pursuing steady resources are certainly nothing new to public school superintendents and principals. The need for such boundary-spanning activity will become increasingly important, but more rigid budgetary constraints will lead to reduced resources for administrative capacity. While states such as Washington will likely retain their basic education funding, these state-generated resources are generally insufficient to effectively operate the ancillary activities contributing to academic excellence and staff retention.

Whether full-scale voucher programs come to fruition in Washington or in other states is largely a function of institutional actors (i.e., elected officials and judges), interest group pressures (e.g., teachers unions, citizens' groups), and general public opinion. In Washington, the 1996 governors' race was won by Gary Locke, a pro-public school Democrat. The 1996 State Superintendent of Public Instruction race was also won by a Democrat who ran against the privatization plans of her Republican opponent. Currently, the State House of Representatives is evenly split: forty-nine Democratic and forty-nine Republican members, while the State Senate is controlled by a Democratic majority. Divided control within the legislature means that dramatic efforts to introduce private school alternatives at public expense will not be forthcoming in the near future. Teachers' unions will also serve to limit the possibility of dramatic changes in educational policy in the state.

Public opinion, however, has shifted and continues to shift, favoring various private school options. Nationwide, privatization plans are beginning to gain voter support. While Washington rejected two privatization alternatives in the 1996 general election, it is not inconceivable that such options will be reconsidered very soon.

Initiative 729, which would have made charter schools a viable option in the state, appeared on the general election ballot in 2000. The ballot initiative, which was not approved by a majority of voters, was supported by Paul Allen, one of the most prominent co-founders of Microsoft Corporation. Allen had pledged over two million dollars to the initiative campaign (Stiffler 2000: B2). Charter school bills were introduced in both the state Senate and the House during the 1999 session (SB 5663, SB 6483, HB 1861, and HB 2415), but all four measures failed to emerge from legislative committee. The initiative process is the most potent and expedient tool for privatization proponents.

Direct democracy relies heavily on the ability of initiative proponents to appeal to particular values, opinions, and beliefs ultimately shaping individual voter choice. Public opinion is a critical factor in determining the future of public school finance and the establishment of private school competition via vouchers and charter schools.   Through the local and state-level election process, public opinion potentially serves as a *direct* constraint on public school organizations.   The status of public school boundary-spanning activities, the legitimacy of public schools in the minds of local voters, and the output of the organization (i.e., student academic excellence) are likely to have a *direct* impact on voter approval or rejection of privatization alternatives.

Public schools, therefore, must seek to further legitimize organizational goals, technologies, and performance if they wish to retain their existing resource base.   Responsiveness to public concerns is an extremely important administrative   function,   which   could   conceivably   necessitate   greater organizational receptivity to changing educational goals as defined by school clientele. Community-based education might be one strategy to filter clientele demands while simultaneously coopting local voters, school boards, parents, and school-aged children.   The goals of the Schools for the 21st Century program was primarily guided by the need to consider the role of human capital in shaping educational outcomes.   Family social capital and community social capital, however, have been eschewed by public school policymakers, concerned that introducing any form of uniform social value or civic education would be at odds with the goals of ethnic and racial diversity education. Additionally, social value and civic education might violate the Establishment Clause and therefore be unconstitutional.

In fact, the attempt to avoid discussion of social value and civic education will in the long run cause significant problems for public school organizations Except for the very basic factual education offered in schools, curriculum and pedagogical choices are largely based on organizational and educator values.   Value-based decisions are continually made in any organization—particularly in school organizations—and value-based decisions frequently leads to the promotion of particular values. The failure on the part of school organizations to fully recognize that values play a substantial role in the education process is a serious problem, alienating voters, parents, and school-aged children who hold different value priorities. If the option to exit the public schools becomes more attractive and feasible for alienated clientele, public school organizations ultimately lose resources and fail to accomplish one important aspect of their mission. Public education helps individuals of different backgrounds establish some form of common ground, identifying those values they hold in common, while simultaneously understanding and respecting diversity, is one method of retaining public school students.

Generally, public schools have done a fairly good job of discussing our nation's social, cultural, and racial diversity, and the strength of diversity education has grown tremendously over the last thirty years. It is a credit to our public education system that schools and teachers have made a tremendous contribution to greater cultural awareness and sensitivity.   From an organizational perspective, the growing emphasis on diversity serves as one method of boundary spanning—legitimizing the educational process in the minds of individuals and groups who have been historically disenfranchised in the educational process specifically and the political, social, and economic realms more generally. As with all things, there is a need to strike a balance between the promotion of diversity in education (the contemporary paradigm) and earlier systems focusing on a narrowly defined vision of social virtue in American society.

Through greater boundary-spanning efforts, administrators and teachers need to recapture the dialogue of communality—what do we share in common and what do we want to teach our children about common values and social and political institutions? Our diversity is certainly an important strength, but within the context of diversity, there are general principles which unite us as people in our local communities, states, and nation. A renewed dialogue focusing on unifying values and beliefs would serve to expand the role of public schools in a way that would offer them new and greater legitimacy as public organizations. It would simultaneously offer school organizations a chance to cultivate family and community social capital—two important contributions to educational effectiveness, both of which often serve as significant organizational constraints.

If public schools choose to expand their core missions to include social value and civic education, there are a number of dilemmas which must be dealt with in a manner which will be equitable to concerned denizens.   The stakeholders in the public education arena are both numerous and varied, ranging from federal, state, and local agencies to elected officials, interest groups, civic organizations, administrators, teachers, concerned parents, and school-aged children. Each of these stakeholders—groups and individuals—will likely approach the establishment of social value and civic education from a different normative perspective, and the clash of viewpoints may create a serious impasse, which must be overcome if new educational goals are to be successfully adopted and legitimized.

The history of education policy in the latter half of the twentieth century has been largely top-down. The Cold War and the education-as-a-weapon (an economic, political, and cultural weapon) paradigm has seemingly remained a part of the public elementary and secondary educational system. We still tend to see education as critical element in sustaining American political and economic hegemony worldwide in the post-Cold War period. I have not encountered any author who has challenged the view that education is critically important to America's future success, and could not conceivably challenge the generally accepted perspective.

It is important to consider, however, how the two driving forces in American education today—namely, the pursuit of equality of educational opportunity and the search for a uniformly high quality educational system—have led us towards uniform top-down strategies. If the last forty years are any guide, Procrustean solutions have not proven to be the panacea for perceived or real educational woes. The strength of the American education system has historically lay in the fact that while we pursue policies which tend to unify our schools in terms of general goals, with notable exceptions we have tended to eschew rigid uniformity in policy.

The contemporary school district has so narrowly defined its core mission that uniformity is encouraged. The standardized test itself assumes that the central goal of public schools is narrowly defined, and pedagogy and curriculum must conform to uniform expectations. Teacher testing, reduced student-teacher ratios, and classroom technology are generally focused on the pursuit of higher student performance as measured by the standardized examination. As the models reported earlier in this book would indicate, the strongest factors explaining aggregate district level student performance represent environmental constraints and organizational staff experience and professionalism (as measured by educational level). Internal change tends to disrupt the school organization, and environmental constraint takes on a more significant role in shaping outputs.

If environment is so important in explaining outcomes, then it is likely that bottom-up approaches to building a new consensus regarding the reintroduction of social value and civic education are necessary. State and federal level administrators and elected officials have a role in setting strict guidelines delineating what is acceptable and unacceptable in terms of the legal boundaries to education policymaking in these two highly sensitive areas, but these levels of government should not so narrowly define the limitations as to entirely constrain local level policy diversity.

In *Organizations in Action* (1967), James D. Thompson argued that an organization's primary strategies in dealing with its organizational environment are *compete*, *collaborate*, or *coopt*. I contend that it is not an either-or situation for public school districts. Rather, school administrators should employ approaches to dealing with environmental conditions when de' organizational strategies designed to produce improved organ̲ performance. Nevertheless, there are serious organizational constraints that must be considered in adopting this strategy to improving our public schools. First, schools must stabilize their core technologies and administrative personnel systems. High quality teaching staffs must be acquired, promoted, continuously trained, and ultimately retained—hopefully, for the length of a career. Administrative personnel turnover must be held to a minimum. The average school district superintendent serves in his or her position for a little over two years before either retiring or being forced out by local school boards who are dissatisfied with school district organizational performance and policy choices. Short administrator tenure is likely to put school organizations in a vulnerable position with less experienced organizational boundary-spanners who may lack a thorough understanding of their jobs and the informal norms and organizational culture.

Stabilizing administrative leadership is critical to building trust between teachers and administrators. New administrators frequently arrive at their positions with new goals and procedures in mind. Organizational change may be an important part of improving organizational performance, but change can create a unique internal organizational dynamic. Organizational culture and informal organization will likely be dramatically altered by the adoption of new standard operating procedures, goals, and norms. Therefore, a transient administrative leadership could produce many unintended organizational outcomes, particularly if the changes in leadership lead to uninformed or ill-considered policy choices.

Organizational outcomes can be considered in a variety of different ways, but we currently spend a great deal of time and effort studying student performance on standardized examinations, dropout and graduation rates, and narrowly defined policy successes or failures. In Washington State, for instance, a statewide effort to increase local school autonomy—Schools for the 21st Century Program—led to a series of state-level policy evaluations to determine the relative success or failure of the program. In most instances, the evaluations employed narrative case studies and personal interviews with administrators, teachers, and parents. Such analyses, however, tend to be *policy-oriented* rather than *organization-oriented*. In essence, the impact of a new organizational mission or a new method of accomplishing existing organizational missions must be judged in terms of the impact on the organization—in most cases, organization can serve as a mediating variable in explaining policy outcomes.

Organizational core technologies are primarily people-oriented. In a formal sense, policy or process changes affect personnel acquisition, position descriptions, personnel evaluations, training programs, and budgets. Informal relationships may also be radically altered by changes in policy or process that are a result of either federal or state policy changes or more directly by changes in organizational leadership. If organizational change is easily measured and leads to demonstrable improvements in organizational performance, then it is more likely that such change will be deemed legitimate or successful by organizational personnel and environmental actors. Public school organizations, however, do not have uniformly accepted organizational output. Parents and concerned citizens look to test scores as a global measure of organizational success, whereas teachers and administrators tend to view the *quality* and *responsiveness* of the organization to individual learners' needs to be a critical measure of success or failure. The result is that organizational change may produce greater unease among organizational personnel and reduced levels of trust in administrators who act as agents of change.

Administrators with long tenure are more likely to have greater success in leading their organization through a change process. Ironically, administrators with long tenure are frequently organizational conservers (see Downs 1967), who tend to be less interested in change. Nevertheless, alterations to organizational goals and processes produced with the guidance of an experienced and respected school administrator will more likely be viewed as legitimate in the eyes of teaching staff. Teaching staff who trust the administrative leadership are less likely to adopt adversarial approaches to resisting change—approaches that frequently involve terse teachers' union-school management encounters.

Successful organizational change cannot be a radical process. It must occur over time and in a well-considered manner. All interested stakeholders—organizational and extra-organizational—must be involved in the process of change. Organizational stakeholders include teachers' unions and administrators, both of whom must act responsibly in the interest of the organization and clientele. Win-win outcomes must be pursued if the organization and its personnel are to offer a coordinated vision of the school and its goals to citizens and elected officials operating in the organizational environment. A divided organization is likely to further delegitimize public school systems and should be avoided if at all possible.

One method of reducing the chances of division within the ranks of organization personnel is to pursue leadership styles that place less emphasis on classical employer-employee relationships. Well over a half century ago, Mary Parker Follett (1926) and Chester I. Barnard (1938) argued that communication patterns between employers and employees were two-way: the *giving* of an order by management also involved the *accepting* of an order by labor. Since that time, the human relations model of cooperative management-employee relations has been a carefully honed element of effective organizational leadership.

Robert Denhardt's (1993) *Pursuit of Significance* provides a well-considered analysis of successful organizations. The author explores the need to pursue collaborative management styles, through the development of employee ownership in the decision-making process and collective responsibility for outcomes. In the turbulent and highly competitive modern organization, administrators must legitimize themselves and their authority in the minds of their employees by offering part of their authority to the individuals who actively produce organizational outcomes. In other words, relationships of trust must be pursued, but trust is not quickly developed.   Building intra-organizational and extra-organizational trust, establishing collaborative policymaking bodies beyond the formal school board environment, and team-building strategies take time and require stability within personnel systems.

In times of adversity, organizations can choose to be either conservative or innovative.   Innovation frequently involves the expansion of core goals and technologies and/or the addition of new boundary-spanning functions.   What is being proposed here involves the expansion of both areas. There is a need to enlarge the scope of core goals and technologies to include an inclusive version of social value and civic education, emphasizing common values and a whole host of methods of public participation in civil society (way beyond the hum-drum discussion of voting rights).   In order to achieve legitimacy, social value and civic education will involve an enlarged role for organizational boundary-spanners, who will become actively involved in establishing goals through community-school collaborative decisionmaking. Boundary-spanners will serve to protect the school organization from undue environmental influence, while simultaneously responding to the demands of environmental actors—serving in the "through-put" role (Katz and Kahn 1966).

There are serious threats to the public school organization in adopting the strategy outlined. First, the education reform would involve the expansion of public school goals beyond the current basic skills curriculum. Conceivably, it would involve a 200 percent increase in curricular goals and create an infinitely more complex organizational atmosphere.   The addition of teaching staff and expanded curriculum would require greater fiscal resources. The organizational culture would be constrained by the reform, which could lead to the need for an expanded administrative capacity.   The implications of such change could be considered by critics to be almost nightmare-ish.

In his book *The Limits to Organizational Change* (1971), Herbert Kaufman concluded that theoretically, organizations will resist change, but as a practical matter change does occur.   His central focus then relates to *how* organizations change.   He found that organizations will resist *rapid* change, preferring incremental approaches. Not all personnel are resistant to change. Regular turnover of personnel frequently involves older possibly more conservative organizational members being replaced by younger individuals, who are more likely to embrace innovative organizational change.

Based on Kaufman's evidence, it is unlikely that the proposed reforms will occur rapidly or evenly.   The introduction of expanded civic and social value education requires a unique mix of established well-experienced teaching and administrative staff and young enthusiastic organizational members. As a bottom-up reform effort, change and resources for the reform may experience some difficulties in implementation; but what is being proposed is not intended to be a quick-fix solution to the crisis of legitimacy facing many public schools. Rather, the reform requires a long-term approach to implementation and evaluation.   Successful reform will necessitate organizational and community commitment to the new goals and methods of accomplishing them.

In the long term, it is anticipated that the cost of public education will actually *decline* as a result of these reforms. Environmental constraints on the public school are likely to decline as the legitimacy of public school goals rises. As communities become more actively involved in creating school organizational goals, social capital will likely increase, which is a critical prerequisite to the building of strong public institutions. Desired outcomes are a function of environmental *and* organizational conditions. Public schools and local communities will more likely reach desired outcomes if they work in unison, fully committed to the process as well as the purpose of elementary and secondary education.

WORKS CITED

Barnard, C. 1938. *Functions of the Executive.* Cambridge, MA: Harvard University Press.

Denhardt, R. 1993. *The Pursuit of Significance: Strategies for Managerial Success in Public Organizations.* Belmont, CA: Wadsworth.

Dewey, J. 1944. *Democracy and Education*, Second Edition. New York: Free Press.

Follett, M. 1992. "The Giving of Orders" [1918], in J. Shafritz and A. Hyde (eds.), *Classics of Public Administration.* Pacific Grove, CA: Brooks/Cole, 66-74.

Katz, D. and Kahn, R. 1966. *The Social Psychology of Organizations.* New York: John Wiley & Sons.

Kaufman, H. 1971. *The Limits of Organizational Change.* University, AL: University of Alabama Press.

Simon, H. 1976. *Administrative Behavior: A Study of Decision-Making Processes in Administrative Organization.* New York: Free Press.

Stiffler, L. 2000. Paul Allen to give $2 Million for I-729." August 23 *Seattle Post-Intelligencer*, B2.

Thompson, J. 1967. *Organizations in Action: Social Science Bases of Administrative Theory.* New York: McGraw-Hill.

Tiebout, C. 1956. "A Pure Theory of Local Expenditures," *Journal of Political Economy.* 64: 416-424.

Wilson, J. 1989. *Bureaucracy: What Government Agencies Do and Why They Do It.* New York: Basic Books.

Suggested Further Reading

Altenbaugh, R., ed. 1999. *Historical Dictionary of American Education.* Westport, CT: Greenwood Press.

Bacharach, S., ed. 1981. *Organizational Behavior in Schools and School Districts.* New York: Praeger.

Chubb, J. and Moe, T. 1990. *Politics, Markets, and America's Schools.* Washington, DC: The Brookings Institution.

Coleman, J. 1990. *Equality and Educational Opportunity.* Boulder, CO: Westview Press.

Cremin, L. 1976. *Traditions of American Education.* New York: Basic Books.

Crews, G. and Counts, M. 1997. *The Evolution of School Disturbance in America: Colonial Times to Modern Day.* Westport, CT: Praeger.

Cubberley, E. 1919. *Public Education in the United States: A Study and Interpretation of American Educational History.* Boston, MA: Houghton Mifflin.

Darder, A. 1991. *Culture and Power in the Classroom: A Critical Foundation for Bicultural Education.* New York: Bergin & Garvey.

Dewey, J. 1944. *Democracy and Education,* Second Edition. New York: Free Press.

Downs, A. 1967. *Inside Bureaucracy.* New York: Little, Brown.

Hanushek, E. 1994. *Making Schools Work: Improving Performance and Controlling Costs.* Washington, DC: Brookings Institution.

Hardaway, R. 1995. *America Goes to School: Law, Reform, and Crisis in Public Education.* Westport, CT: Praeger.

Katz, M. 1975. *Class, Bureaucracy, and Schools.* New York: Praeger.

Lindblom, C. 1991. *Inquiry and Change: The Troubled Attempts to Understand and Shape Society.* New Haven, CT: Yale University Press.

Linowes, D. 1988. *Privatization: Toward More Effective Government.* Washington, DC: President's Commission on Privatization.

Linton, R. 1969. "Society, Culture and the Individual," in J. Johnson, H. Collins, V. DuPuis, and J. Johnson (eds.), *Foundations of American Education.* Boston, MA: Allyn & Bacon, 9-19.

Lisman, C. 1998. *Toward a Civil Society: Civic Literacy and Service Learning.* Westport, CT: Bergin & Garvey.

Lutz, F. and Iannaccone, L. 1978. *Public Participation in Local School Districts: The Dissatisfaction Theory of Democracy.* Lexington, MA: Lexington Books.

Meade, E. 1972. *A Foundation Goes to School: The Ford Foundation Comprehensive School Improvement Program (1960-1970).* New York: Ford Foundation.

Mungazi, D. 1999. *The Evolution of Educational Theory in the United States.* Westport, CT: Praeger.

National Committee on Excellence in Education. 1983. *A Nation at Risk.* Washington, DC: U.S. Government Printing Office.

Piele, P. and Hall, J. 1973. *Budgets, Bonds, and Ballots: Voting Behavior in School Financial Elections.* Toronto: Lexington Books.

Putnam, R. 1993. *Making Democracy Work: Civic Traditions in Modern Italy.* Princeton, NJ: Princeton University Press.

Rothstein, R. 1998. *The Way We Were? The Myths and Realities of America's Student Achievement.* New York: Century Foundation Press.

Simon, H. 1976. *Administrative Behavior: A Study in Decision-Making Processes in Administrative Organization.* New York: Free Press.

Smith, K. and Meier, K. 1995. *The Case Against School Choice: Politics, Markets, and America's Fools.* Armonk, NY: M. E. Sharpe.

Spring, J. 1986. *The American School: 1642-1985.* New York: Longman.

Thompson, J. 1967. *Organizations in Action: Social Science Bases of Administrative Theory.* New York: McGraw-Hill.

Verba, S., Scholzman, H., Brady, H., and Nie, N. 1993. "Citizen Activity: Who Participates? What Do They Say?" *American Political Science Review.* 87(2): 303-318.

Wilson, J. 1989. *Bureaucracy: What Government Agencies Do and Why They Do It.* New York: Basic Books.

Index

About the Author

CHRISTOPHER A. SIMON is Assistant Professor of Political Science at the University of Nevada, Reno. Professor Simon has authored or coauthored numerous articles on education and public policy issues.